1019

CRUISING
AS A WAY OF LIFE

CRUISING
AS A WAY OF LIFE

THOMAS E. COLVIN

Seven Seas Press

NEW YORK

Copyright © 1979 by Thomas E. Colvin

Library of Congress Catalog Card No. 79–66980

ISBN: 0–915160–22–6

PRINTED IN THE UNITED STATES OF AMERICA

Book Design by Tere LoPrete

To MY FAMILY—Karen, Kevin, Kenneth and, especially, Jean; they often must endure what may not be of their choosing in order that I may enjoy what is of mine.

"The time has come," the Walrus said,
"To talk of many things:
   Of shoes—and ships—and sealing wax—
   Of cabbages—and kings—
   And why the sea is boiling hot—
   And whether pigs have wings."

      ——LEWIS CARROLL,
         Through the Looking-Glass

Contents

Preface

Ocean cruising encompasses many things. There never was, is or will be a moment when one can say, "There's nothing more to learn." Perhaps a better term would be "to relearn," for that, in essence, is what we must do, and adapt already existing knowledge to what later experience teaches us.

Some of what is in this book may be familiar to the reader, and understandably, because parts of it appeared in my monthly column, "Blue Water Sailor," in *Rudder* Magazine, and other portions appeared in *Pacific Yachting, Sailing, Practical Boat Owner* and similar periodicals. The notes at the end of each chapter derive from courses I have taught in Ship Design, Advanced Ship Design, Ocean Voyaging and Advanced Navigation and Shiphandling. The notes reflect, summarize or state facts pertaining to the preceding chapter—which facts may or may not be included in the chapter's text. When preparing this book, I did not find it necessary to alter what I had previously written but, when necessary for clarification, I did add dates and portions of the articles that, due to limitations of magazine space, were not previously published.

Material on *K'ung Fu-tse* is new, but the chapter on Chinese sailmaking was previously published by me and was either included as a part of each of my designs that incorporated the Chinese lug or sold as a package to those who wished to incorporate the rig in other designs.

Should the reader find some brevity in my dealing with a subject, it is because the subject was covered in my book *Coastwise and Offshore Cruising Wrinkles* (Seven Seas Press, New York) and I have nothing further to add at this time. Portions of one chapter may overlap or restate portions of another: This is intentional and once again proves that in life—especially life at sea—the entwining of all facets of a subject makes up the whole, and the truth of any fact is predicated on its context.

When one lives aboard and cruises an ocean-sailing vessel, one's priorities differ from those one has when living ashore, and it is impossible, while transporting oneself back and forth, to keep track of every minute detail of each existence. I must ask the reader ashore to accept what I have written while afloat as truths I have learned; always remembering that, as I continue to relearn, I reserve the right to modify or even change my convictions.

T.E.C.
Aboard the junk *K'ung Fu-tse*
May, 1979

"It is only right to say, though, that to insure a reasonable measure of success, experience should sail with the ship. But in order to be a successful navigator or sailor it is not necessary to hang a tar-bucket about one's neck. On the other hand, much thought concerning the brass buttons one should wear adds nothing to the safety of the ship."

——JOSHUA SLOCUM, *Sailing Alone Around the World*

CRUISING
AS A WAY OF LIFE

1

---◆◆---

Reflections

THE OCEAN CRUISER

"Short stay, Captain," calls the mate.

"Very well. Loose headsails; back staysail and foresail to starboard; bring the anchor up and down; helm hard left." Slowly the vessel's head pays off and the captain continues, "Break out the anchor, Mister."

"Aye, aye, Captain," replies the mate. Then, "Anchor aweigh, and anchor clear."

"Cat your anchor; ease the helm; let go and haul. Trim all sheets full and bye."

This was the departure procedure aboard a three-masted schooner, with everything going well. Today, in small vessels, the procedure is the same; however, today the crew may consist only of a husband and wife and their family. There is less protocol and very often some confusion—even to the point of shouting—but the end result is the same: The vessel is underway and proceeding to sea.

The old adage of "wooden ships and iron men" is hogwash. In the old days, many vessels were poorly equipped, undermanned and often in dire need of repair, but with a paying cargo and a philosophy of, "A profit if we can and a loss if we must," vessels plied the seas. Today, at least in ocean cruising vessels, there is little or no excuse for this irresponsible attitude toward crew and vessel. The proper blue-water vessel should be fully found and in want of nothing, with every precaution taken to insure that the voyage will proceed without mishaps caused by negligence.

The acquisition of an ocean cruiser should never be undertaken lightly:

The sea has not changed over the centuries, even though those who go to sea have. First and foremost, a well-found vessel is usually more seaworthy than her crew and, if left to her own devices, will normally weather the worst conditions; however, an inexperienced crew can destroy a well-found vessel simply through ignorance.

The primary consideration in selecting an ocean cruiser is to make certain she is properly constructed and outfitted for the rigors of ocean cruising. There are several ways to go about this. First, you can have a vessel designed and constructed just for ocean cruising by designers and builders who have good reputations for producing this type of vessel. Second, you can purchase an existing vessel already endowed with these desired qualities, as certified by a competent marine surveyor: It matters little what a vessel has done; the important thing to determine is what the vessel is still capable of doing. Third, you can modify an existing vessel with alterations that make her a proper ocean cruiser.

Today, there are few available stock vessels that will not require some modification in their gear, equipment, rig and possibly their hulls, if they are to endure sustained off-shore passages and the permanent living aboard of a small crew. We may safely assume that there is no "ideal" building material, rig or hull configuration. All such ideas of perfection depend on the experience of the individual who, often lacking familiarity with a variety of materials, rig and hull forms, expresses his own prejudices— sometimes rather vociferously. So, beware of generalizations and weigh carefully the depth of experience that permits a person to praise or condemn any vessel simply "because."

Wood is an excellent material; a wooden vessel properly constructed of seasoned material, closely fitted and maintained, has a life expectancy of about 20 years before refastening (by the way, hot-dipped galvanized fastenings *are* good), and then at least another 20 years of hard driving. There is precedent for even longer life than that, but then maintenance becomes rather formidable. There are several vessels in the Chesapeake Bay area that are over 60 years old and still sound; they can pass, and have passed, rigid surveys.

Fiberglass-reinforced plastic construction, when properly done can result in long life, great strength and less initial cost since this form of construction lends itself to mass production. This latter fact is often the drawback to accepting this medium for an ocean cruising boat, as it is the integrity of the builder and not the volume of advertising that determines the quality of the hull. One has no right to assume that any builder must incorporate the qualities of an ocean voyaging vessel in a daysailer, weekend cruiser or around-the-buoys racer. Unless the builder or manufacturer specifically claims the vessel is designed and constructed to go to sea, it is unreasonable to criticize the vessel because of her inability to meet extraordinary conditions. Areas to be strengthened in a fiberglass-reinforced plastic boat would be the keel, bilge and deck edges. The cabin and decks should be strong enough to withstand a capsize or being swept by a sea. Cockpit scuppers should be extra large, and small windows and ports should be of tempered glass; large openings should be avoided. The hull-deck joint not only should be heavily reinforced but must be sealed and bolted at close intervals. In many areas of the world, pilotage is compulsory; and the pilots, accustomed to boarding large merchant vessels, often come alongside with a heavy thump that can crack frames, splinter planks or split deck hull joints even on well-found vessels.

PHOTO I-I. *Kung Fu-tse.*

Steel and aluminum hulls, properly constructed, will have either transverse or longitudinal framing or a combination of both. For transverse framing, 19 inches is the maximum permissible for ocean-cruising vessels 30–50 feet on deck; while six foot four inches is the maximum spacing of web frames in longitudinal construction in which longitudinals will be spaced 12–18 inches apart. In the combination frame, 38 inches transverse frame centers, and 12–18 inches longitudinal centers are the ideal for interior arrangement purposes. The heavier the plating, the wider apart the framing centers; however, in steel this is self-defeating as the increase in thickness of plating adds more weight than it does stiffness. Thus it is best to use more frames or longitudinals and thinner plate. Eleven-gauge plate at 5.0 lbs. per square foot is minimum for ocean cruising vessels 40 feet or less on deck; however, 10-gauge at 5.63 lbs. per square foot is better. The use of Cor-ten steel is best for plating as it has about 1½ times the yield strength of mild steel and does not corrode as fast. Beware of the builder who does not weld both sides of a seam. Aside from the structural weakness of welding only one side of a seam, there is every probability of corrosion in the unwelded seam which will accelerate because of the crevice. Properly maintained, a steel hull has an indefinite life span. Most steel hulls, contrary to popular belief, corrode from the inside out due to the builder not properly preparing and/or painting the interior of the hull. If the builder has done his job well, then the owner must be blamed for not maintaining the integrity of the inside of the hull.

Aluminum hulls, on the other hand, will use heavier plating to advantage since aluminum has less yield strength but greater stiffness than steel. The minimum plating in aluminum is 3/16 inches in vessels under 40 feet, and ¼ inches is better. Choosing the correct alloy is most important, as is the filler wire used for welding since aluminum alloys, if improperly selected, can cause severe electrolytic corrosion. Aluminum, like steel, depends on the builder's integrity, and then on the owner's providing proper maintenance. There exists no cheap way in which to build a metal vessel or, for that matter, an ocean cruiser of any material.

Regarding ferro-cement, little can be said since as a boatbuilding material it is still in its infancy. In ocean cruising, it has yet to prove its durability or suitability. Some vessels once cited as prime examples of ferro-cement construction developed many faults after a few years of hard sailing. Properly engineered, it is possible that ferro-cement can be a satisfactory material for an ocean cruiser; however, more precautions are required in its use than any other material, and there are no shortcuts that will do anything but cause grief in the life of the vessel. It is far from the strongest material, yet it is one of the heaviest.

In designing and constructing an ocean-cruising yacht, it is impossible, in the beginning, to isolate any one feature as being the most important because, like the rim of a wheel, every segment is as important as the remainder. One must deal with generalities before details, major or minor, can be considered and analyzed. In general, therefore, one must determine the vessel's proposed cruising grounds, the number of people to be accommodated, the material of construction, the length of intended voyages or individual passages, the rig and the general hull style. Still talking in generalities, 1½ to five tons is the displacement range of a cruising vessel per person to be accommodated. For an around-the-world cruise, 2½ tons per person is quite modest, and five tons per person, very comfortable. Overall length of hull (LOA) is directly proportional to persons to be accommodated. My rule of thumb has been 10 feet per person—say, two or three persons for 30 feet, four for 40 feet, and five for 50 feet. I realize there are many vessels on the market today that sleep two to three times the number allowed for in my rule, but so do tenement houses!

Draft and length overall are important because they also determine the hull configuration. There are more cruising areas in the world that are suited to six feet or less of draft than to, say, eight feet of draft. If one were to reduce draft to four feet, there is a tripling of bays, sounds and rivers available for shelter or anchoring. When draft is restricted, length

PHOTO 1-2. A stern view of Kung Fu-tse on her mooring.

should increase in order to achieve a faster as well as more commodious hull for a given displacement. True, beam can be increased without increasing length; however, the result is often less than satisfactory except that you gain stability quicker with increased beam than with increased length.

Rig is, to some extent, independent of hull form. In the past, many famous vessels started life as sloops or cutters and were later successfully altered to schooners, ketches or yawls. Occasionally a hull will be so specialized that nothing but the original rig will work with any degree of satisfaction. (Examples: the Cape Cod cat and the Gloucester fishing schooner.) In the past, most ocean cruising was done with multimasted rigs—yawl, ketch, schooner—with only an occasional cutter or sloop. The gaff rig predominated. Since World War II, the jib-headed rig has gained popularity and now outnumbers the gaff rig on cruising vessels. Light displacement hulls utilize the jib-headed rig well. The heavy hulls are often undercanvased with this rig and, therefore, are slow. There is a growing belief that an ocean-cruising vessel is and should be undercanvased. This is not true; she should have a *larger* rig than her racing counterpart. The racing vessel needs numerous headsails because of penalties imposed by racing rules for sail area. But why penalize a cruising vessel when there is no rule to which it must conform? Many people are also of the opinion that gaff rig is passé. This is not so, the gaff-rigger is still more efficient off the wind than a high-aspect-ratio jib-header. When one is bound for the trades, fair winds are to be expected—only a glutton for punishment would attempt to beat against the trades. I have sailed both jib-headed and gaff rigs in sloops, cutters, yawls, ketches and schooners, both coastwise and offshore. The gaff was always handier than the jib-headed rig as it was so easy to set extra canvas, especially on a schooner. Having been dismasted both in a sloop and a ketch, I found it easier to restep a stump mast and jury rig the ketch—hence my leanings toward a multimasted rig. Another gain was that spars, not critical in staying, could be shorter. The handiest rig I have ever sailed, without exception, is the Chinese lug rig; once hooked on it, I have never gone back to any other.

A voyaging ocean cruiser can, in three years, have more hard usage and sail more miles than the average weekender, vacation cruiser or round-the-buoys racer will in 20 years. Thus consideration of sturdiness, comfort and all-around sailing ability are of paramount importance.

Long keel versus short keel has again blossomed into a sometimes heated argument. For ocean cruising, a long keel usually reaches and runs steadier than a short keel; and, should one err, I suggest it be on the long side. It is true that a short keel tacks faster, but it also sags off before hanging onto the new course; whereas a long keel fore-reaches in tacking and hangs on with little if any sagging-off. The long keel can be hove-to, can ride to a sea anchor, and can lay ahull closer than 90° to the wind. The long keel is usually associated with shoaler draft and, thus, when hove-to, provides a better slick to windward and has less tendency to trip. The short keel has to be run off in heavy weather. Often these hulls have short waterlines for their overall length, with long overhangs aft, which have too much buoyancy for the fine bows necessary to drive them to windward. This is the cause of the increasing frequency of tripping and either pitch-poling or capsizing. Before a following sea, the short keel lacks directional stability and, if fitted with a spade rudder or a very long skeg that stalls out when the vessel surfs, runs an increased risk of capsizing.

So, "you pays your money and takes your choice," and you live with it. All vessels, even sister ships, have their own peculiarities. There is no "ideal" ocean cruiser except the one with which an individual is the most comfortable and familiar. No matter how bad the weather or how rough the seas, the knowledge that your vessel was designed and constructed to survive such conditions and that you *are* safe provides great mental, if not physical, comfort.

THE OCEAN CRUISERS

Confucius said, "In all things, success depends upon previous preparation, and without such preparation, there is sure to be failure. . . . Everything has its beauty, but not everyone sees it."

Thus with the smashing of the champagne bottle and the lighting with joss sticks of firecrackers to ward off evil spirits, *K'ung Fu-tse* slid into the water at 1130 August 20, 1974, 23 months after the laying of the keel. In the process of moving aboard, it was quite evident to us that Confucius was astute in his observations, for it became apparent that all our prior planning had resulted in the hoped-for convenience and livability so necessary to ocean voyaging.

The basic difference between those who live aboard and those who plan to is that the former are adapting themselves to an existing vessel, whereas the latter are still searching for the ideal vessel. In reality, each vessel is her owner's momentary dream. Whether the dream becomes a nightmare depends on the eventual compatibility between owner and vessel. The overall problem is complex and defies any logical sequence to arrive at the final solution. However, since the sum is always equal to its parts, one need not try to establish an order of importance.

At a given moment, one decides to have a live-aboard vessel and, at that moment, what was first a hazy concept must be logically implemented. Any serious error in the logic results in the death of the dream.

PHOTO 1-3. The main companionway, approximately amidships. The black tank holds sea water which is heated by the sun for use in the galley. The deck box holds the Avon dinghy, plus spare timber, and sails for the hard dinghy. The turbine vent leads to the galley. The black vent under the companionway porthole exhausts the diesel galley stove and the dorade vent forward of the turbine sends fresh air down into the galley.

Some fundamental considerations include the age of the crew, their habits, finances, abilities and experiences, the intended cruising grounds, and whether the vessel is to be the only home, or if it will be used in conjunction with shoreside facilities. Only when these facts have been ascertained can a vessel be selected.

The smallest vessel I have seen as a permanent home for a couple was 21 feet. Not only was it a home but also it had sailed over 55,000 miles, including a circumnavigation of the globe. The largest vessel I have seen manned and maintained by two people was 65 feet; however, a majority of the vessels are in the range of 30 to 45 feet, with at least 80 percent being 40 feet or less on deck. There are many reasons for this size being popular, of which purchase cost, maintenance, ease of handling and availability are foremost.

Young couples are often on a low budget and are likely to own a minimum-size sparsely outfitted vessel, to which they add items as finances permit. The middle-age group tends toward the larger sizes—i.e., 35–40 feet—especially if more than two persons must be accommodated. Linear length, of course, gives more room for berths, galley and head; however, the true size is the amount of cubic feet alloted to each person accommodated. This can be estimated from displacement. Two and a half tons is about minimum per person and five tons is palatial. If calculated on a cubic foot criterion alone, the USCG documentation figure is a useful rule of thumb: length on deck times beam times depth (deck to keel amidships) divided by 200 = gross tons of 100 cubic feet internal volume; or $L \times B \times D \times .5$ = cubic feet. This fits the average vessel that has a waterline about 75 percent of the overall length, but it is inaccurate for vessels with short overhangs or very full decks. For example, a double-ended of the Colin Archer type would best be $L \times B \times D \times .6$, and a Chinese junk would be $L \times B \times D \times .75$.

Application of the same rule to all vessels yields the illusion that for a given gross tonnage there are "big" and "little" tons. About 250 cubic feet per person is a minimum allowance for comfort and 500 cubic feet is not excessive. At this juncture, one is led to categorize hulls, which is

PHOTO I-4. The after deck box sits atop the cabin trunk, showing the coral anchor stowed on its forward end, but easily accessible. The three cowl vents on the port side lead, from aft forward, to the engine room, to a berth, and to the W. C. The two outboard motors hang on the after end of the box, safe but handy.

dangerous. So, the assumption for this discussion is that while a vessel is best adapted to one type of living aboard and cruising, it is also implied that she can serve in other categories and, under no circumstances, will she lack seaworthiness or seakeeping ability.

1. THE OCEAN ROAMER. This vessel is a type unto it itself in specialization. There is no one hull type that is ideal, nor is length, displacement, rig or outfit uniform. People who own these vessels usually distinguish themselves by their almost complete independence of shoreside facilities. The criteria in selecting a vessel for this purpose lean heavily toward self-sufficiency, thus she is often of heavy displacement and generous beam. If she is fitted with an engine, it is usually of low horsepower for its size. Also, the vessel seldom accommodates any extra persons. (Out several years.)

2. THE OCEAN VOYAGER. This type of vessel, while making long passages, is also used for coastwise cruising. Often as independent as the Roamer, it usually has less displacement and higher horsepower. Extended voyages are interspersed with many of short duration. (Out one to two years.)

3. THE COASTWISE CRUISER. This hull is usually outfitted with more electronics than the Roamer or Ocean Voyager, carries less food and stores, especially water, but carries more fuel. Quite often this type of vessel is capable of accommodating several extra persons for short periods of time. (Out a few months to one year.)

4. THE LIVE-ABOARD CRUISER. While making blue-water voyages as well as long coastwise cruises, she spends a great deal of her time in ports. Often couples living aboard this type of vessel have semipermanent shore jobs. These vessels are of the three categories listed above, but need to be outfitted extensively. Those that anchor out except for brief dockside stints are capable of quicker conversion than those that spend the majority of their in-port time secured to a dock.

5. THE INTRACOASTAL CRUISER. Some vessels on the U.S. East Coast cruise southern waters in the winter and northern waters in the summer, the passage between the two being made via the Intracoastal Waterway. These vessels, depending on other factors, are, nevertheless, seagoing vessels; however, they should have larger engines than desirable on a vessel that makes this trek only once or twice a decade. They should be capable of six knots (seven m.p.m.) minimum, under power. Many make less speed than this, but their progress can be nil if faced with strong currents or headwinds. For the extremely low-powered vessels, 12- and 14-hour days are not uncommon. Oddly, those capable of higher speeds seldom do more than the 50 to 80 miles per day covered by the low-speed vessels, but usually start later and anchor earlier.

In final analysis, we come back to three questions: Which vessel? What must she be? When does one start?

Some attributes a vessel should have, as compiled by those who live aboard and are content with what they have, are:

1. Sea-kindliness, i.e., comfortable in a seaway with a generally easy motion.

2. Good passagemaking—not necessarily fast, but consistent in that the overall average of performance in light, moderate and heavy weather is balanced.

3. Ability to stand up to her canvas and not sail on her ear—most sailors feel that 20°–25° of heel in Force 5 winds is proper.

4. Ease in handling and convenience in sailing.

5. Comfort, with livable space below as well as on deck—compartmenting is desirable but not through gimmicky cubbyholes.

As to which vessel, she must be pleasing to the owner's eye, have accommodations and carrying ability to meet his requirements, and be within his budget.

To answer the third question—when? "Tomorrow, today is yesterday!"

LIVING ABOARD

What are the chances of living aboard permanently? Very slim—less than 50 percent of those who try it get past the first year; less than 30 percent make two years; only 15 percent make it through the fifth year, and only 5 percent to 7 percent remain for many years. There are many reasons for this:

1. The inability of a couple to live in constant close contact. That means 24 hours a day, seven days a week, 365 days a year—always with the same person. The marriage vow is "for better or for worse," but often the general attitude toward total mutual confinement is, "There must be something better and there is certainly nothing worse." Several things begin to happen, often with the result that the marriage is on the rocks and a choice has to be made—the boat or the marriage. The fault is not necessarily the woman's although she frequently gets the blame. Despite the attractions of the new life, she has been removed from accustomed conveniences such as unlimited water, hot water, refrigeration, ice, electricity, communication, space and ample storage, to mention only a few, but is expected to carry on the same duties as she had ashore, under—at

best—quite "primitive" conditions. Furthermore, she now lives in a home that not only continuously moves from place to place, but also up and down and sideways, and also pounds, jerks and heaves—often simultaneously. Then she is expected to endure hours of steering, rain or shine, and to adapt to being awake or asleep on irregular time schedules. From the time she was a little girl, she was taught to play house and to expect the security of family, community and permanence in one location. Had she been taught to play boat, maybe the adjustment would be easier.

(NOTE: Making the statement to a man, "It's me or the boat," may be a poor ultimatum. Sometimes the boat is not the loser!)

2. Wrong kind of cruising chosen. This occurs mainly through inexperience, and then being unable to acquire the proper skills or to overcome fears resulting from early bad experiences. The mature solution to this problem is to accept a limited cruising goal until experience dictates going farther afield. I know many people who have sought out, purchased or built a vessel for an around-the-world cruise only to find out that life at sea was not for them. Some then altered their goals and found they enjoy coastwise and short foreign voyages and living aboard. Others found that even this was too much, and have settled for a style of cruising which provides a secure port at the end of every day with no night sailing.

3. Wrong type vessel for the kind of cruising chosen. Those who have hiked, biked and camped before moving aboard have a better understanding of close confinement than people who have known only space and comfort. It behooves couples to select their vessel on the basis of their past habits rather than on the vague hope that they can adapt to radical changes of life style. (We should remember that most people suffer claustrophobia to some degree.) If too large a vessel is chosen, the physical demands are such that it becomes all work and no fun. For some reason, many try to work equivalent shoreside facilities into a vessel— which proves disastrous nine times out of ten. Deciding that a 40-footer of moderate displacement is too small, the family changes, say, to a 60-footer in the belief that it is 50 percent larger. Nothing can dissuade them from this goal and they remain blind to the fact that what they have chosen is not half again as large, but 350 percent larger than the 40-footer! That's right, 3½ times *larger!* The reason: such increases progress geometrically, not arithmetically! A more common mistake is to select a vessel on past performance—i.e., a sister ship sailed around the world or doubled Cape Horn. Certainly the vessel that accomplished that has merit, but to her crew must go the credit of getting her there and back.

4. Required finances are underestimated. Here again, those who can adapt to a simple way of life—which, in essence, means anchoring out, not requiring shoreside conveniences such as electricity and unlimited

water—and who can eat local foods, especially fish, can reduce their budget to a minimum. The vessel *does* have constant requirements that must be met such as fuel, hauling, repairs and replacements, but savings in other areas can be made. Minimum use of lights and engine reduces fuel costs. An occasional light scrubbing of the bottom stretches the time between haulouts. (This may become the most costly item in the budget if one cannot do the work himself. Sometimes it may be necessary to sail 500 to 1,000 miles to an area where it is possible to do the work yourself or to where the tidal range is adequate to permit beaching.) The self-sufficient and adaptable crew can reduce costs, but those who insist on maintaining the same life style as they had ashore often find that living afloat is more, not less, expensive.

5. Improper equipment for the type of cruising undertaken. This results in needless hardship that discourages many. Usually it is not just one item, but a combination of so many that the problems seem insurmountable. Lack of heat in cold climates, necessitating everyday life spent in heavy clothing, even to sleeping in everything normally worn on deck, certainly does little for comfort—or morale. Lack of ventilation not only in the tropics but also during storms at sea result in a damp, clammy interior which promotes mildew. Inability to work the deck because of poor design or clutter; difficulties in handling ground tackle; complicated electrical systems without alternate nonmechanical back-up systems; inadequate natural light so that life below is akin to living in a cave, and lack of comfort on deck where the crew spends a great portion of its time, not only at sea but also especially in the tropics where almost all activity occurs on deck—all these are discouraging factors to be considered.

6. Communications problems with the home base. These are aggravating at best, and never entirely satisfactory. People dependent on regular mail are always trying to find safe forwarding addresses and are constantly frustrated by having mail missent, returned to sender, delayed en route or impounded by zealous officials. To operate a business while cruising requires either a trustworthy partner at home or an organization that functions independently of you. Some become so worried by what they left behind they can never enjoy themselves. If a business requires frequent returns to work, then finding secondary transportation and insuring the vessel's security are vexing and costly. The inability to cut apron strings plagues many. Prolonged ill health in the family or the welfare of elderly parents is frequently a major concern; hardhearted as it may seem, there is little that can be done if trouble comes, regardless of where one is located, so cruising must be planned on contingencies and one must accept these conditions as facts of life.

7. Inability to adapt to local food and customs. This is more psychological than physiological. Fortunately, cruising does toughen one to almost

PHOTO 1-5. A junk in port—and most other cruising vessels, for that matter—is usually a clutter of lines and gear, and may look a mess, but the opposite is true at sea, as a matter of safety and efficiency.

anything, but some people never do adapt, and insist on the same diet at sea as they had ashore. When the impracticality of achieving it becomes apparent, their only solution is to give up. My own philosophy is that if the natives can live on it, or without it, so can I. This especially applies to ice: We have found that when ice was a necessity for local food storage, it was always available at a reasonable price; when it was not needed locally, we did without it, too.

8. Travel not fun and new places not exciting. To some, the reason for travel is the joy of getting there; to others, it is the sights, the people, the beaches, the climate, etc.; but, in all cases, there must be some good reason to travel—otherwise, one will rot in one locality. We have met many who told us voyaging would be fun if it were not for the foreigners! Others couldn't handle foreign languages, and many don't even try to learn them. Many flagrantly abuse local customs, their attitude apparently being, "Here I am; aren't you happy?" This attitude only leads to confrontation with authorities and natives and unhappiness on both sides.

9. Resentment of never-ending maintenance. When maintenance is neglected, there comes a time when no matter how hard one works there is no catching up. Some people are naturally lazy, shirking everything to

the point where other crew members can no longer tolerate their sloven-liness and quit. We can recall many examples, but one extreme case comes to mind. On this boat, lifelines frayed and then parted but were never replaced; toilets clogged, so a bucket had to serve; anchor lines chafed through, so knots were tied in them; paint peeled off the deck house and spars, and rot set in, but was ignored; the engine leaked oil through the various gaskets but nothing was done; the stove did not work so the crew ate cold food from cans, and so on—until the owner's wife and children just left. Eventually the vessel sank at her mooring with no loss of life but little if any value in salvage. Some pass up deck maintenance because of a shortage of fresh water, not realizing that salt water not only is a bleach, but also, on wooden decks and vessels, acts as a preservative. Heavy salt encrustrations can be diluted by washing and scrubbing with salt water, then be wiped down, at which time the surface is suitable for painting. There is never an excuse for bypassing maintenance, waiting for "ideal" working conditions which seldom if ever exist.

10. Frustration with the cruising life. This occurs when things go from bad to worse in spite of all precautions. Some call it luck, but there are times when headwinds, gales, sickness, equipment failures, general bad weather and close confinement occur so frequently or simultaneously that no sooner is one problem solved than another occurs. The crew becomes physically and mentally exhausted, and is about ready to quit. However, sooner or later, if one just sticks it out, everything is bound to improve.

NOTES

THE HULL

A. SIZE:

1. Dependent on number of persons to be accommodated.
2. For short cruises, about 1½ to three tons per person.
3. For long cruises and permanent living aboard, three to five tons per person.
4. About 10 feet per person to be accommodated is comfortable.
   a. Size has little to do with additional numbers as galley require-ments, food, water capacity, heads, etc., all increase in propor-tion to the number in the crew.

B. SEAWORTHINESS:

1. Depends more on the crew than on the size or shape of the vessel.
2. Certain features, if incorporated in the design, such as heavy con-

struction, short overhangs, wide uncluttered decks, are usually inherent in a good ocean cruiser but of themselves are not essential for seaworthiness.

3. Seaworthiness is a combination of many factors and not influenced by current fads.

    a. *Tilikum* and *Spray* are extreme examples of successful cruisers. It is instructive to compare them.

        Tilikum: LOA, including figurehead, 38 feet; length on bottom, 30 feet; beam, five feet, six inches; beam at WL, four feet, six inches; beam on bottom, three feet, six inches; draft, about 24 inches aft, 22 inches forward; sail area, 230 square feet.

        Spray: LOA, 36 feet, nine inches; LWL, 32 feet one inch; beam, 14 feet, one inch; beam at WL, 13 feet, 10 inches; freeboard, 22 inches; draft, four feet, one inch; sail area, 1,161 square feet; displacement, 35,658 pounds.

C. COMFORT:

1. Requires a safe place to sleep, sit, eat and a certain degree of privacy.
2. Also derives from the motion of the vessel which, to some degree, can be controlled by the placement of consumable stores.
3. The shapes of hulls contribute directly to comfort; so do rigs.
4. Cooking is of paramount importance as is the ability to relax off watch.

D. SPEED:

1. Depends on length on the waterline. A good sailing vessel will do well to "average the LWL," let's say, five knots for 25 feet, six knots for 36 feet, etc. In nautical miles per day, this amounts to 120 and 144, respectively.
2. Most vessels will average around .8 of the WL (square root), which means a 25-foot WL averages 96 miles per day, and a 36-foot WL averages 115 miles per day.
3. Short bursts of speed are less important than sustaining an average.
4. The ability to carry a press of sail is most important for, in heavy weather, constant reefing below Force 5 increases the voyage labor and time, especially if heaving-to is required at Force 5–6.

E. STABILITY:

1. Depends either on hull shape or ballast or a combination of both.
2. A hull that is too tender is hard on the crew's nerves.

3. A hull that is too stiff is hard on her rig.
4. If the deck edge immerses at a 22½° angle of heel in 22 knots of wind the vessel is a good heavy-weather sailer.
5. Proper stowage has much to do with stability, and rearranging stowed gear forward or aft, up or down, can alter the motion of the hull.

F. DISPLACEMENT: $\quad \Delta / (\dfrac{L}{100})3$

1. Light—18,000 pounds or less for 33-feet WL $\qquad$ 223
2. Medium—28,000 pounds medium for 33-feet WL $\qquad$ 349
3. Heavy—35,000 pounds heavy for 33-feet WL $\qquad$ 435
4. Displacement/Length Ratio $\quad \dfrac{\Delta}{(\frac{L}{100})3} = \dfrac{\text{Tons}}{\frac{(\text{WL Length})3}{100}}$

example: $\quad \dfrac{25.13}{(\frac{41}{100})3} = \dfrac{25.13}{.0689} = 365$

5. Light displacement often costs more per pound to construct than heavy.
6. Light weather often is more favorable to heavy displacement.

G. BOWS:

1. Short overhang; clipper; long overhang.
2. Freeboard at bow, 2 or 2.3 × minimum freeboard.

H. STERNS:

1. Short overhang; counter; transom; round; double-ended.
2. Freeboard at stern, 1.40 × minimum freeboard.

I. FREEBOARD:

(Minimum) 2.33 inches per foot of Waterline Beam

or $\quad \dfrac{\text{cubic foot}}{\text{LWL} \times \text{WLB}} \times 1.35 \qquad$ 15 tons

$\qquad\qquad\qquad$ 1.25 $\qquad$ 15–30 tons
$\qquad\qquad\qquad$ 1.20 $\qquad$ 30 tons

$\Delta \quad = \quad$ Displacement
WL $\quad = \quad$ Waterline
WLB $\quad = \quad$ Waterline Beam

1. Example: KFT 2.33 (Const.) $\times$ 12.80 (WLB) = 29.82 inches

   or KFT $\dfrac{880 \text{ cubic feet}}{41.08 \times 12.80} \times 1.25 = \dfrac{880}{522} \times 1.25$

   = 2.11 feet or 25.34 inches

(35 cubic feet = 1 ton salt water.)

Actual freeboard: 27.62 inches

Average of both methods:

$$\frac{29.82 + 25.34}{2} = \frac{55.16}{2} = 27.58 \text{ inches}$$

J. RAIL HEIGHT: .25 $\times$ minimum freeboard is average; .50 is about maximum.

Rail at bow, 1.5 $\times$ Rail

Rail at stern, same as bow

1. Reasons for Rail: safety; stanchions; securing; sheet leads, etc.
2. Toe rails can be dangerous without lifelines.
3. Lifelines: 27 inches minimum; 36 inches best; always two wires.
   a. Rig clearances have much to do with final lifeline heights in ocean cruisers.
   b. Stanchions must be bolted or welded to deck and rail.

K. RIGS: SAIL AREA

1. Jib-headed. 2. Gaff. 3. Junk (lug).
   All are based on area of lateral plane including rudder, and ratios are 6–7. Most ocean cruisers are 6.2 to 6.8. Centerboard hulls are 7.0 to 7.8, not including centerboard. Also area of ⟊ $\times$ 4.0 to 6.0 = amount of lateral plane including rudder.

L. RIG TYPES: (Divide the sail areas into percentages as follows):

1. Ketch: 18 jib....55 main....27 mizzen.
2. Yawl: 20 jib....64 main....16 mizzen.
3. Sloop: 20 jib....80 main.
4. Cutter: 30 jib....70 main.
   Double Headsail: 15–13....61.
5. Schooner: 18 jib....27 fore....55 main.
6. Junk: 31 fore....57 main....12 mizzen.

M. BUILDING:

1. Time element; cost; availability of a builder.

N. BUYING:

1. Ascertain true value—view vessel as scrap value of hull for price, and add condition of sails, engine, rig and hull.

O. SURVEYING:

1. Fee for this job is cheap compared to the loss (or cost) incurred by buying an unsound hull.

2

---•---

Interior

It is usually during the first three months of cruising in a new vessel that 60 percent of all equipment failures occur. One should accept the fact that the failures are not always due to the manufacturer, designer or builder, and should learn to take them in stride—even though each one seems catastrophic at the time.

Equipping a vessel is difficult. Much of the information needed by new or potential cruising people must be gleaned from advertisements which are often misleading and encourage purchases of gear that cannot take the hard usage (not to mention abuse) that it commonly suffers aboard a cruising vessel (although the same gear might last for years on a week-ender).

The best method of determining reliability of equipment is to ask the advice of people who have cruised for years on the same vessel. They usually can be persuaded to tell you (often emphatically) what gear they have found good or bad. Question several people because each one you ask will have his own prejudices. And always remember that the difference between first and second class is about 10 percent in cash, and 75 percent in peace of mind.

One should keep in mind three things: First, nothing is perfect and is, at best, only adequate; second, almost every piece of equipment installed is not only limited in function but also must often be modified to be useful, to eliminate excessive maintenance, to increase safety or to correct outright flaws in its manufacture, and, third, that nothing is free, not even the wind, but at some time the price in energy and inconvenience of a piece of equipment will be so great that if one is to continue cruising, either the equipment must go or one's life style must change.

STOVES

The galley stove is one of the most difficult pieces of equipment to select, all types having advantages and disadvantages. For some reason (and mostly for wrong reasons) a stove mounted in gimbals is widely popular. As manufactured, none of these stoves will perform in rough, let alone violent, seas without extensive modification. And since such a stove has to be installed so that it faces into the heeling motion of the vessel, I know of none that is equipped with an oven that will remain balanced when the oven door is open. Of course, we all realize that proper sea cooks have four arms, but for those of us who have only two, an overbalancing oven is not much use except when the vessel is at anchor or sailing on placid seas. Furthermore, the placement of the stove often denies access to the space outboard of it, and, worst of all, usually has the cook lurching into the stove or "climbing" to reach it. When the stove is out of synchronization with the motion of the vessel, which happens quite often, pots begin to slop over, and the cook risks serious burns from scalding liquids. All seagoing stoves should face fore or aft, be firmly bolted down and *not* be set in gimbals. Liquids on stoves properly positioned spill to port or starboard, away from (not on) the cook, and the oven can be used to control them. Also, one's feet can be braced firmly against rolling and be clear of the stove.

The closer the stove is to the centerline of the vessel, the less it will be affected by motion. This position is virtually impossible on small vessels.

I realize it is contrary to almost all present-day arrangements, but the best area for the galley is still in the foc'sle: Minimum floor space is required by the galley; the normal counter height (about 30 inches) permits generous width; lockers above the counter can be large because of the increase in hull depth due to the sheer of the vessel; more space can be allocated to chain and rope lockers (which are usually an afterthought), and the forehatch can be over the stove, removing cooking odors as well as cooling the galley. The foc'sle is much worse for sleeping than it is for cooking and, if one is content to sleep there, one can certainly bear to cook there! More importantly, the widest part of the vessel is now open for living and lounging. If one assumes two days in port for one day at sea (a fair assumption), then there is not much sacrifice involved in cooking in the foc'sle unless the days at sea are all in gale force winds. (If this happened to me, all I would get would be peanut butter sandwiches!)

Probably the kerosene primus-type is the most popular stove. Some models incorporate an oven, but most vessels use the two- or three-burner table-top model. Many of the new models have burners that use kerosene for preheating, whereas the older models have to be primed with alcohol. Primus stoves are clean, efficient and easy to repair. Kerosene produces a very hot flame and is an inexpensive fuel. In some areas of the U.S., kerosene is difficult to obtain and may be of a poorer quality than the white kerosene that is used as lamp fuel. Some people use Varsol and special lamp fuels, but these are five to 10 times as expensive as kerosene. A further advantage of kerosene is that it can also be used in lamps, and often in running lights, as well. Moreover, it is excellent for cleaning paint brushes, the topsides after sailing through an oil spill or dirty harbor or oily bilges, and it is a good wood preservative. The fumes of the alcohol used for preheating some models do cause queasy stomachs in some people, however.

Alcohol stoves with a primus-type burner are now seldom used because of the high cost of fuel. They are identical in appearance to the kerosene stove. As mentioned, the odor of alcohol does bother some people. The alcohol stove has less heat (British Thermal Units) per gallon, and is somewhat less of a fire hazard than the kerosene stove, since an alcohol fire can be doused with water.

Coal and wood stoves are almost passé, which is unfortunate: The whole top of such stoves could be used for cooking and provide many temperatures to choose from. The top plate, since it could be used for direct frying of meat, fish, pancakes, etc., eliminated the use of a pan; the whole stove heated the cabin which was fine in cold climates, but, unless the galley was well ventilated, could be frightful in the tropics. Suitable wood for burning is now expensive; anthracite coal is impossible to buy in most areas; and soft coal causes too much soot, not only in the stack but on deck. Also, coal and wood require more cubic space for stowage than exists on most cruisers.

Diesel stoves are of two categories—gravity-feed pot burners and fuel-injection burners. The former are simple, and if enough flue height is provided (six to nine feet), forced draft can be dispensed with and they do not need electric blowers. Most diesel stoves have hot-plate tops, like their wood and coal ancestors, and cannot be rapidly cooled. There is an English type that has an insulated "bolster" that closes off the hot plate after use and eliminates the radiant heat. These stoves are quite heavy and best suited for vessels of over 20 tons displacement. The advantages of the diesel stove are that the fuel is available almost everywhere, and if one has a diesel engine no additional tanks for stove fuel are required.

Bottled-gas stoves are widely used and well liked. Gas is the cleanest fuel and the fastest to use, but the stove installation requires very careful attention and several safety precautions. These include external as well as internal shut-off valves on the fuel line, and having the bottles secured in a well-ventilated deck box which has no opening into the hull. It is also important that the fuel-line run should be external, entering the hull as close to the stove as possible. At the point of entry, an external shut-off valve must be installed, in addition to the one on the bottle. This insures that any rupture in the fuel line from the bottle to the valve will be outside and will not present an explosion hazard. On one of my father's vessels (in the late 1920's), we used acetylene gas which we generated on board—even our lights were "gas" lights. However, we children were never allowed to light the lamps or to tinker with any part of the system.

Many of the bottled-gas stoves used today are manufactured by marine stove companies; however, those manufactured for the trailer industry and, with slight modification, some designed for homes, are also used. These have the advantage of variety in sizes and colors, and some offer ovens with rotisseries and broilers. They are less expensive than those designed for marine use, but they are not constructed to withstand the corrosion of the marine environment. In most areas, bottled gas is available. However, if small bottles are being used, there may be difficulty in having them refilled in areas where the filling is done by gravity from a larger bottle. Some proprietors are reluctant to fill small bottles because the large bottle is never completely emptied by gravity and he must return partially full bottles to his supplier, thereby losing money.

Occasionally one sees an electric stove aboard a sailing vessel. This requires that the vessel have a generating capacity of at least 3,000 watts. An electric stove consumes more fuel than, say, a diesel stove and adds another engine to be maintained. The maintenance of complex electrical equipment in a salty environment requires a talented mechanic rather than the jack-of-all-trades handyman that most seamen become. However, who can deny the convenience of a microwave oven, with no open flame and of consistent, repetitive heat produced by an electric stove? At this point, we might add that the generator supplying the stove is usually called upon to provide power for several other pieces of equipment such as lighting, electric coffee pots, toasters, fryers, dishwashers, washing machines, dryers, hot water heaters, refrigerators, ice makers—each, perhaps, desirable in its own right, but further enlarging the possibility of generator failure and a forced change to another method of cooking.

Charcoal is so expensive (and inefficient) that it is rarely used on the wandering cruiser except under the same circumstances as on shore—for the occasional barbecue or cook-out.

HEAT AND HEATERS

Many newcomers to permanent cruising and living aboard must occasionally wonder what's so great about the life when they find themselves cold, wet and just plain miserable, either underway or at anchor. If they are moving southward early in the autumn, extra clothing often suffices for warmth, but since most vessels are not equipped with adequate heaters except at dockside where 110-volt current is available, *real* comfort is usually lacking.

The days of sailing in unheated foc'sles when a change of clothes was to something "less wet," and foul-weather gear was oilskins (oiled linen for the affluent; oiled canvas for the ordinary seaman), which had to be treated frequently in order to retain any semblance of "waterproofing," is not so far in the past—actually a mere 30 years. Perhaps the only pleasure of sailing in steam vessels during the period of World War II was the steam-heated foc'sle, a fiddley to dry one's clothes on and a warm wheelhouse in which to steer. Yachts in those days had heat, not necessarily in the crew's quarters but certainly for the owner and his guests; today, the majority of owners seem content to live like foc'sle hands.

One of my own requirements for living aboard is that I can stay warm and keep the interior of the vessel dry regardless of where I cruise. I am not suggesting a return to coal and/or wood stoves for cooking (in spite of their virtues), but I can say that our diesel stove, even in the tropics, is not uncomfortable. Even a good galley stove on a large vessel is not capable of heating the whole vessel by convection alone. If it were, it would make the life of the cook unbearable. Thus we must rely on space heaters. Every proper seagoing heater has three common features: first, it can be securely fastened by bolts and/or turnbuckles to the cabin sole or bulkhead; second, it has a vented flue (smokestack) to a proper smokehead that prevents both down-drafts and turbulent air from affecting the flame; and third, its fire door faces forward or aft or, in the case of liquid fuel, the major axis of the tank is fore and aft.

Since heat rises, the lower the heater is located the better it will heat the space. Unless a specially insulated back is fitted, care must be taken in siting the heater and the stack, which should be clear of joiner work and fitted with a proper wet or dry deck iron. Perhaps the reason so few vessels are fitted with vented stoves is not only the permanent loss of cabin space but also, more importantly, the difficulty of locating the smokehead where it is high enough to achieve the proper stack draft yet cannot be immersed by a sea or fouled by any of the vessel's working gear.

While I have been shipmates with liquid-fuel heaters (kerosene, diesel and bunker oils) and have not found them wanting, my preference is for solid fuels (wood, coal and, possibly, charcoal), as the latent heat of their embers makes them efficient at drying out a vessel. Often these heaters are of cast iron—some are even firebrick-lined—and, while this increases their heating efficiency, it also makes them heavy to the point that many small vessels would find the weight intolerable, and so they must turn to the lighter, sheet-metal type.

Fuel for any heater is always an "extra" to carry, even when the same fuel is used for the cooking stove. Finding room for this additional fuel presents a problem, regardless of the vessel's size. Perhaps some of the reasons solid fuels are so often chosen are that a smaller amount by weight (but not volume) can be carried; they are readily available, and are often cheaper per BTU, than are liquids. However, they *are* dirty.

Island cruising usually turns up an abundant supply of wood. Many people use driftwood, but, because of its salt content, it corrodes gratings and should be avoided in cabin heaters. Dead wood found away from the water's edge makes good firewood, unless it is from one of the poisonous varieties of trees!

In many areas of the world, charcoal is available and inexpensive. It does provide great heat. The carbon value ranges from about 100 percent for sugar charcoal to about 10 percent for bone charcoal. Absent is the roaring flame of wood, but charcoal does not burn up as rapidly as wood or produce as much ash or smoke. Briquettes sold in the United States are expensive and of lesser carbon content than many South American charcoals.

Coal, when available, is to be preferred—but not just *any* coal. The best, without doubt, is anthracite, although it is usually difficult to find. Anthracite coal is almost smokeless, produces little or no soot and only a small amount of ash, something much appreciated by all hands.

Coal is classified by rank, which is based on the geological age of the deposit as indicated by the percentage of carbon, volatile matter and heat content in BTU's (British Thermal Units) per pound.

Rank	% Fixed Carbon	% Volatile Matter	Average BTU
Lignite (brown coal)	—	—	7,000
Sub-Bituminous	—	—	10,000
High Volatile Bituminous	69 or less	31 or more	12,000
Medium Volatile Bituminous	69–78	22–31	*
Low Volatile Bituminous	78–86	14–22	*
Anthracite	86 or more	14 or less	*

* Classified by fixed carbon. The higher the carbon, the greater the BTU value.

The volatile matter of coal is composed of the coal molecules that are converted to gas or liquid when the coal is heated; the greater the percentage of volatile matter, the smaller the percentage of heat-producing fuel. Also, low-grade coal containing too much volatile matter *can* cause stack fires and *does* cause soot accumulation which will eventually plug up the stack. Furthermore, some of the volatile elements are very corrosive and will, for example, attack Dacron and nylon as well as the heater itself.

In 1976 I purchased anthracite in 12-pound bags at 75¢ per bag. This is convenient both for stowage and use. In freezing weather, consumption is about one bag per day to maintain a 75° temperature below decks. It is convenient both for stowage and use.

What about nonvented heat? All heat, with the exception of electric heat, consumes oxygen. If oxygen is restricted, then carbon monoxide forms. As little as .00001 percent of carbon monoxide in the air may produce symptoms of poisoning, and as little as .002 percent breathed for 30 minutes may prove fatal. Carbon dioxide, which can cause suffocation if inhaled in large amounts, may also accumulate in an unvented space. Therefore, the heater space must be well ventilated and, as a necessary corollary, a large heating unit is required to achieve the desired warmth.

Stowage of any type of solid fuel should be in a dry, well-ventilated compartment because all are subject to spontaneous combustion. Coal and charcoal should be stored in metal-lined containers. The preferred area of storage would be on deck; the least preferred area would be the bilge or engine compartment. Split logs are bulky for storing, especially in short lengths. The advantage of three- to four-foot lengths is that a bundle of them can be lashed on deck, covered with a tarp, and left there to be sawed when needed.

I know of no area in the world where heat is not needed at some time. June nights, in the Atlantic south of Cape Hatteras, are sufficiently cold to require heavy jackets on deck and heat below. Plan for and lay out a place for your heater at the building stage of your vessel!

REFRIGERATION

Those new to living aboard and cruising are usually so accustomed to refrigeration that it never occurs to them they *could* do without it. A vessel cruising the Intracoastal Waterway has two choices—to tie up to a marina dock every night or anchor out. In either case the engine will be in use enough to operate almost any type of mechanical refrigerator at an insignificant cost per day. If shoreside electricity is available, many mechanical refrigeration units have an alternate 110-volt capability which is little bother and requires no fuel. However, if one departs from the U.S. mainland and cruises the Bahamas, Caribbean, South Pacific, etc., he will find marinas not only scarce, but usually nonexistent, and even when available, almost prohibitive in cost. They are not just a day apart, but weeks or even months apart, so refrigeration requires the use of an engine, bottled gas or kerosene for hours per day. Now, "hours" for good installations is usually two hours in the semitropics, and three hours in the tropics; some of the less efficient installations use *double* that amount of time, and that is not an exaggeration!

Sometimes a freezer unit is also used, but this changes nothing other than making it possible to spill over some cold from freezer to refrigerator, thus achieving two or three extra days of refrigeration without starting the engine. This, of course, prevents anything from staying frozen. Most of the time, owners of mechanical refrigerators and freezers blithely assume *no* mechanical breakdowns will occur. We've heard of cases where as much as 500 pounds of frozen food was lost and everything refrigerated was spoiled. So, however reluctantly, one must consider refrigeration as a chancy luxury that is expensive to operate while cruising in remote areas. The best installation I've seen (1976), running two hours per day, with four to six persons aboard, works out to two gallons of diesel fuel @ .85¢ per gallon; two hours on the engine at 12½¢ per hour for lube oil and depreciation, or $1.95 per day or $511.75 per year. If one depends on marinas, then for a 40-foot vessel, the cost of being at a dock averages out to $12.00 per day or $4,380 per year. The rationale for this expense is, "Well, I also get electric lights and showers, eliminate the need for anchor lights, and have the convenience of working ashore." All this means that refrigeration depends not only on first cost but also on maintenance, operating costs and one's budget.

The alternative to refrigeration is the ice chest. The most efficient will have a glass of ice left from a 50-pound block at the end of 15 days. The average cost in the United States is about 4 cents per pound, or, say, 40 cents a day. If the ice is in a separate container from the food, the ice water can be used for ice tea, drink mixes, etc. The ice box takes about five days to warm up after the last ice is gone. But before you say, "Oh, that's the way to go," let's depart from the United States. In the Bahamas, for example, you pay 13 cents *per pound* in Nassau for *soft* ice, which lasts only one-third as long as hard ice; 12 cents per pound in Staniel Cay for excellent hard ice, and 14 cents per pound in Georgetown (Exumas) for soft ice. And, we have been to places during our cruising where it was five cents a cube!

I am constantly asked about kerosene refrigerators. I have used them on several vessels and have made conversions for several others. Here is how to get a standard kerosene unit and convert it to a marine unit.

The refrigerator may be purchased from the Instamatic Corporation of Elkhart, Indiana. The model number is 154, which measures 26.37″ x 53″ x 28″. Under no circumstances should you tell the company that you want the refrigerator for installation on a boat; if you do, they will not sell it to you! The unit is not sold for marine use because it will "catch fire," "explode," and do other things that give manufacturers nightmares.

Conversion is fairly simple in that all the controls and the burner unit are retained, but the burner itself must be cut out of its container and reinstalled in a 3″ x 3″ x 3″ stainless steel box that is fitted with baffles and stuffed with stainless steel wool. The intake spout to this box must not be over 5/16 inches above the bottom of the box. To it is welded a coupling into which is fixed a flexible neoprene high-pressure hose that leads to a service tank of not more than two-gallon capacity. The outlet from the service tank is on the bottom of the tank. It is a gravity feed, and does not have any venting holes; it must be absolutely airtight.

The principle is that the wicking of the burner absorbs the kerosene, causing the level of kerosene in the tank to lower below the spout, thus allowing more kerosene to escape from the service tank after the air bubble goes up to replace the liquid. As soon as the air bubble rises above the bottom of the spout, it shuts off the kerosene; the same principle is used in a chicken feeder or office water cooler. As mentioned, the small box has a baffle in it, and this goes down to within 1/16 inches of the bottom. This arrangement prevents the kerosene from having any free surface-effect, or sloshing. The whole unit, other than the service tank, is then *reinstalled* in the original container because that has the control knob for the wick and a mirror to adjust the flame, as well as guide rollers to remove the burner unit.

Such an installation is good for angles of heel up to about 30° maximum, at which point the flame will no longer enter the flue of the refrigerator. However, in most ocean cruising, the majority of sailing is done at less than 30° angle of heel—in fact, normally about 20° or less—so the unit, by and large, can function at any time.

It's worth remembering that many items used by cruising sailors may not be suitable for the average sailor who is not perhaps as handy and does not live aboard his boat. Unless the vessel is to be used for extensive ocean cruising where the kerosene refrigerator can be kept in operation all the time and be *watched,* I would not recommend it.

Such a unit is used generally by people who either have no engine or very limited horsepower, and have no batteries or generator (hand-starting engine), so this is the only alternative. However, for the "average" yachtsman with ample horsepower and electricity, the built-in cold plate would be safer. On vessels without electricity, i.e., only starting batteries, but ample engine power, a compressor-brine type of system running off the main engine would also be good.

Until such time as solar energy can be used, I believe the ice chest is the best choice for refrigeration, but better yet is to use no refrigeration at all. The majority of sailors take the attitude, "When ice or refrigeration is convenient, we will use it; otherwise, we will do without." For those who can stick to this rule, life is certainly less complex. There are ways to make lack of refrigeration seem less drastic. For example, soft drinks and beer can be kept in the bilge where it is usually 10° to 20° cooler than on deck. (An *olla* jar or jugs wrapped in towels soaked in sea water will serve the same purpose, although not as efficiently.) Ice chests, opened at night and closed at dawn, will probably remain 30° cooler than if opened during the midday sun. Ice chests and top-opening mechanical refrigerators are excellent for dry storage of foods.

It's not really practical to save leftovers in a refrigerator or ice chest in the tropics as they will spoil from one day to the next. If there *are* leftovers, they should be put in a pressure cooker and brought up to heat and left with the top screwed on until the next batch is added, when the process is repeated. After a few days there will be enough for a meal, affectionately known as "garbage stew." Every edible scrap is added— salad included. At worst, it's very good and, at best, it is a blend of flavors that a cordon bleu chef would praise.

Most of the time, vegetables and fruits can be purchased daily or weekly so do not need refrigeration. In the case of meat and poultry, they should be consumed the same day if fresh, or can be thawed overnight, if frozen. Remote cruising is quite similar to life in the United States about 75 years ago, when frequent shopping was a regular routine. Although sometimes frustrating, it is a pleasant job for those cruising: What better way to meet the people, learn the language, and really see the area you are cruising?

LIGHTS

Few cruising vessels can afford the luxury of using only electric lights as the cost is prohibitive, and few use kerosene lights only because of their inconvenience. Most people use a combination of both, blending the convenience of electric lights with the simplicity and minimum expense of kerosene lights.

Once again an example illustrates that nothing is free. Let us take a short passage of say, 72 hours, with four persons cruising in mid-winter. We come up with the following averages:

Item	All Electric Lt. hrs.	All Electric amps.	Kerosene/Electric Lt. hrs.	Kerosene/Electric amps.	All Kerosene Lt. hrs.	All Kerosene amps.
Running lights (port, starbd and stern)	108	124	108	—	108	
Compass light	36	9		9		9
						(hot-shot battery (dry cell) is usually used for the compass. Kerosene-lit compass is quite rare now.)
Galley lights	8	16		16	8	
Saloon lights	18	38	28		28	
W. C. lights	6	6		6		
Berth lights	30	39		18		
Misc. & Chart lights, etc.	8	8	8	3	8	
TOTAL	214	240	144	52	152	9
Amp. hours		240	144			9
Battery charging time—40 amps. per hour		6 hours	1 hr. 18 min.			13 min.
Fuel req. @ 85¢ per gal. per hour (no deprec. or lube)		$5.10	$1.11			$0.18
Cost of kerosene @ 40¢ per gal. for 130 light hrs. . . .		—	.44			.47
Cost of lighting		$5.10	$1.55			$0.65

Without question, kerosene is the least expensive source of light, but it is somewhat limiting. Unless one is engineless or totally without electricity (hand-starting engine only), there are no reasons why you shouldn't have the advantage of using *some* electric lights, especially if the engine can be only started electrically. We have only a hand-starting engine and we find that our electrical requirements average about eight amps. Thus, about every fortnight, we charge the battery; sometimes this can be accomplished by motorsailing.

The convenience of instant (electric) light is unchallenged, especially over the chart table, in the galley and for the berths. The most frequent need for electricity is for running lights at those times when there is going to be only an hour or so of running in darkness. If kerosene running lights are used, it takes about 20 minutes to light and hang them, always provided they were cleaned, fueled and trimmed after the last use. For this reason, a dual running-light system is often used aboard cruising vessels —kerosene for long periods of usage; electricity for short periods.

Kerosene lights are expensive. The best light is produced by the round, circular wicks. The lights are large and give off a good deal of heat, which is easily dissipated when a breeze is blowing but quite uncomfortable on a still summer night. The bulkhead-mounting type must be double-gimballed and have a smoke bell. The open arrangements so common in today's interiors permit a minimum of bulkhead-mounted lamps, so the hanging type is often a better choice.

Candle lamps give off about as much light as the average small bulkhead kerosene lamp and use odorless sperm oil candles—now becoming difficult to obtain. Regular nontapered candles might be an acceptable substitute, but I have never tried them.

Fluorescent lights are the most economical for the amount of light they produce. Great care must be exercised in their purchase as some emit a noise that is not only audible but interferes with radio reception.

Finally, since, when cruising, 9 P.M. is way past bedtime and 5:30 A.M. brings coffee, lights are really not needed very much.

MISCELLANEOUS EQUIPMENT

There is enough Scotch in me—without drinking—to make me thrifty and abide by the old adage "Waste not, want not." Thus, when the time arrived that I had provided *K'ung Fu-tse* with all the necessary equipment and we looked around for items that enhance life afloat and lengthen the time we can remain away from sources of supply, we shopped carefully for each item. Here are some of them.

GRINDERS

The first item which came to mind was a grain grinder (flour mill). The one we have owned for years is the type used by French peasants— *petit broyeur a grains*—and was highly recommended to us by Peter

Tangvald. While I am more than satisfied with this French grinder, Jean likes the Corona Corn Mill she bought from a company in Medellin, Colombia, S.A. The French mill has two milling stones while the Corona has two milling plates. There are several mills made in the United States which have come to my attention, such as the Quaker City hand grain grinder. Like the French and Corona mills, this one produces flour directly in one grinding. The large size of the Bell Mill is reported to be excellent. As you know, refined flour is prone to weevils, and while I doubt that the addition of such protein is harmful, many object to it. Whole grain is easy to store in comparison with processed flour, and furthermore contains no additives. Grains which can be ground are corn, wheat, barley, rice and soy beans.

SEWING MACHINES

Sewing is a sailor's art. Over the years, I have hand-sewn not only sails but also clothes and shoes. Nothing really wears out on a boat—it just becomes something else. Thus, when their knees wear out, dungarees become shorts; shorts become bathing suits and so on. There is nothing like a pair of pants or shorts made from 13-ounce Vivatex—they're almost impossible to wear out. Hand-sewing, of course, is slow compared to machine-sewing. There are many electric sewing machines on the market; however, light-duty machines are not suitable for the fabric weights used aboard cruising vessels. On the other hand, hand-operated and foot-treadle machines are suitable, although the latter are usually too cumbersome to stow aboard most vessels.

The Singer Company makes a hand-operated sewing machine that can still be found in many parts of the world. This máchine is suitable for sewing new sails, awnings, dodgers, and doing other heavy work, provided the material used does not exceed 20 ounces to the yard. The only hand-operated machines I have seen in the United States lately have been sold as antiques, but usually are still serviceable.

In Europe, there is still a demand for hand-operated machines. The *Modele Portatif OMNIA a Commande a la Main* from MANUFRANCE is excellent. Parts are easy to obtain, and repairs are not difficult to make. If you order one from MANUFRANCE and your French is less than perfect, have someone write the order for you in French; it saves a lot of time and trouble.

We have aboard an excellent hand-operated "Sailmaker" sewing machine which we purchased from J. J. & J. Read (Sewing Machines) Ltd., Southampton, England.

SPROUTING—SALTING—ETC.

There are two things I miss on an ocean passage: fresh salads and ice cream. The latter I have learned to do without, but we have found a substitute for the former by sprouting our own seeds. I remember that Chinese cooks aboard various vessels or which I have sailed had their own bean-sprouting gardens in the pantry or lazarette, but few of us ever ate them. With age comes understanding if not wisdom, so now the Colvins enjoy a variety of fresh food while at sea. With careful tending, a continuous supply is available, each tray producing a crop every day. Because of the different sprouting times, it is best to have about six trays for a family of five, with several different varieties in each tray. Sprouts such as radish, alfalfa, soy bean, mung bean, garbanzo, mustard, cress, rice, wheat, bamboo, flax and lentil are all good.

A steady diet of canned food makes one crave more flavor, and for me, at least, this means the food must be highly seasoned. I enjoy Tabasco sauce and seasoned pepper in particular. We frequently can our own food, which is superior to what can be purchased, especially meats. We do our canning when we can get a good supply direct from a farmer. A word of caution—canning is not a spare-time job. We feel that putting up less than two or three dozen cans at a cooking, or less than 50 pounds of meat at a time, is not worth the effort. I grew up on salted meat and fish, but my family doesn't like it, so the old harness cask is now filled with coal in our living room and remains ashore. But for those who enjoy it, six weeks in brine can soften the rump of a most ancient steer to calflike tenderness.

Everyone who served in the armed forces in World War II remembers powdered eggs, usually with a lump in his throat. However, you may be pleased to learn that a new type is excellent, and I defy anyone to note a difference between them and eggs from the shell—except that they can't be cooked sunny-side up. Jean discovered them about six years ago and we have used them ever since, sometimes even ashore. They are canned by the Nutri-Egg Company, Sleep Eye, Minnesota. We have opened three-year-old cans and found them unspoiled.

Only too often, cooking aboard a vessel involves using a large number of cast-offs from the house ashore. Like others, we have tried all kinds of utensils. Jean prefers her old Revereware to the newer stainless steel pots and pans because hers are of lighter weight. I guess this preference is shared by our three children, each of whom can prepare a complete dinner without assistance from us. I still have a fondness for cast-iron skillets, in spite of having been told by various cookware salesmen that I am always eating a little of each meal that has ever been cooked in them. I call it seasoning—they call it sure death!

TANKS

If fuel is carried in more than one tank, the tanks should not be cross-connected so as to equalize the load, and both tanks should not be used at one time. There must be at least two large filters in the fuel line *before* the filter on the engine. If the engine is supplied by a day tank, then there should be an additional pair of filters between the main tank and the day tank. The day tank should also be fitted with a sump which can be drained. If large fuel capacity is needed, it is advisable to achieve this with several tanks.

Water, unlike fuel, *must* be in several tanks, even on the smallest of vessels, and they should not be cross-connected except through a manifold. The whole system should be connected through a double-locking valve to a bilge pump so that one or all tanks can be emptied and flushed without too much effort in case of contamination. Be sure to bolt the handles of the cross-over valves with a bar so as to prevent accidental opening.

A good rule of thumb for any tank size would be .02 x displacement of the vessel as the maximum weight of liquid in any one tank. Thus, for a 25,000 pound vessel, the maximum weight for a tank would be 500 pounds, e.g., about 60 gallons of water or 70 gallons of fuel. Tanks should be designed to be narrow athwartship, with capacity gained through length and/or height. This is desirable because of the free-surface effect of all liquids. Many believe that fuel and water form ballast. This is true only if the tanks are pressed full. The precise effect of liquids in motion within tanks is as follows: They cause a rise in the vertical center of gravity of the vessel equal to the amount of inertia of the free surface, times the weight per cubic foot of the liquid contained, divided by the displacement of the vessel in pounds. Therefore, with two tanks of the same capacity, the wider tank will have the greater surface—thus the greater moment of inertia and the most reduction in the stability of the vessel. In extreme cases, free surface has been known so severely to alter the stability of the vessel as to cause it to capsize. To prevent a sharp list as tanks are emptied, it is common to have a port water tank opposed by a starboard fuel tank. This is not a perfect plan, to be sure, but so long as the tanks are of moderate capacity for the size of the vessel, there is seldom more than perhaps 2° list, and that only for short periods of time.

THE PILOTHOUSE

Upon the great oceans of the world which are traversed by sailing vessels, one is witness to spectacular sunrises, sunsets, clear starlight, moonlit nights, gentle breezes—all very poetic. But, one also experiences scorching sun, bone-chilling cold, rain- and snowstorms, squalls and gales. Bliss and misery are often only hours apart. Yet we must endure all of this and persevere despite it if we wish to accomplish our primary aim of sailing from one place to another. At bad moments I have often wondered if it was worth the effort.

A few years ago, I thought it perfectly natural to place a pilothouse aboard a trawler, freighter or tanker. Although I do not design motor-boats, I suppose I would also concede them pilothouses if I thought about it. There was the so-called motorsailer which had a pilothouse, deck saloon, or "something" up there. This type of vessel is rated by its ability to sail versus its ability to use power, which I have never fully under-stood, such as 60–40 (60 percent power, 40 percent sail), 50–50, or 40–60, etc. My preference was always 100 percent sail, and if I wanted an engine, one was put in. If one wanted to go fast under power, then put a bigger engine in. The engine was an entirely separate entity—a nuisance!

Oh, well, I have an engine in *K'ung Fu-tse*—20 horsepower—and it does everything it is supposed to do—turns the propeller, uses fuel and

PHOTO 2-1. A quartering view of *Kung Fu-tse*'s stern, showing how the new pilot house blends into the stern. Note the after windows which look right down off the stern. These can be seen in other photos of the pilot house interior.

lube oil, and occupies a space that would have been a small cargo hold. It is convenient; it more than satisfies my requirements, and I have enjoyed using it. But, this does not make *K'ung Fu-tse* a motorsailer.

Now, everyone "knows," especially *I* know, that sailing vessels may have awnings but not a pilothouse. Well, sir, in vessels that went to sea professionally, comfort for the crew didn't make money. The reasoning was that anyone could stand a two-hour trick at the wheel in any weather —even six hours if necessary. After all, that was one of the things the crew was paid to do. Today, we go to sea for pleasure, so if we are to have our pleasure, why shouldn't we be comfortable? First, a bench built on either side of the wheel permitted us to sit rather than stand; and then an awning overhead kept the noonday sun from baking us and also kept off some of the rain and snow. That was quite a bit of comfort. Even with those improvements there were still things we found irksome.

K'ung Fu-tse has an exceptionally comfortable interior. During the first part of our first voyage, we added a settee in the saloon to replace two chairs, and two settees aft to replace two more chairs. The saloon table

PHOTO 2-2. The new pilot house seems to flow right into the lines of the stern, growing right out of the after trunk cabin, and is not as obtrusive as one would have expected, because of the natural bulk of junk design. The rising sheer aft resulted in a pilot house whose windows have excellent visibility in all directions.

which could seat 12 comfortably for a sit-down dinner was altered to seat six. We added a writing desk in the aft cabin. In short, we had plenty of space and lounging area below. However, Jean and I enjoy having our morning coffee, reading and lounging, on the aft deck on the benches that flank the wheel. There, we get a fine view of the anchorage and usually a nice breeze. This area was denied us, however, in rain, snow, fog, strong winds (either hot or cold) or when the bugs began to fly. We accepted these inconveniences when sailing. We did think of drop curtains, port awnings, etc., but not seriously.

Then one day at sea, after spending most of it at the wheel in oil-skins, I crossed tacks with a Baltic trader. As we passed, the helmsman lowered the window of his *pilothouse* and gave me a cheery wave. As I waved back, rain water ran down inside my sleeve. I noted the shriveled skin on my hands from many hours of being wet, and said to myself, "Next year *I* will wave back from a pilothouse!"

The pilothouse became my obsession. No, I did not go back to the drawing board. Instead, I got oars, boathooks, boards, sticks, marline,

PHOTO 2-3. A view of the pilot house interior, showing the small settees to port and starboard of the jigger mast, and flanking the lazarette vent. The seats are also lockers, and there is a deep shelf aft of each back rest. The centerline window is fixed, but the two abaft the settee open. This photo was taken from the starboard forward window.

crates, boxes, buckets and any flotsam I could find, and mocked up a pilothouse. It was not a question of *"Should* I or *Will* I or *Can* I add a pilothouse?" The only question was how large a pilothouse and what would be incorporated into it? Nothing else mattered; the pilothouse would be added—period. Furthermore (and by now I was adamant) I would have openings with screens, seat cushions, backrests, lockers, a place for my radios, jump seats, a coffee table, doors to port and starboard, etc. This was going to be an all-weather, all-purpose "house" on top of my vessel, and she would just have to accept it.

Soon, several things became apparent. There would have to be other changes. The main boom interfered with the proposed pilothouse, so it would have to go. This did pose a minor problem since I had not blessed the *K'ung Fu-tse* with excess sail. On the other hand, I did not like the 29-foot boom and the five to eight minutes it took to raise the 800-pound mainsail, or the fact that the mainmast was tabernacle-mounted. So the simple solution was to remove the mast altogether and move it forward, pierce the cabin top, and build a mast step on the keel. If I was going to do that, I reasoned, why not lengthen the mast, thus giving more luff, and

PHOTO 2-4. The pilot house has a clear passage across it from port to starboard, to facilitate working the vessel's decks without having to negotiate "roadblocks."

shorten the boom, thus reducing the *weight* of the sail to 400 pounds, without reducing the *area?* This plan left a nice big gap between the main and the mizzen—plenty of room for the pilothouse. The appearance of the hull suffered marginally, but since the rig could use more sail area anyway, why not add a *fourth* mast right through the big deck box I had built when in the islands? The mast would then clear the deck, and its gallows frame could be mounted on top of the pilothouse. The solution was simple. The pilothouse solved all kinds of problems without creating any new ones.

I don't want to run this into a shaggy dog story, so it must suffice to say that the changes in the rig, thanks to the added pilothouse, improved what was already an excellent ocean-cruising vessel; the added sail area improved light-weather performance, and the increased luff added more driving power, especially in short, steep seas.

Well, what has this to do with the interior? The new pilothouse is eight feet wide by eight feet seven inches long, with full headroom forward of the wheel. The cushioned seats and backrest, to port and starboard of the wheel, are atop a locker, and four can sit comfortably on these seats. Behind the seats, running full-width, is one shelf, and at the

PHOTO 2-5. In the pilot house the typing table creates a really comfortable corner in port, but is never used at sea.

after end of the house; another shelf, where I keep my Zenith radio, is recessed between two opening screened windows. Below this shelf, the after end of the pilothouse has five windows, four of which open, but are not screened. On the overhead is sited the AM and VHF radios, along with the switch for the electric running lights (not for ocean passages) and the switch for the compressed-air foghorn. Aft of the jigger mast is a fiddled coffee table. The forward corners of the pilothouse contain jump seats with cushions, each of which comfortably seats one, or two very friendly people. The door sills, port and starboard, are extra wide and provide comfortable seating. The *piece d'resistance* is a portable typing or writing table. One end hangs from the overhead and the other end is pinned between the jambs of the starboard door. It gets continuous use in port, especially for breakfast, family hour, visiting friends, etc., but is never used at sea. We have added, in reality, another nine linear feet of living space. There are eight opening and screened windows, four un-screened windows, two fixed windows, and two doors—making our pilot-house practically a solarium. Hot or cold, rain or shine, it is a comfortable addition. The visibility is excellent at anchor, under power or under sail.

The pilothouse serves as coffee house in the morning, tea house in the afternoon and, when the sun is over the yardarm, as grog shop; but, at sea, it is a pure pilothouse that has quadrupled our comfort and pleasure under way. Had it stopped here on *K'ung Fu-tse,* one might rightly conclude that it was okay for a junk or okay for a heavy 48-foot vessel. You know, "If my boat were as large as yours . . ." or, "If my boat were as small as yours . . ." or "If I only had your draft . . . I could do what you did." Not so. Several people who have seen our pilothouse are now alter-ing their vessels to add one. Several of these vessels are only 34 feet on deck. To be sure, not all the pilothouses will be as large or sumptuous as ours, but I feel certain that if all of them provide even a fraction of the benefits we have, the owners will conclude that they were well worth the effort.

NOTES

ENGINEERING FOR HUMAN DIMENSIONS

Berths: Six feet two inches to six feet six inches long; 21–28 inches wide. Foc'sle Vee berths, because of length to centerline, are often close to seven feet long, yet occupy only six feet three inches or six feet four inches of fore-and-aft space. Cold climates require a width of 22 or even

24 inches to accommodate bedding. Double berths are great in port but not at sea. Space between upper and lower berths should not be less than 19 inches and 21–22 inches is better. Athwartship berths are bad. Mattresses should not be a tight fit—about one inch less in length and width than the berth to provide space for sheets and blankets.

Seats: Width 16 inches minimum; 18 inches maximum; a minimum of 12 inches above the cabin sole—16 or 17 inches is best; three feet three inches is minimum headroom above a seat; 42 inches is better. A sitting person requires 23 or 24 inches of frontage. At table, hearty eaters often require more. Space between seats should be 22–24 inches; if seats face each other, 30 inches is about minimum. The higher the seat, the less foot space is required. Sitting and sleeping space are more important than standing space.

Never pinch dimensions. Allow at least one inch for thickness of bulkhead.

Galley: Solid fuel stoves require at least two inches more clearance all around than catalogue dimensions. If there is full headroom, the stove top should be a minimum of 30–38 inches above the cabin sole, for the comfort of the cook. Thirty-five to 36 inches is about right for people five feet eight inches to six feet tall. Over the stove, 15 inches is the minimum clearance needed. A gimballed stove requires lead weights in its base to make it usable in seaway—4 pounds per burner, approximately. Some additional detachable weights are required when double boilers are used and pot height increases.

Stow pans under a kerosene stove, coal and wood under solid fuel stove. Chimney on stove must be well clear of galley woodwork and sited not to foul anything on deck. Stove pipe should be about six feet long for a good draft.

Icebox top opening should be 12″ × 15″ × 15″ minimum. Insulation; three inches for sides and top, and six inches for bottom.

Sink—10″ × 10″ × 6″ deep minimum (plates are usually 9-9½ inches diameter. *Sink height* 36 inches is standard. Best criterion is hand touching bottom of sink without stooping.

Lockers—40 inches high, 17 inches wide or deep.

Tables—24″ × 18″ per person is ideal (22″ × 12″ minimum); 29 to 30 inches above cabin sole is average height; *always* 12 inches above seats. Height of fiddles—two and one half inches maximum, 1½ inches minimum.

Work tables—36 inches above sole; 16″ × 20″ surface, minimum.

Dressers—40 inches above sole; 12″ wide × 17″ deep minimum.

Cupboards: Clearance between upper and lower cupboards in galley—15 inches lower counter × 21 inches wide; upper lockers 11 inches wide.

Dishes should be measured beforehand for a cruising vessel: 10½″ × 10½″ × 10″ is minimum stowage of place setting for six, minus cups, but including silverware drawer.

Water Closets: Can go up side of hull somewhat (raised sole), but still require 15″ × 18″ space for bowl and pump. A man requires 17 inches width (clear) to sit on seat; a woman 19 inches. Be careful about location: fore and aft or athwartships? Is bucket simpler? Sanitary bucket? Holding tanks? Headroom over toilet: 42 inches is best. (Men go to lee rigging half the time.)

Drawers, in general—9 inches deep maximum; 18 inches × 28 inches maximum practical size. Heavily loaded ones can be roller mounted if they open fore or aft.

Stairs: Two times rise + tread = 24 inches, nine inches rise is a comfortable step up.

Ladders: 16 inches total width minimum; pitch of 15° very steep; 30° comfortable; watch headroom. Athwartship ladders bad, unless semi-circular.

Companionway: 18″ × 24″ long minimum; my normal is 21–22 inches × 24 inches long. Sills on companionway must be higher than bulwarks and/or cockpit coamings. *Cockpit scuppers* should have one inch diameter drain per cubic feet of volume. *Deck lockers* leading below hull must have positive battening arrangement.

Compass base. Locate about 27 inches above cockpit for wheel steering; one inch to three inches less for tiller; check heights with mock-up before construction of pedestal.

Spreader lights are dangerous and not really necessary. Paint the decks white and there will be sufficient light to see them, even on the darkest nights. Wear sunglasses for glare in daytime. White decks produce less glare than the sea, and are cool in tropics.

Hatches: 18″ × 18″ minimum; 20″ × 20″, or 22″ × 22″ are better.

Walkway between cabin and deck edge, 12 inches minimum; 19 inches, ocean cruising minimum; 24–27 inches or even more is desirable if possible.

Lifelines, 27 inches minimum; 30 inches desirable for ocean cruising; 36 inches or more if possible. Always double lifelines; use fish net to keep children aboard.

Rope and chain—Allow five cubic feet, more in cruisers. Stow rope and chain in separate lockers. Chain—30 fath.; 45 fath.; and 15 fath. Rope—use six fathoms of chain with anchor.

Clearance in passageways—at shoulder height to 22–30 inches; at waist height, 19 inches minimum.

3

A Sailor's Life

DISCIPLINE/ROUTINE

For the blue-water cruising vessel no formal regulations regarding discipline have been established. Either Navy or Merchant Marine customs are frequently observed, depending on the background of the owner/master. The ability to navigate is easy to come by; seamanship is a matter of experience and judgment; but full command is not possible without, first, self-discipline and, second, complete command over the crew so that orders are carried out faithfully and cheerfully.

Today, with almost everyone feeling he must always "do his own thing," and that everyone is equal, sailing often becomes chaotic. What should be a pleasant voyage turns into confusion, extra work and uncertainty. This is sometimes the case with family or husband/wife crews. It's often said, "There is, and can be, only one master on a vessel; only one who can legally take the blame; only one who can make the final correct or incorrect decision. Going to sea is not democratic."

I have always found that by doing one's "share" and a little bit more, responding promptly to all commands, and doing so courteously, the natural result is less apparent discipline and a happier ship.

Everyone in the crew should be responsible for some department. With small crews, of course, each will have multiple duties. (For example, all standing and running rigging, all lifesaving equipment, the engine room, etc.) Then, if something goes amiss, the master knows whom to seek out, and the excuse "I thought Charlie did it" can never arise. The greater each one's competence, the less burden on the master. I have seen a few blue-water cruising vessels that operate this way: They are immaculate; apparently always ready for sea; and all hands are free to go ashore when port is made. When you see the opposite extreme you wonder how crew and vessel ever made the passage at all.

A few simple rules can make life better for all. On an ocean passage, if it's necessary to tack ship at night, doing so at the change of watch (if more than the watch is needed to tack) is a small kindness both watches will appreciate. The first watch starts at 8 P.M. (2000) of the first day at sea, and is the master's watch. The following watches are set on either the Swedish system or, with larger crews, the American system, using "dog watches." In any case, there should be an odd number—except when there is sufficient crew for three watches. Often on short cruises only hours of darkness are set in watches. The one I have used is 8–12 (2000–2400); 12–3 (0000–0300); 3–5 (0300–0500); 5–7 (0500–0700). Breakfast is at 8 A.M. and the daily routine includes the children's lessons, baking, maintenance, navigation, etc. The children take their daylight trick at the wheel and also stand one of the first two night watches with a parent—the 8–12 watch alternating.

When the ship's bell clock can be heard from the helm, the bell is not struck except on very large vessels. The new watch is given the "good news" (what to expect on deck) 15 minutes before they turn to, and are on deck about five minutes before, at which time they adapt their eyes to darkness, check out weather and wind conditions, how the vessel is steering, and get any other needed information—such as other vessels in sight—that will enable them to assume the watch. At the hour they say, "It is my wheel; you are relieved." The relieved watch then answers "Your course is ————"; and this is answered by "My course is ————."

When the crew is working the deck, any order, such as "Ease the main sheet," should be repeated by whoever is in charge. Repeating indicates that the order is understood. When the task is done, the crew should say, "Main sheet eased." The reply then is, "Very well."

The command, "All hands on deck!" means *now,* not after one dresses, gets into boots, oilskins or whatever, or after a cup of soup. Any slackness here cannot be tolerated, and, needless to say, the command should never be given unless an emergency exists. "All hands, make sail," or "All hands, tack ship," does not allow for stragglers but at least permits one to dress for the weather before going on deck.

When coming about, the command, "Stand by to come about," is repeated by the watch leader as the crew goes to stations. On the command, "Ready about," everyone does his job without repeating. From that moment on, it is incumbent on the person at the wheel (or whoever is in charge of the maneuver) to give progress reports so that the others can judge the rapidity with which they must accomplish their own tasks. These reports, all of which are self-explanatory, are terse: "The wheel is over"; "She's coming up"; "She's through the wind"; "Wheel's amidship"; "Trim your sails." Total concentration on one's own job is possible because, in the mind's eye, everything can be seen in proper sequence. Once the sails are trimmed to the new course and all sheets are coiled, then the word is passed aft, "Sails are trimmed, coiled down, ready to run," to which is answered, "Very well, watch below go below."

All of this may sound pompous, ridiculous or even archaic to many; however, one must admit that there is no ambiguity, no chance for mis-understanding or doubt in this time-honored procedure. The helmsman need not wonder if a command is understood or is being executed, and his attention is not diverted or divided. Imagine working your way amongst coral heads or through a reef entrance and the sheets need to be hardened. Which would you rather do—attend to your piloting or have to check to see if the crew is doing what it was told to do?

I can hear some wives saying, "If he made me do that, I'd kill him." But consider how many times wives are blamed for a mishap because of lack of clarity in the command given. It's worth emphasizing that, unlike on land, at sea one should comply first and question later. The polite way would be to say, "If you are so disposed, perhaps you would be so good as to bow your head to prevent a collision with the main boom." Would anyone disagree that it's better to yell, "Duck!" and save someone a crack on the head? It's at such moments, when the crewman obeys reflexsively, rather than muttering, "Who, me?" that discipline pays off for the crew-man as well as the vessel.

Many singlehanders follow the repeating routine by giving the order aloud and then answering it themselves. I find this no stranger than a landlubber talking to a dog or a cat.

ROUTINE/MAINTENANCE

Cruising is a fine life for those who survive the early adjustment, which requires, contrary to popular belief, a great deal of physical and mental activity.

The number of miles covered annually by cruising vessels depends on so many variables that it's nearly impossible to make reliable estimates, but between 2,000 to 20,000 miles per year covers the range of about 90 percent of the cruising live-aboards. Our own cruising averages about 7,000 miles per year. We find that for each day under way we spend two days at anchor, thus our junk averages about 20 miles per day. On long passages, one accumulates many lay days on mileage alone—i.e., a 1,200 mile passage in nine days yields 60 20-mile days and 51 lay days, obviously not used all at one time—since in any island group, perhaps 50 to 100 anchorages may be visited and the distances sailed between them are but a few miles.

The never-ending maintenance and routine is always a shipmate. This is fortunate for there is seldom time for self-pity or monotony, which is the bane of most lifestyles. This is a list of various "chores" which I consider necessary aboard my own vessel, and the reader can pick out those which he feels apply to his.

Daily: Maintain logbook; wash down decks; make up bunks; cook; wash dishes; clean up below. Miscellaneous odd jobs include: renew whippings, fill salt-water tank (for dishes); check chafing gear, etc., give lessons to children, fill kerosene lights. In addition, at sea: stand watch, do navigation or piloting, check compass via azimuths twice, light running lights, sail vessel. In port: check anchor, light anchor light when required, polish lamps, refill founts and trim wicks.

Weekly: Check all running rigging; wipe off engine and clean bilge under it; bring accounts up to date; check inventory of consumed stores recorded; check lifeboat (dinghy).

Fortnightly: Charge battery; up-date charts; drain fuel filters; add vinegar to toilets (this breaks up accumulated salt and bacteria).

Monthly: Grease steering gear and deck machinery; do general maintenance on outboard; oil all interior woodwork.

Quarterly: Scrub bottom (lightly) if scum or grease is accumulating; check anchor chains, shackles and pins; inspect life jackets; set up standing rigging if necessary; check fire extinguishers.

Semi-Annually: Slush down rigging; overhaul blocks; end-for-end halyards; check engine for proper torque on hand bolts, etc.; clean fuel filters; inspect and repair stove firewalls if required and do whatever other stove maintenance is required; end-for-end anchor chains; clean bilges; paint dinghy exterior if beached frequently; overhaul toilets.

Annually: Paint decks and deckhouses; paint topsides if necsesary; prepare bottom for painting with a good scrubbing if cruising area has been foul; paint bottom; clean chain locker; paint dinghy interior; renew lube and fuel oil filter elements; paint spars; overhaul sails, awnings and dodgers.

Two years: End-for-end all sheets; inflate and repack life raft; overhaul emergency radio, loran, transmitter and other electronic equipment; dismantle and repack propeller (if variable pitch); check all electrical circuits.

Five Years: Pull shaft; flush water tanks; overhaul engine; strip all lockers and re-inventory; paint and varnish interior; sand down all rigging; renew all halyards; regalvanize anchor chain and anchors; renew all window gaskets.

From the above it can be seen that in a year's cruising time one will anchor 75–150 times; change oil in the engine two to four times (every 125 hours of operation); raise sail 300 times; secure to a wharf five times; prepare 1,700 meals (including night lunches); charge battery 25 times; stand 1,800 hours on watch; probably never be sick; have a healthy tan; and read 50 to 100 books.

KNOTS

From the earliest times, blue-water sailors have been accomplished in the arts of knot-tying and splicing. It's often asked, "How many knots and splices does one use?" The answer, of course, is, "As many as one knows *how* to use!" On *K'ung Fu-tse,* perhaps a hundred different hitches, bends, knots and splices have been used during her construction, outfitting, and rigging. Those who have not yet developed a store of knots might consider some of the following:

The *bowline* needs little introduction. It never jams and never slips if properly tied. One could safely say, "If in doubt, tie a bowline." There are several types of bowline other than the common bowline. The *bowline on a bight* has a limited use; however, the *running bowline* (also known as the *French bowline*) is worth mastering because it is the only safe way of working aloft in a seaway since, unlike the bos'n's chair, it is impossible to fall out of this knot even if injured or unconscious.

The *square* or *reef knot* is often used for purposes other than for which it was intended and is not very reliable in these uses unless both ends are seized. Under no circumstances should it be used for bending ropes together for purposes of hauling when a *sheet* or *double sheet bend* would be better.

The *round turn and two half hitches* are frequently used, but the end must be seized if left for any period of time.

The *clove hitch* is an excellent hitch that is often misused. It can jam, which makes it excellent for ratlines or stopping off sails on yards and gaffs. When needing assurance of easy release, a *rolling hitch* should be used.

The *reeving line bend* should be learned by all who work aloft, and it must be taught to those on deck to prevent oddball knots being sent aloft.

The *fisherman's bend* is, of course, used to secure mooring lines to a buoy or a warp to an anchor.

Seizing is often omitted nowadays in favor of heat-shrunk tape or dipping in solution, neither of which works well aloft except under ideal conditions. Since I use deadeyes and lanyards for our shrouds, a *double Matthew Walker* is the traditional three-strand knot for this purpose. I also use it on the ends of all halyards and sheets instead of *seizing,* and the *figure eight* for a stopper since, after reeving, there is always sufficient extra length for shortening the end when freshening the nips is required.

Eye-splicing is a must and is always put in over a thimble, a heart, or a lizard, as well as in mooring lines with an eye of about 30 inches in length. With synthetic lines, I use four, five or six tucks, except in mooring lines where five, six or seven tucks are standard. This allows the ends to be on one side, which not only looks better since it is tapered, but eliminates an abrupt change in line diameter.

The *long splice* is used mostly in sailmaking on bolt ropes, and only under emergency conditions would I use it in running rigging because synthetic line has a tendency to become "long-jawed."

Not so many years ago, when we used chain for jib bridles, as well as on parts of halyards, manila had to be spliced in so it would run through the sheaves without hesitating or jamming. Frequently today one can see a short eye-splice in anchor chain which chafes one strand, or a thimble put in which, while preventing chafe, will not run over the wildcat. The standard chain splice has all three strands bearing and should be used on beckets, on safety nets below bowsprits, over wire or chain, and always when a warp is spliced into an anchor chain.

Baggy wrinkles, in the past, were often made using a *railroad sinnet.* This was easy and quick. In synthetics it is expensive, so sisal or manila would be a better choice. Being inexpensive, they can be discarded after a long passage or removed and stowed after a short one. Very often nowadays they are seen as status symbols on the good vessel *Never Sail.*

If *ratlines* are required, there are several methods of making them. On small vessels, wood rungs are most common; however, tubing and solid, round steel staples are also used—all of which are seized to the shrouds. The old-fashioned rope ratlines are reserved for very large vessels where the weight of a man going aloft will not squeeze the shrouds together; however, even on some larger (over 100 feet) schooners, wood is often used because it is easier on the feet than rope. Steps are used on the masts of many jib-headed vessels to eliminate the necessity of ratlines. Steps lessen windage, maintenance and first cost. However, on the negative side, the difficulty of going aloft on steps in heavy weather, and the impaired visibility when conning shoal waters, seem to favor ratlines. To save weight, one could alternate wood and rope, using, say, one wood and two rope, with 15–16 inches between.

Years ago, *wire splicing* was one of the basic skills of an able seaman.

Splicing 1 × 9 wire is very difficult, but when 7 × 7 wire is used, splicing is easy to do, especially with preformed wire. The use of Nicropress RTM sleeves is not only an acceptable substitute for splicing but also is actually stronger than a splice. Emergency repairs can be made with hand tools through the use of this sleeve, on wire sizes up to ¼ inch. Larger wire sizes require a hydraulic tool to obtain full strength. Many people use wire rope clips for emergency repairs, but they should be used with care or the wire's holding power will be diminished. Also, clips can kink and permanently deform the wire on the U-bolt side of the clip. This is one instance where, on a long voyage, one would, if possible, try to save a shroud or stay by fitting a temporary tackle to replace the wire while it was *long spliced* to a spare piece, or completely replaced. One reason ocean cruisers are often overrigged is to reduce the possibility of such a failure.

Frequently, on small vessels, a single size of wire is used throughout so that the amount of spare wire carried can be limited to the length of the longest shroud or stay.

COMPROMISE

There are words in common usage that should not be used in mixed company, from the pulpit or in the presence of children. There is another word that is used ashore by all manner of lubbers, statesmen, politicians, preachers and others of that ilk, but has no place at sea. The word is "compromise." Compromise may be a way of reconciling different points of view ashore, but it is totally unacceptable as an approach to practical matters at sea.

If a bargain is struck, no compromise is involved because each party to the bargain has a limit: The seller wants a high price but will settle for less; the buyer wants a low price but will pay more. But if the buyer will not pay enough more, or if the seller will not take enough less, there can be no agreement—and no compromise. As soon as the seller and the buyer agree on a price, we can assume that from the beginning each party was prepared to retreat from the first-stated position; therefore, the proper word for this transaction must be "bargain" and not "compromise."

Many people are wont to apply "compromise" to the discussion of the design and construction of vessels. Again the word does not apply. A ketch is *not* a compromise between a schooner and a yawl. Medium draft is *not* a compromise between shoal draft and deep draft. In short, when a mare and a male ass are crossed, there is no compromise—there is a sterile hybrid called a mule!

For a sailor, the decision is that he must always do the best he can with what he has on hand. He must never do less. There can never be a compromise between a good repair and a bad repair. The sailor learns to live with a "temporary" repair until he reaches a port where he can do a proper job. In the Army, this is called "field expediency." It is small wonder that, when ashore, the sailor is confused by the varying shades of "grey" he confronts when his life at sea depends entirely on telling black from white.

Oh, well. I hear many things ashore that make little sense—such as that shore people cannot understand sailors because what the latter say *can't* be true. Sailors may exaggerate a little, but I have yet to meet one who has asked me to believe, as shore people have, that there is such a thing as being "a little bit pregnant."

HEALTH ABOARD

Sickness aboard an ocean cruising vessel is rare, especially after a week at sea. Yet, occasionally a crew will come down with headaches, nausea, abdominal cramps, fever, vomiting and diarrhea—leaving the victims washed out and weak. Unless the vessel has just departed a port, one should suspect Salmonellosis, a common type of food poisoning caused by Salmonella bacteria, which, fortunately, is rarely fatal.

There are a few precautions that can minimize the hazard of Salmonella, since odor and/or an off-flavor are not reliable guides of detecting its presence. They are: (1) heat food to temperatures above 68°C (155°F) which destroys the bacteria; (2) maintain clean counters and clean hands when preparing food; (3) do not reuse utensils that were used for raw food without washing; (4) always wash counters with a detergent or soap and hot water after preparing raw meats or other raw foods; (5) always pour boiling water over a cutting board after preparing raw foods (this sterilizes the slits caused by cutting); (6) do not eat meat or poultry that has been at room temperature more than two hours after cooking without first reheating to 68°C (155°F). Bacteria thrive and multiply at temperatures 7°C–60°C (45°F to 140°F). If carrying frozen meats to be consumed during the first few days of the voyage, do not allow the defrosting meats to come in contact with other foods. Insects as well as pets are known carriers of Salmonella.

NOTES

I. HEALTH.

    A. International shots and vaccination card.

    B. Thorough checkup by doctor and dentist prior to departure.

C. Adequate medicine chest aboard. Have your doctor prepare it.

D. Exposure to water:

Temperature	Maximum survival time
32°F.	15 min.
36½	30 min.
41	1 hour
50	3 hours
59	7 hours
68	16 hours
79	3 days or more

E. Hypothermia:

91.4°—Temperature regulation of body fails.

90°—Shivering; response ceases; muscular rigidity commences; speech becomes difficult.

88–83°—Drowsiness occurs.

83°—Unconsciousness occurs.

77°—Death occurs.

Rate of cooling depends on the thickness of the fat. Fat people survive longer than thin people, women longer than men, whites longer than blacks, yellow race longer than either.

F. Diving with underwater breathing apparatus (SCUBA) very dangerous.
   1. Should be professionally trained.
   2. Should always dive with buddy.
   3. Should be in good health.
   4. Should know the decompression times required.

G. Attack by sea creatures.
   1. By birds—when in life rafts or boats, in life jackets in water, or unconscious on beach.
   2. Fish, sharks, some large schools of fish, jellyfish—are dangerous only to the swimmer.
   3. Mammals—seals, whales, porpoises, etc., are usually harmless except if wounded or being hunted.
   4. Shellfish such as crabs will attack a stationary person such as when in a life jacket in the water or hanging onto a lifeboat or raft.
   5. Mollusks—squid and octopuses are normally harmless on the surface.

H. Exposure to cold—requires adequate clothing and warm food.

I. Exposure to heat—keep clothes damp or wet during day; let dry a couple of hours before sundown.

II. SLEEPING:

   A. Watch systems provide regular rest; quality, not quantity, is most important.
     1. Four-and-four watch system is most tiring.
     2. Navy system (dog watches) is good for large crew but tiring when combined with item 1.
     3. Sailing-ship system—best: provides most rest.
   B. Dry bedding essential in all but "survival" situations.
   C. Full stomach helpful to good rest.

III. PEST CONTROL:

   A. Remove labels from cans (roaches lay eggs in label glue, in store)
   B. Jean's recipe to eliminate or prevent "bugs"—mix sweetened condensed milk and boric acid powder into paste; spread along cracks or doorways or wherever any "habitation" is noticed.
   C. Screens.

IV. HUNTING AND FISHING:

   A. Guns—small caliber sufficient.
   B. Fishing equipment—spears, Hawaiian slings, poles and large hooks.
   C. Trolling—40-pound line is best; not sport; food.

V. VOYAGE STORES—SHELF LIFE:

   A. Canned foods—two years plus.
   B. Fresh foods—five days.
   C. Dehydrated foods—two years plus.
   D. Dry stores—grains, six months to one year.
   E. Sprouting and gardens—pick daily.
   F. Consummables—toothpaste, paper products, etc.: unlimited.
   G. Weight of stores, per person, per day: food and cans, three pounds, water consumption, five pounds. Total—eight pounds per person, per day.

4

Seamanship

GROUND TACKLE

After 14 years ashore, we resumed our full-time cruising life, this time aboard our 48-foot aluminum junk, *K-ung Fu-tse*. Before moving aboard, Jean and I both had extensive physical examinations, which required our remaining in the hospital for several days. The result of these checkups was our doctor's assurance that we were in excellent health and had the stamina of an age many years less than our calendar total. Had the results been different, our cruising plans would have been altered but not abandoned.

Extensive sailing trials came next. Then the stowing and restowing of our personal belongings, stores and ship's gear—for convenience and availability. In other words, we began developing habits, or "the routine," which is sometimes considered pretentious by those who live ashore, but is vital to those who go to sea. Once the habits are firmly established, there is no difference between day and night, fair or foul weather, as everything has —and is in—its place and there are no exceptions. We also came to understand the traits of our vessel—what she likes and dislikes. Once this is accomplished, neither she nor we will try each other's patience.

One would suppose that after 35 years of cruising, moving aboard would be "old hat." Not so. I find that while living ashore many of the commonplace bits and pieces of everyday seamanship are forgotten because of infrequent usage. We now anchor out 99 percent of the time (as we did in the past) and this naturally brings to mind examples of what has to be relearned. Not so much the "art" of anchoring—with experience (especially of dragging), that is seldom forgotten. And not *types* of anchors; I had and still have my favorite type. No, ground tackle *in general* is what should be reviewed. Recent events have reminded me of certain rules regarding ground tackle that should be kept in mind when preparing a vessel for ocean voyaging.

Most vessels we meet while cruising carry inadequate ground table. It is inconceivable to me that the U.S. Coast Guard requires signs, numbers, personal floatation devices, a bell, a horn (not necessarily reliable), etc. (all of which have some value), and yet does not require a vessel to have adequate ground tackle, or the gear to handle it. Loss of vessels and lives can and does result from inadequate ground tackle.

Chain has so many virtues that many cruising vessels use it exclusively. However, most stock boat designs must be altered to accommodate its weight and stowage requirements. A vessel rides easier to chain because its weight reduces the pitching, and the resulting catenary repose of the chain reduces the angular pull at the anchor. In deep water, chain requires less scope than rope warps; chain does not chafe; it stows compactly; it does not rot or mildew; it serves nicely as trimming ballast; and it is easy

PHOTO 4-1. *Kung Fu-tse* has an easily worked foredeck. Note the windlass foundation which elevates the chain pipes and almost totally prevents sloshing seas from running down into the chain locker. The anchor chains run in wooden troughs which have metal runners inside them to prevent wear. The cowl vent on the bow ventilates the rope locker.

to clean. It has some disadvantages: weight in the bow of light hulls, difficulty of handling without a windlass, and the need to stow each anchor rode in its own compartment. The proper size of chain needed is not easy to determine, although there are numerous tables that supposedly cover all situations. However, the resulting choices are usually inadequate. My observation is that light displacement vessels need chain heavy in proportion to their displacement because of their usual tendency to sail about, whiplash and jerk, all of which wear out and break chain. Heavier displacement vessels usually lay back, keeping a steady strain, which is easy on chain. A vessel with a deep forefoot and a short overhang forward rides easier than one with a cut-away forefoot and a long overhanging bow. This reduces the amount of lift in a swell which in turn lessens scending and plunging. Except in small hulls—say, under 30 feet LOA light displacement—the minimum size chain should be 5/16 inches, even though calculations indicate ¼ inches is adequate. Lightweight anchors require heavier chain than the Fisherman or Herreshoff. If, because of a vessel's size and displacement, it's not feasible to use all chain, then good practice suggests using five fathoms as a lead chain, in one size heavier than the size needed when all chain is used. In all cases, a swivel shackle *must* be used at the anchor.

The displacement-length ratio (D/L) is the only valid comparative measure of hulls, and is derived from the formula: $\dfrac{\triangle}{\left(\dfrac{L}{100}\right)3}$.

$\triangle$ equals displacement in long tons (2,240 pounds); L is the waterline in feet. This is a *nondimensional* formula, thus one can compare a 20-foot waterline vessel with one having a 100-foot waterline. When this D/L ratio is combined with length on deck, an immediate value comparison can be made. It's widely accepted that light displacement is a D/L ratio of 200 or less; medium displacement is D/L 200 to 350; and heavy displacement is D/L 350 and above.

I do not know of any anchor that is trouble-free if it is overridden. With the Fisherman, Northill and Herreshoff types, the elevated fluke can be fouled, but proper design of the flukes reduces this possibility. The CQR Plow and the Danforth types *can* break themselves out. Often both will reset themselves, but if the vessel is anchored in a spot where surrounding areas are unsuitable for anchoring, there may not be sufficient room to take the chance that these types will reset themselves. Kelp, weeds, clay, rocks, shells, etc., often render the CQR Plow and Danforth anchors useless when tripped, so the best practice seems to be to sheer the vessel—i.e., turn the rudder toward the anchor—so that on a change of tide or wind, the vessel will tend to sail a large circle about her anchor, working it deeper into the holding ground and thus preventing the elevated fluke from fouling. The stronger the breeze, the less sheer required.

The number and weight of anchors and size of chain are dependent on the vessel's length on deck and its displacement-length ratio. A well-found ocean voyager will have two bowers, one of which is usually one-third heavier than the other, plus a spare that is equal in weight to the heavier bower. Larger vessels will carry a kedge about one-half the weight of the large bower and located aft. Smaller vessels will usually find the spare bower serves as a kedge if it does not exceed 75 pounds, thus eliminating the fourth anchor. When an anchor is used as a kedge, a nylon warp is usually bent on, as it is difficult to row out chain.

The amount of chain carried varies in relation to cruising grounds. Forty-five fathoms on each bower is the usual minimum. Some use 45 times the draft if it exceeds six feet, and this seems to be a good formula. Many of us split one of the bower chains into two sections—15 fathoms and 30 fathoms—that can be shackled together or used separately. For example, 15 fathoms is usually enough in the shallow waters of the Bahamas for drafts of six feet or less, and 30 fathoms is enough for a 10-foot draft, leaving the unused shot to be shackled to either anchor, yielding either two of 45 fathoms or the combinations of 15 and 75, or 30 and 60.

Scope is dependent on the type of anchors used, the state of the wind and sea, the range of tide and the freeboard of the vessel. Here's a useful guide which covers most situations, using all chain:

	Minimum	Normal Swell	Storm with Sea
Fisherman, Northill, and Herreshoff (broad sharp flukes)	3:1	5:1	10:1
CQR Plow	5:1	8:1	15:1
Danforth	7:1	10:1	20:1

With each of the above, in strong tidal areas, the use of a second anchor is desirable if not mandatory, especially when swinging room is restricted. In narrow rivers, often one anchor is set from the stern to keep the vessel's keel in line with the current. Claude Worth's "anchor ballast shackle" was a popular wrinkle in the past, permitting one to send down 40–120 pounds of extra weight (pigs of lead) on the anchor chain, which prevented the anchor rode from snubbing. One must recognize that weight is the insurance of safe anchoring. No anchor can be continually snubbed without being dislodged if there is any upward force. Further, it is hard on the vessel and her rode. Windage is not as important as many theorists would lead us to believe. While ballasting a rode is seldom done today, the reduction in scope would be about 30 percent in a storm sea. Any reduction in scope is desirable when the amount of chain or warp is limited, as it permits anchoring in great depths with safety. The anchor ballast shackle is very

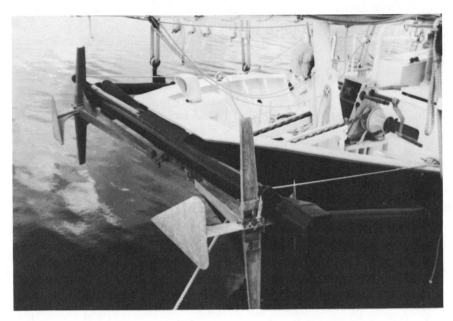

PHOTO 4-2. The two Northill anchors in their normal stowage positions. Note on the starboard anchor a reinforcing gusset welded between arm and stock, which had to be added to correct a flaw in the basic design. Both anchors had failed to hold on several occasions until this modification was made.

hard on warps because of chafe. It's worth noting that sending down the extra weight is a difficult maneuver and requires proper gear plus personal agility and strength.

The tables below show the difficulty of making selections from published tables:

L. FRANCIS HERRESHOFF——FOR HERRESHOFF TYPE ANCHOR

Boat Displ. Tons (Short)	First Bower	Second Bower	Chain	Approx. Warp Circum.	Warp Diam.
2	15 lbs.	——	——	$1\frac{1}{2}''$	$\frac{1}{2}''$
5	35 lbs.	20 lbs.	——	$2''$	$\frac{5}{8}''$
10	55 lbs.	45 lbs.	$\frac{1}{4}''$	$2\frac{1}{2}''$	$\frac{13}{16}''$
15	75 lbs.	60 lbs.	$\frac{5}{16}''$	$2\frac{3}{4}''$	$\frac{7}{8}''$
20	90 lbs.	70 lbs.	$\frac{3}{8}''$	$3''$	$1''$
25	110 lbs.	85 lbs.	$\frac{3}{8}''$	$3''$	$1''$
30	120 lbs.	90 lbs.	$\frac{7}{16}''$	$3\frac{1}{4}''$	$1\frac{1}{16}''$
35	130 lbs.	100 lbs.	$\frac{7}{16}''$	$3\frac{1}{4}''$	$1\frac{1}{16}''$

Length	Danforth Standard	Hi- Tensile	CQR Plow	Fisherman 1st	(Broad sharp flukes) 2nd	Storm
25–32	13-S	12-H	15 lbs.	60 lbs.	45 lbs.	90 lbs.
33–38	22-S	12-H	20 lbs.	90 lbs.	60 lbs.	120 lbs.
39–44	40-S	20-H	25 lbs.	110 lbs.	75 lbs.	135 lbs.
45–54	65-S	35-H	35 lbs.	135 lbs.	80 lbs.	165 lbs.
55–70	85-S	60-H	45 lbs.	150*	100*	200*

(*calc. for 60')

Lloyd's Rule L $\dfrac{(B + D)}{2}$

Equipment Numeral	Req. No.	Fisherman Less stock	With Stock Approx.	Chain	Warp. Circum.	Warp Diam.
300	2	34 lbs.	42 lbs.	$\frac{5}{16}''$	2''	$\frac{5}{8}''$
400	2	34 lbs.	42 lbs.	$\frac{5}{16}''$	2''	$\frac{5}{8}''$
500	2	45 lbs.	56 lbs.	$\frac{5}{16}''$	2''	$\frac{5}{8}''$
600	2	56 lbs.	70 lbs.	$\frac{3}{8}''$	$2\frac{1}{4}''$	$\frac{3}{4}''$
800	2	67 lbs.	84 lbs.	$\frac{3}{8}''$	$2\frac{1}{4}''$	$\frac{3}{4}''$
1000	2	90 lbs.	112 lbs.	$\frac{7}{16}''$	$2\frac{1}{4}''$	$\frac{3}{4}''$
1200	2	101 lbs.	126 lbs.	$\frac{7}{16}''$	$2\frac{1}{4}''$	$\frac{3}{4}''$

ANCHOR CHAIN—Wrought iron—from Lloyd's

Size	Short Link Tons Proof	Tons Breaking	Stud Link Tons Proof	Tons Breaking
$\frac{1}{4}''$	.75	1.5	—	—
$\frac{5}{16}''$	1.15	2.35	1.75	2.60
$\frac{3}{8}''$	1.60	3.20	2.40	3.60
$\frac{7}{16}''$	2.25	4.50	3.40	5.10
$\frac{1}{2}''$	3.00	6.00	4.50	6.75

This table reveals that stud-link chain has one and one-half times the proof strength of short-link chain, but only seven-eighths the weight.

The tables shown are but a few used by designers. None are valid if based only on one factor—length, displacement, depth, etc. Once the D/L ratio begins to change, then any of such single-factor comparisons quickly becomes a case of comparing apples to oranges. To use length (or any other dimension) alone is as ridiculous as saying that all horses are four-legged animals; therefore, all four-legged animals are horses.

Such a comparison can be illustrated using our last two vessels as examples. It shows why the rules are difficult to use:

	Gazelle	*K'ung Fu-tse*
LOA (Deck):	42'–0"	48'–6"
DWL:	33'–0"	41'–2"
Draft:	3'–10"	4'–4"
Displacement (Tons)	8.15	25.13
D/L Ratio	226	364
1st Bower:	75-lb. Fisherman	125-lb. Fisherman 85-lb. Northill Type
2nd Bower:	50-lb. Fisherman	75-lb. Fisherman 50-lb. Northill Type
Spare:	None	125-lb. Fisherman 85-lb. Northill Type
Coral Hook:	20-lb. 4-prong grapnel	20-lb. & 35-lb. four-prong grapnel
Chain:	$\frac{5}{16}$" short link	$\frac{7}{16}$" stud link
Warps-nylon:	$\frac{5}{8}$" diam. (2" circum.)	$\frac{3}{4}$" diam. ($2\frac{1}{4}$" circum.)
(if manila):	$\frac{3}{4}$" diam. ($2\frac{1}{4}$ circum.)	1" diam. (3" circum.)
CQR Plow:	25-lb.	35-lb.
Danforth:	40-S or 20-H	65-S or 35-H
Herreshoff:	55 lb. and 45-lb. with $\frac{1}{4}$" short-link	110 lb. and 85 lb. with $\frac{3}{8}$" short-link
By Lloyd's:	Numeral 500 56 lb. $\frac{5}{16}$" short-link	Numeral 650 70 lb. $\frac{3}{8}$" short link
Fisherman:	90 lbs./60 lbs./120 lbs.	135 lbs./80 lbs./165 lbs.

Lloyd's, in both cases, is *under* what would be required in anything but a quiet harbor. Herreshoff is right for *K'ung Fu-tse* but light for *Gazelle;* in both cases the chain is inadequate for anchoring in an open roadstead where considerable surge is frequent. The Fisherman is conservative for *K'ung Fu-tse* and much too heavy for *Gazelle*. The Danforth in both cases could be the next size up in the (High Tensile) series. The same holds true for the CQR Plow. With either of these anchors, I would use the next size chain or increase length of chain carried by 15 fathoms per anchor. Both of these anchor manufacturers make claims of superb holding power for their anchors, which are true only under the conditions of the test. It's true they do hold more than the Fisherman, Herreshoff and Navy types under the same test conditions; however, there are many bottoms where they are inferior, as noted earlier. They do not take kindly to tripping and, if too light in weight, will sail through the water and skate across the bottom unless very carefully set—which is not always possible.

As for using a nylon warp, there is no question as to its strength or elasticity. It is the elasticity which, while adding to its strength, also causes the vessel to surge and then snub her anchor. Chafe is nylon's greatest enemy; and the use of ⅜" diameter line on 40- and 50-foot vessels must be deplored. In any kind of sea, nylon frequently approaches its elastic limit. If repeated often enough at close intervals, the friction can soon part the fibers—and another vessel is adrift. In spite of what rope makers assert, there is no way nylon can be compared to chain—other than to say each has its own virtues.

The following table is useful. The size of warps given by Herreshoff and Lloyds are for hemp (manila) rope. Direct comparison cannot be made between natural and synthetic fibers as, for example, ¾" diameter manila is approximately the same strength as $\frac{7}{16}$" nylon. The larger diameter is easier to haul in by hand, and chances are that most owners would change over to the same size. However, the reverse is true in larger sizes: 1¼" manila would probably be replaced with ⅞" diameter nylon.

Anchors, anchor chains and anchor rodes should be tested to insure that chains and rodes run free and clear, and that anchors hold the vessel. Years ago, testing was done under working sail in winds around Force 4. Here's how it went: Coming off a broad reach and letting go with a scope between 3:1 and 5:1, the vessel was jerked into the wind, the anchor drag-

PHOTO 4-3. Two 85-lb. bower anchors are the normal ground tackle. At sea, they are further lashed to prevent any movement and damage to the vessel.

APPROXIMATE STRENGTH OF ROPE IN POUNDS

Circum.	Diam.	Manila	Dacron	Nylon
$\frac{3}{4}''$	$\frac{1}{4}''$	600	2,150	1,950
$1''$	$\frac{5}{16}''$	1,000	3,300	2,960
$1\frac{1}{8}''$	$\frac{3}{8}''$	1,350	4,500	4,200
$1\frac{1}{4}''$	$\frac{7}{16}''$	1,750	6,000	5,550
$1\frac{1}{2}''$	$\frac{1}{2}''$	2,650	7,600	7,200
$1\frac{3}{4}''$	$\frac{9}{16}''$	3,450	9,250	9,000
$2''$	$\frac{5}{8}''$	4,400	11,250	11,000
$2\frac{1}{4}''$	$\frac{3}{4}''$	5,400	15,600	15,300
$2\frac{3}{4}''$	$\frac{7}{8}''$	7,700	20,000	21,000
$3''$	$1''$	9,000	25,000	26,500
$3\frac{3}{4}''$	$1\frac{1}{4}''$	13,500	30,600	41,500

ging very little before setting. If the bitts or windlass (in the case of chain), stayed put and the vessel stopped, the master had peace of mind. Occasionally the anchor did not dig in or, if it did, would not hold the vessel, which meant that the anchor was not large enough. Nowadays, most owners would object to testing this way, fearing to scar their topsides, so they substitute backing down on the anchor under power which, at best, produces only a fraction of the strain of the older method.

Using all chain, or all rope, or a combination of both depends, of course, on the waters sailed, and on the equipment of and size of the vessel. For all chain, I use three lengths of chain—45 fathoms on the storm anchor; 30 fathoms on the working anchor; plus a 15-fathom length that can be shackled on to either chain. When sailing in the Bahamas, I sometimes use 15-fathom chain on the spare anchor with an additional 15 fathoms of nylon bent on.

If the voyaging includes a transit of the Panama Canal, then four lines of 100-ft. each must be on hand to reach the top of the lock walls. They can also serve as warps. For economy's sake, one could have two warps and use two anchor rodes for this purpose if there is also chain for anchoring. While the allure of the South Pacific continues undiminished, the coasts of Central and South America have been neglected as cruising grounds. Should one decide to visit these coasts, frequent transits of the Canal would justify reserving lines solely for lock use.

I notice that few dinghies carry anchors these days. We have always kept a four-prong grapnel (coral anchor) bent onto a ring in the stern sheets so that the dinghy can be kept clear of any wharf, especially during a change of tide. By using such an anchor, more dinghies could use a wharf without much damage to the dinghy's fender rails.

In coral, rock and bottoms covered with unknown debris, one should buoy the anchor. In areas of small tides—less than six feet—the line need not be of much greater length than the depth of the water plus enough to put three turns on the gypsy. Where tides are greater than six feet, there is usually enough current to warrant adding a couple of extra fathoms. Otherwise, the float will be dragged under by the current. This can cause a problem because the surplus line could foul the elevated fluke or chafe on the bottom. A few small floats secured at regular intervals (say, one fathom apart) will keep the line clear of the bottom. When diving to clear an anchor in murky water, the floats help determine the depth as one descends. The breaking strength of this line should be 20 times the weight of the heaviest anchor, but never less than ¼″ in size. The float should be substantial and visible—bright orange seems to stand out best and a piece of reflecting tape shows up in the dark.

Often, when no bearings are available and one is anchored in heavy weather on a bank, it is hard to tell if you're holding firm or dragging. In this situation, there are two methods to determine if the vessel is holding firm. One method uses a drift lead which is cast near the stern of the vessel; the line is secured slack. After an hour, if the relative positions are the same—i.e., the lead and the vessel—one may assume no dragging has occurred.

The second method is to secure a buoy to the lead line, casting it at the same time the anchor is let go. This provides a constant reference point, regardless of the state of tide, and is easier to use than the drift-lead method. A float must be chosen whose buoyancy is not sufficient to lift the lead. Often a second lead is carried for this purpose, with leaders of about 18 inches spliced in at the 10-, 20-, 30- and 40-foot marks, the float being secured to the appropriate leader for the depth of water.

We have watched with amusement and concern the growing practice of "squall baiting," popularly referred to as "rafting," in which a number of vessels cluster together, all on one anchor. The amusement arises from watching the mad scramble to disentangle the vessels and get more anchors down when a squall comes up—all done with much running about, wild shouting and frantic gesticulation. The antics are rivaled only by the Keystone Cops. The concern is not for our vessel, even when they are dragging down on us, but for theirs, knowing as we do that if they do collide with us there may be damage to their vessels and perhaps even injury to the crew. In years gone by, I seldom saw rafting practiced by cruising folk. Visiting between vessels was done by dinghy. Recently, however, I saw 14 vessels riding to the anchor of one vessel. A squall came up and all vessels dragged; several went aground. The danger of fire and explosion is another concern when vessels are moored in a bunch; we have seen such things happen.

Safety and proper seamanship dictate that one's vessel always be secure and safe, and have enough room to maneuver should a sudden need arise to abandon the anchorage. There's much truth in the old saying that "a vessel will take more than her crew!" At times, it's a wonder how some vessels survive the ineptness of their crews!

THE SEA ANCHOR

Sooner or later the blue-water part of a voyage ends and the vessel approaches the land. A first axiom of seamanship must be: *Never under any circumstances approach a coast unless the anchors are bent on and ready for use with chain claws off, or cables cleared for running.* Many vessels are lost through ignoring this rule. Fortunately, most of the time, we are entering well-established ports which pose only the usual problems. Yet, many who explore or gunkhole in remote areas meet very different challenges—cross bars, entering rivers, passes and/or reefs, etc.—to reach a desired anchorage.

Of late, the sea anchor has fallen into disuse because of its inability to bring up modern vessels. With their cutaway underbodies, the tendency of these vessels without sail up, is to put the wind on the quarter or lie stern-to. Also discarded is the use of oil for calming "troubled waters." There are times, however, when either or both of these devices are the best—or *only*—safe way to get in. They deserve to be used with greater frequency. If you have them aboard and know how to use them, and to adapt their use to the conditions of the moment, do so, and let the armchair experts be damned.

When crossing a breaking bar on a flood tide, if the wind is moderate and favorable, reduce sail, put oil bags out over astern and let the oil float in ahead of the vessel. Speed it not wanted and the vessel must be slowed, so a large rudder is an asset in low-speed maneuvering. Spreading oil works well only when the entrance is straight, without doglegs. One should sail past a doglegged entrance and distribute the oil while lying well to seaward so that it arrives at the weather side of the bar as the vessel is crossing. Easy to say, but it takes a bit of seamanship in the doing.

When an ebb tide is running, oil is of no use. As long as the wind is favorable, only a rip tide need be expected. With strong favorable winds, over-falls may be encountered near the bar if there is much speed to the current.

If you are being driven down on a bar, try to arrive on a wave crest—always remembering to subtract one half the wave height as the true depth over the bar. If the sea conditions are such that a vessel may thump heavily in crossing (if a crest is missed), then the best alternative seems to be to use a sea anchor, bending onto it an extra-long warp or spare cable (about five times the vessel's LOA), streamed over the bow on short scope. Work the vessel in so that she nears the seaward edge of the bar in a trough. As the sea anchor begins to drag the bow into the wind, ease off on the warp to keep the keel parallel to the bar. The crest will then lift the vessel over, the warp being kept slack. Should she scrape, the hull will heel, reducing draft, and momentum will carry her across into deep water. Once over the bar, snug down the warp. As the vessel heads into the wind, trip the sea anchor and haul in; then, the vessel can either be anchored or continue upriver.

In straightforward inlets, a sea anchor over the stern is useful in slowing down a vessel, preventing a broach; however, it can be tripped in an instant to allow the vessel to accelerate if necessary—which can't be done when towing warps. In the absence of a heavy swell, this maneuver is impossible if the bar will not accommodate the vessel's draft. Why do we try it? There are several reasons, I suppose. I remember one occasion years ago when we crossed a bar with two feet less water than our vessel's draft to gain entrance to a hurricane hole that we absolutely had to enter at the moment. Indeed, the storm that followed proved it was well worth the risk and the effort we had made.

Speaking of rivers, all rivers follow the path of least resistance. Charts are a convenience; however, one's eyes are usually a sufficient guide because the following rules rarely vary: (1) The fastest flow is always the deepest water, and the water always flows to the outside of a bend in the river; (2) when bends are extreme, the deep water channel will be close to the outside bank; (3) all rivers have a deep hole immediately inside a barred entrance; (4) if there is an inflowing creek and it meets the river at right angles, there will be a bar up and down the river, and the river channel will be well away—probably on the opposite side from the creek entrance; (5) the more of an angle made by the creek to the river, the greater the sandbar will be on the lazy (outer edge) side of the creek, caused by silt deposits; (6) a river never has less depth than that which is found over the bar; (7) it is always best to enter on the flood, although impatience often prompts one to attempt it at other times. By entering at the beginning of the flood, grounding is usually not a catastrophe and provides an opportunity to study most of the shallow areas and pick out the best anchorage; (8) the channel into a river can always be located by the difference in waves and wavelets, even in very calm weather; (9) the direction of fastest flow of the river will be in the channel; (10) the approximate flow will be straight from the river except when the river curves just before the mouth, in which case that curve must be projected as a continued curve to seaward; (11) fast rivers cut straight channels, slow rivers often describe a serpentine path.

A prevailing wind will usually shift a channel in the opposite direction.

For instance, a prevailing northeasterly wind will tend to push a river mouth to the south.

Bars move not only from year to year, but also after each flood or storm; however, radical movement usually occurs only in the event of a major storm such as a hurricane, or severe flooding.

In clear water, color will indicate depth. A clear day and a good breeze shows up the channel, and streaks of foam indicate the shoals. The most difficult situation is a calm, cloudy day when the clouds reflecting the water appear as reefs or shoals.

In murky water, such as jungle streams, there is normally sufficient flotsam to reveal the current. Areas that are congested indicate still water and a probable shoal. If the speed of the current is two or more knots, then the movement of scattered debris will define the channel; four or more knots will produce eddies and occasionally small whirlpools.

Size of sea anchor has, by tradition, been approximately one inch of diameter for each foot of waterline length. For running bars, ¾ inch per foot would be minimum. *K'ung Fu-tse* has a sea anchor with a 36-inch diameter for her 41-foot waterline.

There is wide disagreement about which type of oil to use as a calming agent. Some of the best kinds, such as oil of almonds, sperm oil, etc., are hard to find. The ones that are widely available include turpentine, linseed, fish and petroleum oils, and their relative effectiveness runs in that order. Since it takes very little oil to do the job—only a few drops—the convenient oil bag is sufficient. The amount of oil carried would be about two gallons minimum, 10 gallons maximum. A good substitute material is soap suds; detergent also works but it takes more of it to do the job. Crankcase oil should be saved for emergency use, even though it is the least effective. In U.S. waters close to shore you might have to balance need to use it against possible consequences of polluting.

CASTING

A maneuver sometimes referred to as "casting," should be studied; it has saved my vessel in by-gone years. I used it one time when I was anchored in a cul-de-sac about 75 yards in diameter. Directly astern lay a shelving coral-and-sand beach. To port was a coral reef. Directly ahead was a channel approximately 70 feet wide, with coral on both sides and breakers coming over the windward side of the channel, which meant it was necessary to come up on a tack to get a favorable wind. The wind was Force 6, so I had to get out; the anchorage was becoming untenable.

The procedure of casting went this way: Working sails were set. The anchor rode was payed out until the stern occasionally bumped on the bottom. Since I had my starboard bower anchor over, I went off on the starboard tack without heaving up the anchor and swung her as far to the port side as the scope would allow. (I had previously bent on my longest spring line, passing it through the chocks to the bitts forward.) When I had made as much progress to windward as the rode would allow, I tacked with the rode taut, sailing close-hauled on the port tack until I again ran out of rode and spring line. I then dropped the coral anchor over the starboard side. Paying out all the line possible, until my stern was almost directly over my original bower, I brought the bower aboard, and ranged the chain on deck for emergency anchoring. I then swung her as far to starboard as possible, bringing up the steep-to coral atoll on my starboard side, and laid her close-hauled on the starboard tack. By the time I came abreast of my coral hook, I had good way on, so kept paying out line until I was into position where the channel bent to starboard. I then tacked, and when I was positive that I had enough headway to make the passage good, I slipped the rode, leaving the coral hook down, and sailed out into the open water. (In a few days, I returned to retrieve the anchor.) During this maneuver, at no time before I slipped my coral anchor was I free of the bottom, and if I had aborted any tack, I could have fallen back on an anchor already down.

The last maneuver could have been accomplished by working the anchor from the quarter rather than the bow; however, that creates a rather dangerous situation in a fore-and-aft rigged vessel, in that it places her stern-to the wind. In many ways, it is similar to "club-hauling" in series, except that the anchor is always worked from the bow, and a spring line is not used except in the final maneuver, if necessary. (Club-hauling is normally used only on square-riggers. It has little application in a fore-and-aft rigged vessel.) The danger of falling off, due to lack of headway when room to leeward is limited, makes "casting" preferable. Also, the built-in safety factor is that an anchor is still down and holding in case of an abortive attempt. The best way to sail up past one's anchor is to use a series of half-boards; and on vessels that forereach well, paying out scope on the main anchor rode may suffice without having to drop the kedge. Today, apparently few yachtsmen know this technique. On several sad occasions which I have witnessed, it would have saved a vessel from being beached or destroyed. As indicated in the example, on the last leg of the maneuver, it becomes necessary to leave one anchor behind and return to pick it up another day. If it is buoyed, there should be little difficulty in doing this.

This is not something I would recommend as an everyday procedure, and I hope no one will be foolish enough (as I was) to find himself in a position where it must be attempted. The maneuver of casting is just another of the many arts of seamanship and self-sufficiency that the crew of a cruising vessel should possess.

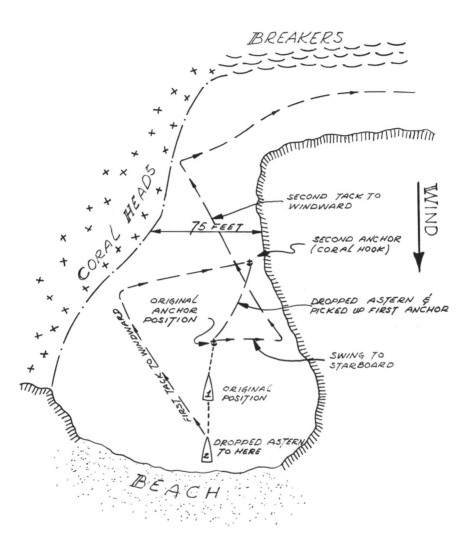

FIG. 4-4. The technique of casting to escape a cul-de-sac anchorage.

GOING AGROUND

Going aground is an art. Such phrases as "on the putty, hard, marle, shingle, beach, sand, mud, rocks," etc. are slang expressions which vary with locality—just different ways of saying that one's vessel is stranded, aground—just plain stuck.

Now, going aground is not always as bad as it may first seem. My adage has always been, "He who never goes aground, never goes anywhere, but he who goes aground with a vengeance becomes a monument." The worst part of a grounding is the all-too-frequent crowd of witnesses to the event who, with muted voices that nevertheless seem to roll like thunder across the water, assess your ability as a navigator, your legitimacy, the quality of your gray matter and—most suspect at such moments—your seamanship.

There are many valid reasons for going aground, among which are: a beacon or buoy is missing; your chart is uncorrected; the channel has changed; the Notice to Mariners has not caught up with you; there is an unknown current; etc. More likely, however, you were not paying attention to what you were doing; you were trying to beat the tide across the bar; you used the wrong date or wrong reference point for the tide; or you were using local knowledge which is usually of little or no use because the person who gave it to you omitted the fudge factors, such as "only on a northeast wind," "never on the dark of the moon," "mebbe in the month of January if it ain't too windy."

There are many categories in which to place the unfortunate mariner who strands his ship, so perhaps we should examine a few. First is the Hard-Case type, the all-too-familiar master, shouting and screaming, "Full ahead; full astern; hard right; hard left," etc. After a few minutes he has worked himself into a frenzy, and the orders come faster, his face becomes redder, his eyes begin to bulge. He is finally reduced to sputtering and then to mouthing unintelligible sounds, all of which provide maximum amusement to the audience.

The second type is the Fearless Navigator who really doesn't know where he is, but has gone aground precisely and with a certain flair, and is absolutely stunned by the apparent error in the location of the channel. He now sets about getting off in proper Navy fashion. His kedge is run out and a strain is taken; he assesses the wind and tide and sets about with a plan of action and reaction to extricate himself from this pickle, usually with the aid of a loud hailer. From him we are supposed to learn some of the fine points of seamanship and judge him by how well he follows the book. He really is sort of a jackass.

The third type, heartily disliked, is The Blamer. He blames everyone but himself: "If you'd followed my orders!" "Why didn't you watch the course?" "Can't you tell *dark* water from *light* water?" If he is taking it out on the mate, who happens to be a meek wife, the show is embarrassing. Occasionally the mate turns out to be a fighter, equally as abusive as the master, and if she can cuss in proper nautical fashion while giving the master his come-uppance, the audience enriches its vocabulary.

Finally, there is the one who presents a show that is long running and somewhat puzzling, particularly if his audience is sure that he ran aground unintentionally. If the vessel is only slightly aground, say at the bottom of the ebb, he drops an anchor and brings out a picnic lunch to await the rising tide. If it is not mealtime, then an awning and a book will do to fill the short period he is aground. If, on the other hand, he has several hours to wait and there is a good range to the tide, he may go overboard to scrub the bottom of the vessel. This confuses the onlookers, who are forced to wonder if the grounding was perhaps deliberate after all. If, at the *height* of the flood, he not only scrubs the bottom but *paints* it, this compounds their puzzlement. Finally, if the next tide fails to take him off, and he heaves her down on the opposite side to scrub and paint the other side, the voices across the water proclaim, "That certainly was a slick way to avoid a haul-out charge." Many are envious, especially if the little woman is seen, up to her knees in muck, helping out. This is The Philosopher—the one who never cries over spilt milk but consoles himself with the thought that it was half-water anyway, and congratulates himself on squeezing advantage out of adversity.

NOTES

I. TIDES:
- A. Definition: Tides are the *changes in elevation* of the surface water and are not the same as tidal currents and tidal drifts.
  1. The tide *rises* and *falls*.
  2. The tidal currents *flood* and *ebb*.
  3. The *stand* is the time of high or low water where no vertical change takes place.
  4. The *slack* is when no horizontal motion takes place.
  5. The *set* is the direction of tidal flow.
  6. The *drift* is the velocity of tidal flow.
- B. Tides are caused by the unequal attraction of the sun and the moon, and act most on the areas of the earth nearest these bodies.
- C. High water occurs on the average of every 28 days—a lunar month —at about the same interval of the moon's transit over the meridian, expressed in *hours* and *minutes*. This interval is known as the lunar interval.

D. The observed interval at any part of the time of full and change of the moon is called the *establishment of the port*.

E. The vulgar (or common) establishment is the monthly observations tabulated.

F. The highest tides do not occur at the precise times of full and new moons, but *one* day after on the U.S. Atlantic Coast, *two* days after on the European Atlantic Coast, and approximately at the time of change on the Pacific Coast.

G. *Spring tides* are the highest of the high and the lowest of the low. Neap tides are the lesser tides of the first and third quarters.

H. To find the time of high and low water:
   1. From Tide Tables (four volumes)
   2. By calculation:
      a. Old method.
         (1) From Nautical Almanac, find time of moon's meridian passage (upper or lower as required) and correct it for longitude (Table 11) 1890–1925/(Table 26) 1938–1943/using the daily variation shown in the Almanac.
         (2) Add the tide hour or establishment of the place.
         (3) Add the longitude west or subtract east longitude which equals local mean time of transit. Add high or low water interval shown in Bowditch.

Note: Local astronomical date must be strictly adhered to, and this often requires use of the lower transit or transit of a previous day to find the correct time of tide.

         (4) Corrections and bases: fourth from three tables in Bowditch (old ones); from old tide tables, establishment may be calculated; from difference of upper and lower transits.
      b. New method.
         (1) Apply lunar interval to times of moon's meridian passage (local).
         (2) Greenwich Civil Time of meridian passage is given in Almanac.
         (3) Let L = Longitude in degrees of station; $+$ if west; $-$ if east.
         (4) Let S = Longitude in degrees of time meridian used; $+$ if west; $-$ if east.
         (5) Then, the correction to account for the difference in transits over Greenwich and local meridian will be $+$ 4.14 L minutes, and the correction to take account of the difference of Greenwich and the standard time of the phase will be $-$ 4S minutes. Total correction (4.14L $-$

4S) minutes or 4 (L-s) + 0.14L minutes applied to the true MHW/MLW lunar intervals.

When applied to GCT of moon's transit at Greenwich, this equals standard time of local high and low water. (H.W.F. and C.) used in older publication.

EXAMPLE:

Longitude of Station (L) = 74°W. approx.

High water lunar interval = 8 h. 44 m.

Low water lunar interval = 2 h. 49 m.

Standard time of station based on meridian (S) = 75°W

Correction +4 (L–S) + 0.14L = + 6 minutes

+4 (74–75) + 0.14.74

−4   10.36

∴ Upper transit time   5h   32m

high water = 8 h 44 m + 6 m   8h   50m
_____

Eastern std. time H.W.   14 − 22 or 2h 22 m
                                P.M.

Lower transit time   18h   01m

low water = 2 h 49 m + 6 m   2h   55m
_____

Eastern std. time L. W.   20h   56m or 8h
                                56m P.M.

5

Ship's Business

REGULATIONS

We're all involved with or subject to the law every day of our lives. Yachting magazines receive many letters from people who are planning to live, retire or cruise aboard a vessel, and want to know what their legal status will be in various localities. I am not a lawyer and am not giving legal advice here, but only offer a few observations based on personal interpretations of regulations as I have experienced them. My primary concern is with blue-water sailing, a part of which includes eventually reaching port and having to cope with often-insensitive, bureaucratic "lubbers."

First, let me make it clear that documentation of a U.S. vessel does not exempt her from taxes and other liabilities. She is subject to all the state and local taxes of her port of documentation, which is the legal residence of the vessel, and of her owners and crew as long as they live aboard. There is little question that yacht documentation is abused by many people in an effort to evade taxes, and this abuse works to the disadvantage of those who have a valid need for the privileges of documentation.

Next, I want to point out that the validity of a live-aboard sailor being a yachtsman is often the bone of contention in interpreting local ordinances. "Living aboard" implies that the owner and crew of a vessel consider the vessel to be their domicile. A yacht is a vessel used solely for pleasure; therefore, a yachtsman is one who sails or operates a vessel for pleasure. Yachting has come to mean weekend and vacation use of a vessel, thus implying that anyone who lives aboard permanently—blue-water sailor, coastwise cruiser, power, sail or houseboat owner—is no longer a yachtsman but a semiprofessional because he has changed from an occasional to a permanent life afloat. In some ways this new "classification" is correct; those who cruise permanently often do acquire the skills usually attributed to qualified professionals. The difference between the former and the latter is that the former do not use their skills for remuneration. Many blue-water sailors have served as professional seamen and now, sailing for pleasure, still consider themselves professionals rather than yachtsmen.

A vessel may frequent an area or a port without any change in the status of the vessel or her occupants providing no stay is so long as to constitute a change of residence. For example, one may enter Hampton, Virginia, ten times a year, leave the state, go foreign, cruise coastwise or cruise the whole Chesapeake without experiencing any problem, whether the vessel is, or is not, registered in Virginia. However, as of 1977, if the vessel is registered or documented in Virginia and is physically in the state on January 1 or for more than 30 days per year, she is then subject to county or city personal property tax.

A vessel registered *out of the state* but moored within a Virginia locality *for six months* is also subject to personal property assessment. While this may not be true for all states, it appears that six months is considered, both locally and internationally, as the maximum permissible stay without declaring residency or paying import duties or penalties. The United States issues six-month cruising permits to foreign yachts, as do many other countries to U.S. yachts. A person living aboard a vessel and employed ashore is subject to state and local taxes. Families with children in school have no right to expect exemption from state and local taxes levied to pay the costs of the school system.

A transient is one who uses the facilities of a port for a period of time— usually *less* than 30 days, unless in that port for bona fide repair and outfitting, in which case a year's stay, while unusual, is not unknown. To avoid personal property taxes in the state of Virginia, such repair or refit would have to be done by established shore facilities, and not be a do-it-yourself project. Material used for repairs, and stores purchased during this period and not placed in bond are subject to state and local sales taxes.

Ports used by cruising vessels for overhaul, outfitting and restocking for a voyage add revenue to the local economy. A cruising vessel with its hauling, painting, general repair and outfitting, plus purchase of stores for a year's voyage, will spend from $1,000 to $4,000 locally—a windfall seldom shunned by city fathers.

Some municipalities enact local regulations to limit the length of time in port permitted to transients for many reasons, some of which are: the port has limited berthing facilities which, overloaded with visiting vessels, would hamper commercial activities such as fishing or fitting-out; harbor congestion, or too great a build-up of a floating community. Many ports rightly enact regulations prohibiting dumping of garbage, oil or sewage into municipal waters. This is particularly valid in congested areas where the drainage by current and/or tide will not flush out the basin. Such laws do not make sense, however, when the municipality drains its own sewage right into the water next to your vessel.

At the present time, to the best of my knowledge, no state or municipality can prohibit transit through a federal commercially navigable salt water area, nor can they prohibit anchorage in areas outside secondary channels, in restricted underwater cable or pipe ways or wild life refuges; nor force a transient to moor or use the facilities of the municipality as a means of levying dues or taxes for the right to pass through.

All of this may change at any time—i.e,. there is talk today of a federal "use" tax and fuel tax on vessels using the U.S. waterways system.

As a transient voyager using commercial ports from Brownsville Texas, to Lubec, Maine, I have not found local officials who were not civil, courteous and helpful if they were met with the same attitude. It's my observation that so long as master and crew accept that they are guests of the port and act accordingly, little friction will result. The same cannot always be said for staffs of marinas or officials of towns that cater to motor yachts —often they discriminate against sailing vessels, and are surly, rude and indifferent. Fortunately, the reputation of these places spreads quickly and they can easily be avoided.

Like a circle of equal altitude, the ever-increasing rules and regulations implemented by the U.S. Coast Guard never approach the Geographical Position, but continue to race around the main issue—which is seaworthiness. The act implemented in April, 1974, permits each district commander of the Coast Guard to terminate an intended voyage if the vessel is "manifestly unsafe for a specific voyage on a specific body of water." Furthermore, his decision may be based on: (1) unsuitable design or configuration; (2) improper construction or inadequate material condition; (3) improper or inadequate operational or safety equipment.

The basis for this ruling is that "there are about four manifestly unsafe voyages attempted each year." I am sure that under this ruling neither Joshua Slocum in his converted oyster sloop, *Spray,* nor John C. Voss in his dugout canoe, *Tilikum,* would have been permitted to sail from these shores.

This line of reasoning could be used to insist that all bridges and multi-storied buildings be demolished because each year many people commit suicide from them. Similarly, the removal of tires from automobiles would stop traffic deaths. Although I am somewhat reconciled to bureaucratic empire-building, I do object to the enactment of "blanket" regulations that only aim at protecting the miniscule minority. Such regulations give powers to administrators who seldom exercise either prudence or justice in enforcing the rules. Written into the law is a provision giving the right to petition the rulings. Ha! A sailor has a better chance of surviving a typhoon in a bathtub than of winning in the courts. Omitted from the law is clarification on this question: If one district commander approves the vessel, and the vessel enters another district, will the prior approval be honored?

If all of the present regulations were applied evenhandedly, the U.S. Coast Guard could not make rescues with their own small craft! So obviously there are exceptions to the rules. It is rather sad that as noble a service as the Coast Guard has to become involved with the administration of Mickey Mouse laws. I believe it has a more important and dignified role.

It's rather unfair to criticize unless one has something constructive to offer as an alternative. A simple alternative suggests itself to me: All vessels would be classified by an independent, non-government agency, such as the American Bureau of Standards, or Lloyds, according to the waters to be sailed. Further, the vessels would: (1) be built to standards equivalent to their scantling rules and regulations; (2) have equipment, machinery, materials and quality of workmanship that were certified by inspection during construction and confirmed by plans; (3) have a certificate of seaworthiness; (4) have a mandatory resurvey every 10 years to insure continuing structural integrity; (5) have a biannual minisurvey of lifesaving, firefighting, etc., equipment, anchors, chain and rig, to determine if they still meet required standards. All active ocean-cruising vessels would be documented (at present, documentation is limited to vessels of five or more net tons) and at the annual renewal of the document, the master would *certify* that his vessel meets the requirements for safety at sea. Vessels not intended for ocean going would not be documented.

In this situation, the master or owner would simply produce his Certificate of Seaworthiness and this would inform the Coast Guard inspector of everything he needed to know, including the certified area of operation. It would eliminate the on-the-spot judgment and policy decision with which the inspector is now burdened. I can hear shouts of protest from the boating industry which, for the most part, has been infested with those who build to the "lowest common denominator." Maybe much of our present dilemma has been caused by the uninformed, but surveys of damaged hulls indicate that sound hulls and sound judgment by owners usually go hand in hand.

I was rather amused at the newest use of Chapter 13 of the Federal Safe Boating Act. The U.S. Coast Guard has devised a formula to determine if the waves are too high for a vessel to leave port. The formula is: length overall divided by 10, plus the minimum freeboard in feet equals the *permissible wave height* to the nearest highest whole number. If the wave heights are over four feet, or the current is over four knots, you can be prevented from leaving port. This rule is applicable to the Pacific Northwest now. How long before it is applied elsewhere? A 30-foot houseboat with nine-foot freeboard = 12-foot waves. A 95-foot cargo schooner with 2½-foot freeboard = 12-foot waves. This law once again proves that apples = oranges!

A new regulation, which is being enforced, also requires the display of a five inch by 8 inch placard which reads:

DISCHARGE OF OIL PROHIBITED
The Federal Water Pollution Control Act prohibits the discharge of oil or oily water into or upon the navigable waters in contiguous zone of the United States if such discharge causes a film or sheen upon, or discoloration of, the surface of the water, or causes a sludge or emulsion beneath the surface of the water. Violators are subject to a penalty of $5,000.

This placard must be posted in the engine room or near the bilge pump, and applies to all vessels over 26 feet.

The time has come to mention a few not-so-happy problems that face the cruising fraternity, even though "happy problems for happy people" seems to be the new vogue nowadays—in print, at least.

Man is the only animal that organizes and wages war against his own species. Until recently, nations have frequently expanded by conquest of land areas. The sea has been seen as an obstacle to conquest by both the aggressor and the defender. Not so today. A battle now rages over who owns the sea and the sea bed.

This dilemma intensified when the United Nations Law of the Sea Conference convened on June 20, 1974, in Caracas, Venezuela. Basically, the major maritime powers—United States, Great Britain, Russia, France and Japan—are *for* the freedom of the seas. On the other hand, archipelago nations such as Indonesia, the Philippines, Fiji, Mauritius and Greece, want total control over their interisland sea bed, regardless of its distance from land. (This demand, of course, involves some of the most important straits in the world.) Still other countries, such as Canada and most South American nations, want economic and other controls covering waters 200 or more miles offshore.

For the ocean voyager, the ultimate impact of the United Nations conference may not be felt for a decade, but if the "right of innocent passage" is abridged in the interests of mining the ocean floor, then the limitations might mean that vast areas of the ocean could not be traversed without prior approval of numerous nations, or perhaps even a permit from the

United Nations. Freedom of the seas might vanish. To date, no firm resolution has emerged.

INSURANCE

Going to sea has been and is a way of life for me; therefore, I accept its benefits and its few inconveniences rather matter-of-factly. Self-preservation is one of the strongest traits I possess—but, while I am cautious, I am not timid. Certain "protections" of life are largely taken for granted ashore. Afloat, these same things are thought of—maybe even wished for—but are not usually possessed. I am thinking of property, liability, personal and health insurance. This subject was raised in a letter I received from a Dr. Peter Hofer, who wrote: "Time and again the . . . (cruising) man runs into problems created through nationalistic customs and regulations requiring static and/or national residence, etc., etc. When this is not a matter influencing the economics of the matter on hand (say, premiums versus benefits), I, for one, have not been able to find a truly open-minded, full-service health insurance with equal worldwide coverage and any residence base."

Many who live aboard and cruise have no other home than their vessel and seldom stay long enough in one country to establish residency. Always on the move, like gypsies, they have lost their right to vote and, therefore, the right to complain about what the politicians do. They also have usually lost the group health insurance, unemployment compensation, workmen's compensation, Social Security and a host of other supposed benefits into which, at one time or another, they have paid hard-earned cash, either directly or indirectly. I confess that, after calculations proved that I would have to live to be 230 years old to collect all of my Social Security, all these so-called benefits, including Social Security, lost their glitter for me. Still, living aboard as I do, all I own is contained in my vessel, and her loss would be a staggering financial blow. Few of us are constituted to feel an "easy come–easy go" attitude toward our vessel. Insurance, therefore, has more than once crossed my mind over the years. Several times I have vigorously pursued the question. The answers I got boil down to the fact that insurance for a true ocean cruiser is usually impossible to obtain at any cost, let alone at reasonable cost, and when it is to be had, the policies contain so many riders that the vessel could no longer cruise.

Over a dozen major insurance companies and many more independent agents, including Lloyds, have been questioned by me regarding coverage of an ocean cruiser for 12 months on *any* ocean. The average suggested premium, with all the small but numerous "extras," amounted to 10 per cent per annum, not including liability. This amount *exceeds* my yearly income before taxes; therefore, such insurance has been impossible for me to consider. Health insurance is so localized that one almost has to gamble that sickness or accident will not occur, *"except. . . ."* Life insurance, with the exception of the G.I. (Veteran's) Insurance, has too much fine print, prohibiting death *"except . . ."* including the suicide clause, acts-of-war clause, etc. Of course, everyone knows that . . . one who ventures out on the ocean has to be suicidal!

There are many vessels that cruise, or rather "voyage" fully insured due to their owners' "blackmail" of the insurance companies. This deal is possible if one owns sufficient property ashore so that the threat of loss of *all* premiums makes the company willing to write coverage of one's vessel. Such are the people who say nonchalantly, "Don't worry, I'm insured," or, "Let the insurance company worry about it." Perhaps it is their experience with these people that has caused insurance companies to raise their premiums to such levels that the average ocean cruiser cannot afford coverage.

The logical solution for the ocean cruiser is to *be his own underwriter*. Really, his risks are small. If he maintains his vessel in a seaworthy condition, keeps his ground tackle in proper condition and *above* the minimum requirements of Lloyds, practices the best seamanship—always trying to improve it with experience—obeys the Rules of the Road and the laws of nature, then his chances of major disaster are small, indeed. It strikes me that insurance companies should take into consideration the competency of each master and the condition of his vessel in determining premiums. In this way, for every year that no claim was filed, a substantial reduction in premium could result. Perhaps such policies *are* available, including public liability and health insurance. If they do exist, many people, including myself, would be eager to investigate them and invest in such coverage.

SHIP'S PAPERWORK

A voyage of pleasure can turn into a nightmare if captain and crew are not prepared to handle the vast responsibilities and paperwork involved in foreign cruising. Often they are not aware of the penalties involved in failure to comply with the laws of each country visited.

It's worth remembering that as you sit aboard your vessel in a U.S. port on the day you depart for another country, *they* are the foreigners; on the day you arrive in that country, *you* are the foreigner.

U.S. vessels documented as yachts enjoy rather unique privileges in most cruising areas. Unfortunately, many vessels abuse not only their own country's leniency but also that of the nations visited. In many cases, this stems from not knowing or understanding the laws.

The basic law, set forth in Customs Regulations (19 C.F.R. 4.94 section (A) states: "A vessel documented as a yacht shall be used exclusively for pleasure and shall not transport merchandise nor carry passengers for pay. A vessel which is so documented and which is not engaged in any trade, nor in any way violating the customs or navigation laws of the United States may proceed from port to port in the United States or to foreign ports without clearing and is not subject to entry upon its arrival in a port of the United States, provided it has not visited a hovering vessel." Thus, a U.S. vessel may travel to or from any East or Gulf Coast port, to or from, say, the Virgin Islands or Puerto Rico, and to or from any West Coast port, Hawaii and Alaska without clearing or entering, *provided* it has not visited a foreign place or port or visited a hovering vessel. This is covered in Section 1433, title 19, United States Code.

4.94, section (b) states: "A cruising license may be issued to a yacht of a foreign country only if it has been made to appear to the satisfaction of the Secretary of the Treasury that yachts of the United States are allowed to arrive at and depart from ports in such foreign country and to cruise in the waters of such ports without entering or clearing at the customhouse thereof and without the payment of any charges for entering or clearing, dues, duty per ton, tonnage taxes or charges for cruising licenses. It has been made to appear to the satisfaction of the Secretary of the Treasury that yachts of the United States are granted such privileges in the following countries: Argentina, Australia, Bahama Islands, Bermuda, Canada, Great Britain (including Turks and Caicos Islands), St. Vincent (including the territorial waters of the Northern Grenadine Islands), the Cayman Islands, and the St. Christopher-Nevis-Anguilla Islands), Greece, Honduras, Jamaica, Liberia, Netherlands, New Zealand and West Germany." (These are the countries that were listed as of May, 1974).

Thus, many U.S. flag vessels feel that they need not formally enter the countries listed because of the statement that the vessels are allowed to arrive and depart without clearing customs. This is as false as the notion that any of these foreign vessels can enter the United States without clearing. So each year, some U.S. vessels are seized and fined in foreign ports because they neglected formally to enter that country. It is wise to make sure that the procedure is carried out correctly, for many Canadian vessels have been fined, say in North Carolina or Florida, because they entered the United States, they did not receive a proper clearance—sometimes due to the fact that the port entered was not accustomed to handling yachts.

Those foreign vessels not having reciprocal privileges will find that contact with U.S. officials involves endless paperwork, often accompanied by suspicion, curtness and displeasure at having to bother with a foreign yacht, as the amount of work involved is about equal to handling a vessel loaded with 100,000 tons of freight. Indeed, most foreign yachts not on the privileged list usually avoid U.S. waters, finding that no other nation can make cruising such a nightmare of bureaucratic red tape.

While section (b) states and implies that no charges are levied, many of the countries listed do have such charges: light dues (which the Bahamas are proposing); or customs inspector's transportation charges (also often used in the Bahamas); or a head tax for entering or departing, or both. So, apparently there are ways of circumventing all laws.

Most countries allow three to six months on a cruising permit, after which the vessel must depart or apply for an extension. Often U.S. yachts, because they don't need U.S. clearance papers, will just sail to another port in the area, saying they have just arrived from the United States or one of its possessions. This does eliminate the necessity of leaving the country; however, some do get caught at this and, of course, complain, particularly since the penalty is usually heavy.

A common mistake occurs in the Panama Canal Zone where all vessels must pass through Canal customs. A yacht, having done so, begins cruising Panamanian waters (anchoring in a nation's waters), but often *without* clearing the Zone, formally entering the Republic of Panama and receiving the necessary permit. It is, therefore, quite possible for such a vessel to be seized and the owner fined. In *all* countries, pilferage is not unheard of, nor is the "planting" of evidence to justify subsequent seizure. Fortunately, such practices are rare in the United States, Canada and the British Commonwealth countries.

Many yacht owners (U.S. and Canadian) charter their vessels in foreign countries in order to supplement their income, and that is illegal without a license and/or payment of a fee. Some are caught; however, most are not. It is done with the idea of getting a paying crew who share the expenses of the voyage, a practice common in Europe. This hardly applies, however, when the "crew" changes daily.

There is only one way a vessel can be reasonably assured of having a minimum of trouble, and that is to meet all requirements of accepted international custom and fill out all the papers necessary.

A yacht must have on board:

1. Her document or certificate of register. This proves the vessel's nationality and gives her description—i.e., her length, breadth, depth, number of masts, gross and net tons, description of propelling machinery and her purpose (yacht, passenger ship, tanker, freighter or fishing vessel.)

2. Radio license.

3. Her official number carved into the hull.

4. Panama Canal or Suez Canal certificates, if they have been awarded. The former may be obtained in the United States from the Admeasurement Office, Department of Transportation, at the time of documentation or prior

to departure for the Canal; otherwise, measurement is done by Canal authorities.

5. Copies of any mortgages or liens against the vessel.

6. Classification certificate (Lloyds or A.B.S.), when applicable.

7. Certificate of anchor-chain proof test, carried by many yachts.

8. Certificate of inspection.

9. Any other papers such as receipts for equipment purchases, life raft repacking, warranties and instruction manuals for all equipment.

10. Receipts for all current purchases (this prevents one from paying twice!).

11. All current contracts involving labor, material and added equipment furnished by third parties for the vessel.

12. Entry and clearance papers.

On the first page of each voyage log, or in an attached or separate notebook kept at the chart table, should be listed the vessel's official number, official call letters, length, beam, draft, capacity of fuel and water tanks, gross and net tons, height of masts, date and time of arrival in the present port, with the amount of fuel and water aboard and where purchased, name and nationality of each crew member (in alphabetical order), number, type and serial number of all guns aboard, anticipated date and time of departure, agent or lawyer's address, mail forwarding address and bonded stores list.

Some larger yachts carry paid crew. In some countries, it is necessary to ship (employ) them in the same manner as a merchant vessel. Ordinarily, members of a yacht crew are assigned various jobs such as master (on document), mate, cook, A.B., engineer, etc. If they are not shown as having an assigned duty, some countries consider them as passengers, and more paperwork results. If someone is to join a vessel in a foreign port, or if a crewman must return home from a foreign port and then rejoin the vessel prior to sailing, it is wise to write a letter explaining the entire arrangement for the person to carry and show, outbound and on his return. Otherwise, upon returning the person may be required by authorities to purchase an "outbound" airplane ticket (to insure his departure) and a refund on it may be difficult to collect.

Consuls in many countries require yachts "from home" to furnish them with a crew list and particulars of the vessels. It's considered proper for yacht owners to pay a courtesy call on their country's consul, but this is not encouraged by U.S. consuls—possibly because of the large number of U.S. vessels cruising, the consul's many other duties and their general lack of interest in yachtsmen. So unless the area is remote and seldom frequented by yachts, or one is certain the consul is a yachtsman, it may be easier just to avoid U.S. embassies and consulates. This is not meant to be derogatory of the consular service, but is simply an observed fact.

The number of copies of crew lists required varies from country to country. A foreign vessel entering the United States must have four to eight copies—i.e., customs (2); immigration (1); quarantine (1); customs searchers (2) if they board; harbor control (1); and water police (1). Some countries require, in addition to a regular crew list, a special crew list on their own form. They may also require a visaed crew list executed by the consul before the vessel's departure from their last port but, in any case, to be visaed prior to arrival in the present port. On U.S. vessels having alien crewmen and on foreign vessels entering the United States, one should check with the United States consul prior to departure to see they have valid entry permits, or passports visaed for the United States. There are exceptions, but they seldom apply to yachts.

When bound for the Panama Canal, send a crew list via Air Mail from the last port to the port captain of either Balboa or Cristobal, whichever is the expected port of arrival.

A crew list should be set up as follows:

CREW LIST

NAME OF VESSEL

———————————— Masted Yacht

Official No. ——————————— Country of Registry: ———————————

Gross ——————————— tons   Net ——————————— tons

No.	Last Name	First	Middle Initial	Age	Date of Birth	Country of Birth	Nationality & Passport Number	Assigned Position
1.								
2.								
3.								
4.								
etc.								

Last Port of Call ——————————— Date of Departure ———————————

Port of Arrival ——————————— Date of Arrival ———————————

Signature: ———————————
                         Master

If the list is alphabetical, it is easier for the immigration officer to check out the names against his "Book" (unwanted or wanted list). The crew list should be typed or hand-printed in BLOCK LETTERS.

While still at sea before arrival in a foreign port, the courtesy flag of that country should be flown from the starboard yardarm (spreader or shroud) of the forward-most mast. From another flag halyard, the quarantine (pratique) flag ("Q," all yellow) should be flown if there are no infectious diseases aboard and one has a clean bill of health from the last port. However, if one does have, say, a case of smallpox or other communicable disease aboard, then one must fly two (2) yellow flags from the same halyard, or a "Q" flag plus first repeater if a full set of code flags is carried.

After entry into the territorial waters of a country, no one may leave the vessel until the vessel is cleared, except the master or other ship's officer to report the vessel's arrival. In U.S. ports, the quarantine officer and immigration officer usually board together, and after they've given their clearance, the customs officer and Department of Agriculture officer will board. The only other persons authorized to board prior to clearance is a pilot, the vessel's agent, a consular official and the U.S. Coast Guard (in U.S. ports), or police, army or navy (in many Latin American countries). In fact, often there are more officials than crew aboard. All countries have become strict in this regard, and more often than not any person boarding prior to clearance must remain aboard until the vessel is cleared. I have known of fines up to $300 per crew member and $1,000 against the vessel for neglect to follow correct procedure. Needless to say, one should arrive during normal working hours or expect to pay overtime to all officials. Also, some countries take a siesta at midday. Should one arrive at this time, it is best to take a siesta oneself rather than risk arousing and irritating an official.

When entering U.S. ports, the customs officer will require the following papers and information:

1. A sealed envelope marked "Customs" which is given to you by the immigration officer.

2. The time of arrival and anchoring at quarantine.

3. Four (4) copies of a crew curio manifest.

4. Four (4) copies of the stores list. This list includes any bonded stores and any narcotics in the medicine chest.

5. Two (2) copies of the crew list.

6. Two (2) copies of Customs Form 3415 if any foreign repairs were made; plus four (4) copies of Customs Form 7535, which details the cost of these repairs. If no repairs were made, only one (1) copy of 3415 need be filled out, marked "No Repairs."

7. Clearance from the last port, if the yacht has been cruising in a

country that does not have reciprocal cruising privileges with the United States.

8. An itinerary showing date of arrival and departure from each foreign port visited. This is not always requested.

When U.S. yachts have been only to Canada or the Bahamas, some of the above are not required, especially a stores list. However, all repairs, new equipment or reconstruction to a U.S. vessel in a foreign port are subject to a custom's tax.

Yachts are normally considered to be voyaging "in ballast," and one may be required to fill the appropriate customs forms to quadruplicate. If so, the phrasing should be: "In ballast—no cargo on board." Then, in the space provided, "nine tons lead and cement in the keel, plus ¼ ton shifting lead ballast in bilge."

The customs officer will then grant a "preliminary entry" permit in the case of foreign yachts, which is then presented to local customs officials when formal entry is made. The formal entry must be accomplished within 48 hours after arrival, Sundays and holidays being excepted. For the formal entry, one takes all of the papers issued by the boarding officer— i.e., those mentioned above, plus the following:

1. Your ship's document (register or other paper proving ownership and the vessel's nationality.

2. The pratique; crew's list (certified); draft on arrival; fuel and water on arrival; date and time of arrival.

This is a lot of paper work; yet, for U.S. yachts, it can usually be accomplished in less than one hour. For yachts from privileged countries, it takes only slightly longer, and they receive a cruising permit usually good for six months. *However,* all yachts from any other country, in order to proceed coastwise, must obtain:

1. One coastwise manifest.

2. Two (2) copies of Form 1385, "Permit to Proceed," one of which is The document or register is surrendered at the Customs House until certified and returned to the master of the vessel. such time as one clears, along with two (2) copies of the crew list, and one copy of "Permit to Proceed," Form 1385. On clearing each port, these documents will be returned, but one must make formal entry at the next port, etc.

In clearing from any U.S. and most foreign ports, the vessel must depart within 24 to 48 hours of midnight of the day the clearance was issued. If, for some reason, this cannot be accomplished, one may receive (by application) an extension provided there have been no crew changes or changes to the vessel since clearance was granted.

A foreign yacht may stop in any U.S. port to take on fuel, water, stores or to make repairs; if she sails within 24 hours, she does not have to enter or clear as listed above. However, she must submit a report in writing and under oath to the collector of customs, stating the date and time of arrival, date and time of departure, the quantity of fuel, water, stores, or extent of repairs made. This must be done within 72 hours of arrival. Thus, to depart within the 24-hour period requires some very careful planning or the help of an agent.

Many countries permit a vessel to seek refuge from the elements (storms) or to make necessary repairs for survival. Most require that this not exceed 24 hours, and there can be no contact with the shore which includes, say, purchasing stores from passing vessels of that country. Some countries do *not* allow this refuge, and one must then make a protest entry. This merely means that one must file a statement noting the severity of weather or accident which caused the vessel to divert from her intended route to seek refuge. In some countries, the "P" flag is flown to indicate this status. More correct would be the flags "IBI"—my vessel is seriously damaged—; "F"—damage cannot be repaired at sea without assistance—, or "XUI"—I will wait until weather moderates.

Without doubt, one of the greatest causes of concern in all nations is smuggling—primarily of narcotics, guns and aliens. Failure to itemize and declare the most innocent narcotic in the ship's medicine chest, no matter how small the amount, or guns and ammunition normally carried, may result in detention or imprisonment of the crew or even confiscation of the vessel. As for transport and landing of aliens, in spite of the often lucrative compensation offered, this is so risky that not many yachts are lured into attempting it, although there are always the few who try. Loss of vessel and heavy fines are the *least* one can expect if caught. The firing squad is specified by some governments. Smuggling for the average yachtsman is a foolish game, for if the item has great value, there is almost certainly an informant at the selling end who can be relied on to share the reward (part of the fine) if the smuggler is caught.

This brings us to vessel search. Not every yacht is searched when entering a port, but it may be. Having a complete inventory or "stores list" often prevents being ransacked. After going through a few dozen lockers that check out with the list, customs searchers usually only spot check the remainder of the hull. If one arrives from a suspect area or if customs has been alerted, a very thorough search is common. Unfortunately, mistaken identity sometimes causes unwarranted harassment and sometimes, considerable damage to the vessel. Needless to say, the logbook should contain the time of boarding and the names and functions of each official. This protects both parties. The "searchers" are professionals and when they are seeking narcotics they are often aided by dogs; there is no immediate redress for damage they may inflict on the vessel.

Visiting foreign yachtsmen normally have passports visaed for the

United States. While the crew is permitted to travel, the same privilege is not always granted the vessel. This same arrangement holds true for U.S. citizens in some foreign countries, some of which requires a bond to be posted for each crewman, or sufficient money deposited for a one-way air fare out of the country to the person's home country. Some ports (or parts of them) are restricted because of defense installations or other reasons, and must be avoided.

Upon arrival at all ports from another country, the vessel must present itself for quarantine inspection. Many countries require an international health card that lists the immunizations received by each crew member and the effective dates. If a vessel has come from an infected area, the port doctor may inoculate the crew at this time. If it has come from an area where the rhinoceros beetle thrives and is entering an uninfected area, the vessel will be required to depart that port one hour before sunset until one hour after sunrise each night, either heaving to several miles offshore or moving to a special night anchorage. Pets are also subject to quarantine laws that vary from country to country. It behooves the master of the vessel to learn these regulations for each country the vessel will enter, *before* cruising to them. Most nations maintain an embassy or consul in the capital city. One should write for information and allow six to eight weeks for a reply.

Many countries prohibit the importation of fresh meats, poultry, vegetables and fruits. Fortunately, most small vessels consume all these foods during the voyage. On short voyages, such as from Canada, Mexico or the Bahamas, it is best not to stock up on these items as they will only be confiscated when the vessel enters her first U.S. port. Other items forbidden to enter the United States include any packing or rope made of grass, seeds, bulbs and plants of many kinds. These laws may seem archaic, but a new species of plant, bug, etc., might accidently be introduced into an area which has no natural defenses or controls against its worst features. This has happened in almost every civilized country, usually with the worthy goal of improving the natural beauty and ecology of the area, and often with devastating effects.

Accidents in port or at sea that cause damage or loss of the vessel, or which cause another vessel to damage herself, must be recorded and reported. The majority of small bluewater vessels are not insured. Some have P & I (protection and indemnity) which covers loss of life, hospitalization, damage to docks, bridges, navigational aids and other movable or fixed properties, etc. Underwriters pay only for what is specified in the policy and only after proof that such loss or damage has occurred and only when substantiated by entry in the vessel's log, the master's report and statement, and often by a surveyor's report.

In the case of an accident, the master should not allow anyone except his lawyer, underwriter, or a bona fide government official to inspect the vessel's logbook. When information contained in the logbook is required, that information is excerpted (a true copy, including errors) and certified by the master or owner. The logbook itself should never be surrendered, nor should any statement be given either by the owner or crew to anyone but the above-mentioned persons. Even in marine matters one can find the equivalent of the "ambulance chaser."

The logbook should contain a continuous record of the voyage—i.e., weather, speed, sea conditions, the events taking place during each watch, and also a record of all occurrences, while entering, leaving, and in port. When the vessel suffers an accident or injury, it must be entered in the log as soon after the event as possible. If the event takes place over a considerable length of time it is best to write a rough draft so that the whole scene is in chronological order with the precise times given if possible. Never trust anything to memory—get it down on paper! The vessel is an entity and the log is the voice (and memory) of the vessel. What is entered *must* be a true account of what has occurred each day of the vessel's life. Never erase an error. Draw a line through the error so it can still be read and initial it; then make the correct entry. Never remove a page or attach any document to the log. Always enter the name (printed) of any official who comes aboard and the time of his arrival and departure. Always record the time when taking on fuel, the time when pratique was granted, when the engine was started and stopped, etc. The general rule is: If in doubt, *log it!*

From the above, it may sound as if one is continuously writing up the log. Quite the contrary—10 minutes a day would be a generous average. Incidentally, the log is best kept in ink. In the merchant service, the deck log is kept in pencil, but is recopied in ink by one of the officers, proofread, and then called the "smooth" log. The log should never be a novel, a guest book, or anything but an exact account of the vessel's routine. A log, properly written, is a legal document, and extracts from it are admissable in court.

MEDICAL MATTERS

Reports of accidents, in general, regardless of country, have often to be made on voluminous forms, and six to 10 copies may be required. Statements should be as brief as possible, but include all details. One thing to be particular about in such reports is that equipment or gear that was involved in the accident was either *new* or *used*—never, never *old*.

Perhaps one of the most difficult reports to prepare for radio transmission or for relay from vessel to shore is a request for medical assistance and guidance. I have had several occasions to seek such assistance. To save time and confusion, my doctor suggests the following information be given:

1. Name of vessel; latitude and longitude; port of departure; port of destination; estimated speed; and course being steered.

2. With regard to patient: his age, sex, whether mobile or immobile, conscious or unconscious, clarity of speech.

3. Pulse rate per minute, labored or easy, noisy or quiet, and if there is pain in breathing.

5. Temperature: state whether oral or rectal, rising, falling or steady, and how long it has been monitored.

6. Cause of injury, or illness (if known).

7. Type of wound, if any: deep, ragged or clean; size and depth.

8. Any associated pain: whether moderate, severe, dull, sharp, widespread or localized, continuous or intermittent; what increases the pain; what relieves the pain; how long the pain has been present.

9. Describe the area involved and locate it from some fixed point on the body.

10. State if bleeding is present or absent in vomit, phlegm, stool or urine. If present, whether it is slight or severe and if it is controlled.

11. Any deformity or abnormal function or movement.

12. Other symptoms such as pale skin, mental dullness, extreme cold in extremities, thirst, nausea.

13. Past history if possible, listing all disease such as malaria, ulcers, heart trouble, head injuries, etc.

14. Any treatment given: name any medicines given; whether the attacks become less severe, more severe, or were unchanged, after medicine.

15. If the patient takes any other medicine with any frequency, such as sleeping pills, laxatives, Dramamine, etc. If so, how long has it been taken, how often and when last taken.

16. Patient's complaint.

17. Any other associated symptoms observed. This is difficult, but best thought of as, "If the patient were not suffering most from the other complaint, I would have described these symptoms."

Reading the medical books normally carried on board ship can be confusing, and if help is available via phone or radio, ask for it. If help is not at hand, you must use the book. Write down the symptoms in one column and, opposite each item, write the book's suggested cause of those symptoms. With luck, a pattern will emerge and chances will be pretty good that you are treating the right ailment.

FLAGS OF CONVENIENCE

In the United States, foreign flag vessels owned by U.S. citizens are politely called "vessels sailing flags of convenience," the implication being that the owners are too cheap to conform to U.S. laws, rules and regulations. This may be true of some, but for many of us it is a "flag of survival," and our vessels not only meet but also often exceed U.S. safety requirements.

There are many countries which offer their flags to bona fide applicants, among them Panama, Liberia, Cayman Islands, British Virgins, Bahamas, Turks Island, Singapore and Hong Kong. Each country has different requirements, but each requires more paperwork for original documentation than does the United States for yachts. To register our vessel, Panama required a Seaworthiness Certificate, Certificate of Equipment, Certificate of Ownership and a Master's Oath that I would uphold the laws of the country, along with other forms and statements, including the services of a lawyer. My vessel, *K'ung Fu-tse,* was then licensed for International Voyages.

When I had completed the forms for Panamanian documentation, I mentioned this to several long-time acquaintances in government and gave my reasons. I was assured that they would never have bothered me as far as inspection was concerned, especially since I had a "grandfather date" for the start of construction. Then a stranger entered and the situation was explained to him. He immediately leveled a 30-minute tirade at me, the gist of which was: "Old Glory will always rule the sea, and only an idiot would sail on any vessel over which the Stars and Stripes did not wave."

This was interspersed with history, both present and past, and his version of what the future would bring. Finally, red in the face, having mentally condemned me as a turncoat, traitor and criminal, he concluded: "Don't you know those little 'monkey countries' change their laws overnight?"

Not having been able to get a word in edgewise during the entire tirade, I answered, "Oh, God, that can't be true!"

"But it *is!* It *IS!*" he shouted.

"Oh, hell," I answered. "Now you're telling me it is just like the United States, and I was looking for some stability for a change!" I turned and walked out.

I must say that I have had no problems flying the Panamanian flag. It has been somewhat inconvenient in the United States as I must officially enter and clear each port where I remain for 24 or more hours, and notify U.S. customs each time I stay in a marina. I am not permitted to go for a daylight sail or even to just cruise around, as Panama and the United States do not have reciprocal cruising agreements. Strange, isn't it? Thus, when traveling the Intracoastal Waterway, I do so on a "Permit to Proceed," and it is from one port to another port—i.e., say, Newport News, Virginia, to West Palm Beach, Florida. With but few exceptions I have always found U.S. customs inspectors friendly and courteous; and while it may at times be inconvenient, I certainly meet many people and get lots of paperwork done for only $2.00 each time I enter and clear.

Why a Panamanian flag for *K'ung Fu-tse?* There are many reasons. Foremost is my objection to the reality that my vessel, if of U.S. flag, could be boarded by the U.S. government on *any ocean at any time* for any supposed or real violation of *any law.* I acknowledge the right of any nation in its own waters to inspect my vessel for proper papers and, in time of war, to determine my nationality on the high seas. But, in peacetime, I am not willing to suffer, say, a German ship to board me on the high seas or in U.S. waters, nor do I grant this right to the U.S. government outside its territorial waters.

Other reasons include the inability of the U.S. government and the individual states to achieve a uniform and realistic sewage law that is both practical and enforceable. Here we find a case of "whose ox is being gored," each side imposing contradictory regulations that are ridiculous. There are double standards for vessels *under* and *over* 100 tons as regards oil pollution. Different numbers of lifesaving devices for under and over x number of feet. An arbitrary change to single sideband radios, only to discover that an organization was not available to monitor the frequencies, and then that the authorized frequencies were wrong—which required a change in crystals (at least two so far and a promise of one more). What is worse, no one else in the world, except Canada, has followed suit—i.e., banned AM radios. How can a fisherman in a "developing" country shell out several thousand dollars for a radio set when he can get an AM set for $25 to $300? The list of problems goes on and on, but it will suffice to say that at the time I laid the keel for *K'ung Fu-tse,* on September 19, 1972, to the time of my first voyage in 1975, the increase in cost of construction in order to conform to all the U.S. regulations would have been $15,000! Prior to our departure, the required expenditures were obsolete and many would have had to be removed if they had been aboard—$15,000 wasted! Now at the beginning of her second voyage, an additional $20,000 could have been spent to keep *K'ung Fu-tse* current, and not *one* expenditure would have increased her seaworthiness or safety.

Furthermore, the State of Virginia would have had many thousands of dollars in personal property taxes, although I personally no longer live there. I no longer live in the United States. I *live* aboard an ocean cruising vessel of *Panamanian* registry and visit *many* countries. I have forwarding addresses in several states in the United States, and in all the countries I visit. I am *permanently* and only domiciled aboard my vessel, and thus I suppose it is my world or country. In it I do my best to achieve law and order by following the traditions of the sea. In port I suffer the laws of each country until our voyage begins again.

One thing I should make clear—I have not given up my U.S. citizenship and do not intend to do so.

What is the status of *K'ung Fu-tse* in Panama? There have been no changes in the law pertaining to boats; there have been no threats or rumors; and the taxes have not changed. We have not been hassled by the Panamanians.

BURIAL AT SEA

(*A Memory*)

"Swede" was a good shipmate—both on watch and off. He more or less understood English, as well as a half-dozen other languages, although he spoke only Swedish, sometimes mixed with a smattering of German. I spoke only English, although I could understand and speak a few words in a half-dozen other languages. Off-watch, we often played cribbage which, if nothing else, taught me to count in Swedish. On-watch, it was a different matter. Swede was a professional and his watery blue eyes missed nothing. In his 40 years at sea, he had forgotten probably as much as I would ever know. I can well remember those great gnarled hands deftly tying a knot or splicing, and how gentle but firm they were as he forced my clumsy fingers to simultaneously twist and push to complete the knot he was teaching me. He was a good teacher, and a *"Ya, das iss goot"* was a trophy, and *"Nein, dass is schitt,"* was almost a mortal wound. We were shipmates for two years, always on the same watch. There were two others on the watch, but Martin, the Belgian, and Frenchie always spoke French so pretty much kept to themselves. In all that time, I never knew Swede by any other name.

During a storm the seas, while large, are not always combing, for the wind is often so fierce that it blows off the tops as they form, and this whips across the sea like hailstones, cutting faces and whipping oilskins. Under such conditions, we were always under short sail, well reefed, and sometimes even under bare poles. Most often, it is after a fierce storm that the waves become mountainous, with heavy combers that occasionally break aboard with just a lot of water and no force. Occasionally, however, the sea heaps up into vertical cliffs of water that crash on deck, spewing tons of water with such force that it carries away lifeboats, stanchions, bulwarks, and even two-ton anchors. Under such conditions, we usually set more sail and, since the wind eases faster than the sea diminishes, we are often under all lowers plus topsails to keep the vessel from rolling, especially to windward.

It was on such a day that I was working the main top and Swede the fore top. The mate and Frenchie were working the halyards, outhauls and down-hauls while I cleared the stops. Swede had some trouble as his outhaul was jammed, and as I started down I saw a wave larger than any I had seen before. Its crest seemed to be level with my eyes and I was 70 feet above the deck. I shouted, "Hang on, Swede!" and pointed to windward. At the same time I saw the mate and Frenchie scrambling up the halyards. Then Swede looked over his shoulder and wrapped those great arms around the gaff on which he was halfway out. It seemed an eternity before the sea smothered the whole of the deck. The schooner lurched, then heeled over onto her beam's end. When I looked down, there was nothing but froth, and the weather rigging seemed to be parallel to the water. I knew then how ships were rolled over and finally understood one's complete inability to do anything about it—except watch.

Slowly—very slowly—she righted herself, water pouring over both bul-warks. Finally the deck cleared and we rose again to the oncoming seas. Just as we crested one of them, the foresail luffed, the vessel lurched, and then the sail filled with a snap. The gaff whipped across. Swede was mo-mentarily suspended in air, and then he fell, arms outstretched, legs spread-eagled, face up. I heard no thud, no cry, only silence. I could see Swede's calm face with his eyes open, then with his impact on the forehatch edges, his body bent backward and his head hit the deck.

That night, "Sails" sewed him up in a tarp. The stitches were even and neat. I found a piece of pig iron for his feet and cleaned it up, which is proper. The mate took inventory and then took his sea chest aft, for tomorrow Swede's possessions would be auctioned off with the proceeds going to his next of kin.

At dawn, with both watches on deck, the captain came to the fore rail of the quarter-deck, prayer book in hand, and in French, said:

"Bjorne Axel Sevenson was an able seaman in the best of tradition." From the prayer book he read: "Unto Almighty God we commend the soul of our brother departed, and we commit his body to the deep; in sure and certain hope of the Resurrection unto eternal life, through our Lord Jesus Christ; at whose coming in glorious majesty to judge the world, the sea shall give up her dead; and the corruptible bodies of those who sleep in Him shall be changed; and made like unto His glorious body; according to the mighty working whereby He is able to subdue all things unto Himself."

As the hatch board tilted, the Swede splashed gently into the sea. The mate then said, "Colvin, stand aft the watch below; go below."

I went aft and the mate led the way to the cabin of the captain who bade us enter. He picked up a letter and, in English, said, "This was in Seven-son's sea chest. It is addressed to me but concerns you also. It says, 'If I die, please forward my pay, if any, and the money from the sale of my belongings to my wife, Marie. Please give my knife and cribbage board to the American, and ask of him if he is in Sweden and near the town of Uudsvall to see my wife and say he was a shipmate of Bjorne."

Some years later, I was able to honor Swede's request.

6

---◆---

The Engine
or
Taming the Beast

As many readers of my other books know, I am not a great believer in the absolute need for an engine in a vessel built for ocean cruising; however, if one is to be installed, my approach is to seek versatility and low horse-power per ton of hull displacement. The ocean voyager realizes that the engine is but one small part of the whole vessel, yet it and its components may cause 90 percent of all the troubles that one experiences at sea.

Most trouble with engines starts either from neglect or, more frequently, from not understanding the nature of the beast. Neglect of one part of the vessel usually means there is other neglect; however, neglecting the engine is usually due to one's having never realized that it has a limited relationship to the vessel in which it is installed.

There are hundreds of reasons given for not learning about the engine, such as: never had the time; it never seemed important; don't use it that much, etc. Only too often the moment arrives when knowing the performance of the hull and engine is the difference between an enjoyable cruise prolonged with safety and certainty, and one that must be cut short, beset by uncertainty and fears of uncharged batteries, shortages of fuel, being becalmed a few hours from port, or being late to arrive at one's destination.

One may calculate this performance at any time; however, if one is tired or under stress, one is subject to cumulative errors that do nothing but increase anxiety and create further frustration. Therefore, it would seem that a precomputed table, chart or nomograph would not only save hasty piecemeal computations but also permit the solving of numerous engine-related problems at any time, with a minimum of mathematics.

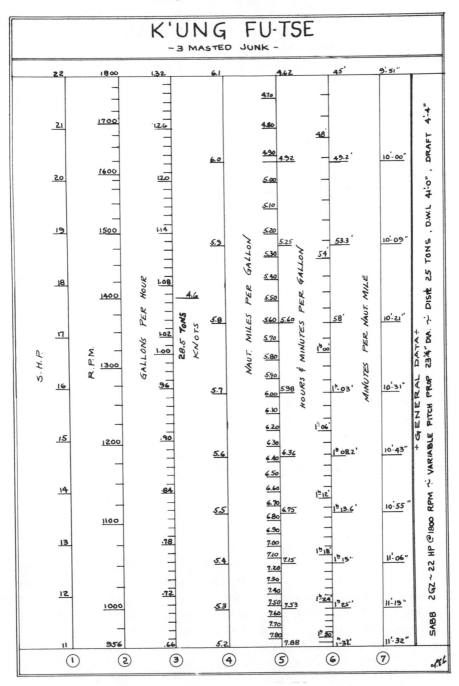

FIG. 6-1. The nomograph prepared by the author for *Kung Fu-tse*.

To construct a nomograph is not complicated, but it does require care and patience, for it must be as exact as possible. From the engine manufacturer, the owner has received or can obtain the information regarding horsepower versus r.p.m. Those two factors provide the information needed to fill in Columns 1 and 2. The charts in engine brochures are too small to use, and should be carefully redrawn to a larger scale, with the information transferred directly to your own chart. For small engines, I use one inch spaces for horsepower and r.p.m. and a smaller scale, say one half inch or three eighths inch for larger engines. There is little value in throttling back to less than half the rated shaft horsepower given by the manufacturer as this may cause carboning or overheating in some engines. As a word of caution, there are many companies, especially in the United States, which "rate" the engine by its brake horsepower. This, except for selling purposes, is a useless number to the owner of the vessel, as losses caused by gear box and accessories must be deducted to get a true continuous h.p. rating.

Column 1 multiplied by .06 will yield the average gallons per hour of diesel fuel consumed. Multiplying Column 1 by .094 yields the average gallons per hour consumed for gasoline engines of that horsepower. Manufacturer's consumption curves are based on a fuel consumption rate of .44 pounds per horsepower per hour for a diesel engine, and .58 pounds per horsepower per hour for a gasoline engine. These figures vary from one manufacturer to another. Diesel fuel weighs about 7.25 pounds per gallon; gasoline weighs about 6.15 pounds per gallon. The weight of fuel oil also varies according to type used—i.e., diesel, or No. 1 or No. 2 furnace oil— and according to the country where it is refined. These figures yield slightly more than the old rule-of-thumb power rating, which was 16 horsepower per gallon for diesel engines and 10 horsepower per gallon for gasoline engines. The resultant information becomes Gallons Consumed Per Hour at various r.p.m.'s, and is labeled Colume 3.

Column 4 is the most difficult to compute. Such a column is normally prepared by the designer of the vessel. For a naval architect, it is laborious and filled with "fudge" factors that are valid only for a given vessel.

From past experience with the same type of vessel, the architect can accurately compute speed ± .02 knots. Such calculations should not be attempted by the average owner. If the designer's calculations are not available, it is then fairly easy to work up a speed table by r.p.m.; using the vessel itself. That way, one can be confident the results are free of guesswork. To do this, one must operate the vessel either over a known distance or have a reliable log that has previously been calibrated. Using a log is the faster way to do it. Distance is run at various r.p.m.'s and elapsed time noted, and from this the speed computed or, in the case of a log, noted. Several precautions should be observed:

1. The hull must have a clean bottom—no barnacles or weed. Speed trials should be made some time *after* a haul-out for bottom painting. If done the same day as launching, a false figure will result that can only be obtained again on another launching day. I prefer to wait 20 days, which gives the general average that would be experienced on a cruise. Bottom fouling is the greatest during the first 15 days, after which the curve flattens out over the next 90 days.

2. Trials must be done at slack water. If any current is known, then runs must be made *with* and *against* the current, and then averaged.

3. There should be wind force "o" and the sea should be "calm."

4. The trials must not be run in a narrow river or shallow water, as either or both conditions will affect the results.

5. The engine must have been on a constant r.p.m. reading for three minutes before timing or reading speed, which allows the governor to settle. Also, it is best to go at minimum r.p.m. first and increase progressively.

This information must be plotted (see Figure 6-2) on the horsepower curve since this relates to horsepower and to r.p.m. Speed must fall on the same line, which is always a curved line. Resultant ratios are: horsepower: speed, r.p.m.: speed, or horsepower: r.p.m. in a calm condition. For power vessels, a second curve for, say, Force 4 winds, and a third for Force 6 winds, would be useful, as would additional information on free running —i.e., with wind and wave.

Once Column 4 is completed, then dividing it by the corresponding figures in Column 3 gives us the Nautical Miles per Gallon and we label this Column 5. If a curve is plotted, more points can be obtained to give, say, tenths of a mile per gallon, requiring less interpolating against r.p.m.

Column 6 is computed by dividing Column 3 by 60, which yields minutes required to consume one gallon. This is then converted to hours and minutes. If labeled every six minutes, then tenths of an hour can easily be read and mental multiplication done; however, each minute should be accounted for. Again, this is a curve and must be plotted.

Finally, Column 7 is Column 4 divided into 60 which gives time required to travel a nautical mile at that speed in minutes and tenths. This can be converted to minutes and seconds if your habit is like mine—to think in seconds.

Some sample problems and solutions follow. EXAMPLE:

1. Given: Flat calm with 10 gallons of fuel remaining; the sea buoy for the next port is 50 miles distant; time is 1000 hours; visibility of land is 14 miles; slack water ebb is 1930 hours.

Required: a. r.p.m. to reach sea buoy with two gallons reserve.
           b. Speed.
           c. Time land should be sighted.

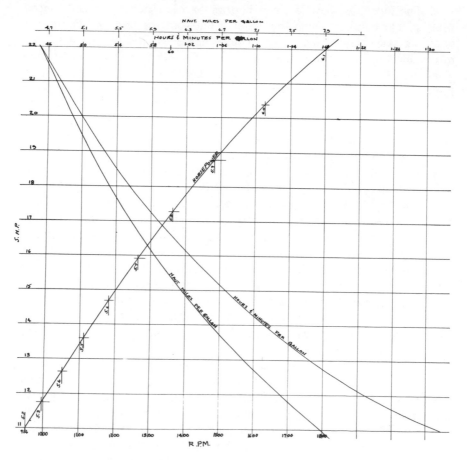

FIG. 6-2. A typical horsepower/fuel consumption/miles per galley graph.

        d. What speed and r.p.m. to arrive at sea buoy at beginning of slack water.

Solution: a. 50 miles ÷ 8 gallons = 6.25 miles per gallon = 1,210 r.p.m.

        b. 5.63 knots (by interpolation).

        c. 50 − 14 = 36 ÷ 5.63 = 6.39 hours or 6 hours, 23 minutes.

        d. 50 ÷ 9.30 = 5.38 K = 1040 r.p.m. (by inspection).

2.   a. At 1,300 r.p.m. how many miles per gallon?
           Answer: 5.85

        b. How long will it take to consume one gallon?
           Answer: 1 hour and .01 minutes.

    c. At this r.p.m. what is my approximate speed and time to do one nautical mile?

    Answer: Approximately 5.74 knots; 10 min. 27 sec. per mile.

    a. Wishing to use only 10 gallons of fuel for battery charging, and this requiring three hours of engine running per week, and on a five-week cruise, at what engine r.p.m. must I charge batteries and gear the alternator? Answer: $3 \times 5 = 15$ hours; $10 \div 15 = .66$ gallons/hours, or 956 r.p.m.

This reminds me that many ocean cruisers have their alternators drive remotely from the main engine via a clutch and differential pulley, which allows battery charging at various r.p.m. to obtain maximum output of the alternator. This is especially useful on hand-starting engines. So, one can see that it *is* possible to make the beast work for you.

There is one further complication and that is the propeller. On *Kung Fu-tse,* I have a variable pitch prop which allows an infinite number of variations in propulsion and fuel economy. A fixed propeller, the most common type, does not have this advantage and is only loaded correctly at one r.p.m. Thus, if the propeller is designed to operate at maximum r.p.m., then any r.p.m. less will mean a loss in speed and efficiency, and a greater fuel consumption for that r.p.m. If, however, the propeller is selected for the maximum torque (which is usually much less than maximum r.p.m.), the reduction to less r.p.m. does not result in a drastic loss in efficiency and is always the best approach in an auxiliary, especially when turning the largest permissible propeller at low r.p.m. One thousand r.p.m. is maximum and less is even better.

It's worth remembering that the engine is designed so that at a given r.p.m. *X* horsepower is the maximum it can deliver. It might give less but never more; that depends on vessel loading. Actually, it is the governor that controls the amount of fuel required to maintain a given r.p.m. Once the engine overloads, the r.p.m. decreases, often resulting in serious harm. (The usual sign of this is a smoking exhaust—the darker the smoke, the worse the overload—often accompanied by higher operating temperatures.)

You will notice that with my engine, by decreasing speed from 6.1 knots at 4.62 miles per gallon to 5.75 knots (a loss of six per cent), I gain a fuel reduction of 29 per cent. My maximum reduction in speed to 5.2 knots is a loss of 15 per cent, while my fuel reduction is 50 per cent.

Using the nomograph, many decisions can be made with accuracy. And it seems likely that the conservation of fuel which has always been a consideration for the ocean voyager will soon become a necessity for others who go cruising.

7

———◆———

Insulation of Hulls

Boat- and shipbuilding is an ancient and honorable trade, steeped in traditions and slow to change. Through the ages, we have been generally content to improve only marginally upon what our forefathers accomplished. Thousands of years of vessel construction has not yet made obsolete a single building material used centuries ago by the boatbuilders of antiquity; nor has any material up to the present shown promise of becoming the universal "ideal," encompassing the best properties of all other materials while being readily available and easy to work. The result is that we are still using ancient ideas and techniques with only slight modifications to achieve the same end result—i.e., to transport people and goods across the oceans.

With the introduction of new materials, builders employed the same basic construction techniques as they had previously used; however, in the process of modification (which usually implies simplification), a loss occurs which must be compensated for by the addition of yet another material to achieve the same or equal quality inherent in the original material. If this were not true, man would now enjoy perpetual motion. These thoughts lead me to the subject of insulating hulls, aluminum in particular.

One sad fact of life is that all materials promote condensation under the right (wrong) conditions. Some materials do this more readily than others. Owners of wooden hulls often cite the sweating of a metal or GRP (glass-reinforced plastic) hull as one of the objectionable features with which one has to contend if his vessel is made of these materials—in spite of the easily demonstrable fact that, if the circulation of air is increased, the probability of condensation would diminish. When it's pointed out that wooden hulls are also plagued with condensation problems, the answer is usually, "Yes, but not as much."

To overcome condensation in our metal vessels, we have used cork sprayed on with an adhesive or, more commonly, have thrown handfuls of granulated cork onto a freshly painted surface. What we really did was to expand the surface of the metal many hundreds of times. This permitted air to surround a greatly increased area, thereby absorbing greater amounts of moisture. Apparently, a simple solution to a rather complex problem. From the Chesapeake Bay southward, and in the tropics, condensation is not a common problem and usually can be tolerated without hardship. In northern climates this is not true, and additional measures have to be taken, such as putting wood sheathing on the inside of the hull. For normal winter operation, corkboard, sawdust or mineral wool can be placed against the metal, inside the ceiling, with varying degrees of success.

Heating and cooking with solid fuels keep most hulls reasonably comfortable. I do not remember what foc'sle temperatures were 35 years ago, but I do remember that longjohns and a wool shirt were not unwelcome, and that going on deck from the foc'sle in a snowstorm was not a great shock so far as temperature was concerned. Times change. Solid fuel is seldom used nowadays, having been replaced with kerosene, fuel oil and alcohol. Often, heaters that use these fuels are installed and used without a flue, thus causing condensation by burning up oxygen and releasing carbon dioxide below decks. Burning solid fuel, vented with a flue, produces *dry* heat.

Condensation occurs when water vapor is added to the air beyond its absorption capacity, and when the air temperature is lowered below its dew point. Condensation is further encouraged by the presence of minute salt crystals—primarily sodium, but also magnesium, calcium chloride, and sulphates, all of which are components of sea water. The higher the air temperature, the more water vapor the air will hold—up to about three percent maximum. At low temperatures, air will "carry" only about .01 percent water vapor. Thus, condensation will always be a greater problem in cold climates than where it is warm. Perhaps for the ocean voyager condensation is most noticeable when the interior of the hull is cooler than the outside air and water temperature, a condition which can occur in any region of the world. In the tropics, increasing the ventilation usually eliminates the problem.

Thermal conductivity of any material is the quantity of heat transmitted per unit of time, per unit of cross section, per unit of temperature gradient. The best heat conductors are metals; liquids are poor conductors; and gases are almost non-conductors. Therefore, to achieve the same degree of comfort from the various materials used in boat and ship construction, it's necessary to consider their conductivity relative to each other. If one material is established as the base—for instance, wood—then any other material, if more conductive, would need another material added to it, in the form of insulation, to equalize it relative to wood.

Table I gives the conductivity of the more common materials and then relates each to wood:

TABLE I

	Conductivity cal/cm/sec/°C	Conductivity Relative to Wood
Aluminum alloys	0.480	3,000.00
Copper	0.918	5,738.00
Cast Iron	0.161	1,006.00
Lead	0.083	519.00
Glass	0.002	12.50
Ice	0.005	31.25
Cork	0.0001	0.63
Fiberglass board	0.00007	0.44
Fiberglass (blanket)	0.00008	0.50
Mineral Wool	0.00009	0.56
Asbestos (board)	0.00087	5.44
Expanded polyurethane foam	0.00005	0.31
Rigid polyurethane foam	0.00005	0.31
Wood	0.00016	1.00
Water	0.00139	8.69

From this table we can see the value of a copper-bottom skillet as compared to one of cast iron. The copper is 5.7 times as efficient in the absorption of heat. The table also reveals that an aluminum vessel will sweat 2.98 times as much as a steel vessel. What this translates into is that when a steel hull shows little or no sign of condensation (sweating), one would have to wear oilskins in an aluminum hull. As previously mentioned, there are areas of the world where this would not be a problem, but one is not always in those areas. Therefore, it has been a practice to insulate or partially insulate steel and iron vessels if they are to be used in northern climates, and aluminum vessels if they are used north of the semi-tropics.

To compound all these problems even further, a vessel is exposed simultaneously to both water and air. Water absorbs 6,250 times as much heat as wood and, fortunately, the absorption varies directly with temperature. With air, however, absorption varies not only with temperature but also with wind velocity, atmospheric pressure and vapor saturation. So solutions to the problem of condensation aboard vessels are not as simply achieved as with land structures.

Ground cork and cork blocks served boat- and shipbuilders well for many years. Indeed, some builders still use them. To me, there appears to be only one drawback to these materials, and that is the fact that cork is organic, therefore subject to rot—deterioration.

Many builders substituted other materials—usually a mica mineral, such as muscovite or potash mica—which are sold under various trade names and are used for insulating houses, in roofing and lightweight cements, and as plant food. These materials are quite satisfactory, especially when applied by blowing them onto freshly painted surfaces; however, they are messy and do absorb water. Fiberglass batts were another good insulator when this material came onto the market, but since it cannot be effectively bonded it has a tendency to shake out, as does mineral wool; so it had to be ceiled. This reduced its effectiveness as a sound absorber (which was a bonus). Also, a few stray fiberglass threads can play hell in an armature or other machinery, and, sifting down into one's bunk, they certainly don't make for comfortable sleeping. The arrival of urethane foams seems to have solved most problems. It is easy to use; provides excellent insulation; is almost voidless; is non-aging; and is immune to rot, fungi, insects or vermin. Also, it is nontoxic, compatible with most coatings, and does not absorb water except in the surface cells.

Is this the ideal material? At first thought, yes. However, as with so many "miracle" materials, one is initially awed by all the announced properties, but until there is some elapsed-time data, one cannot evaluate the long-term compatibility of this material with other materials. Also, if there *is* incompatibility, you can't immediately determine a method of circumventing the problem so the material can be used safely.

In a steel vessel, you rapidly develop a sensitivity to the reality that iron and steel will corrode when exposed to the elements. The degree of corrosion depends on the composition of the metal and the kind of environment. A builder, through habit based on experience, automatically protects the steel first from corrosion, and then applies the insulation. Direct application of *any* insulation to steel without such preliminary preparation is a serious mistake. In spite of announced performance of the insulating material, which he rightfully regards with skepticism, the builder knows that no coating is perfect. This is one of the reasons for using multiple-coating systems—to lower the probability of voids. The installation of insulation aboard metal vessels, therefore, is usually successful. Through trial and error boatbuilders learned the merits of various materials and how best to install them. Today the average metal vessel builder can offer a pretty reliable guarantee on the acoustical and thermal insulation he installs in the finished hull.

On land it is another story. Home builders are quick to change insulation, often not for the better, but because the unit cost of an alternative product drops. Obsolescence is a way of life and of survival. Many can still remember the iceman coming to the house several times a week, the gargantuan ice boxes in the kitchen, or, if on a farm, the icehouse filled with ice cut the previous winter and packed in sawdust. In those fondly remembered but perhaps overrated times, early refrigerator vehicles were sleds or horse-drawn wagons, and were insulated to protect the ice with sawdust between their inner and outer walls. Later, cork or mineral wool was used as the filler; and, by the time long-distance trucking became common, fiberglass, block foam and then sprayed-on foam had come into use. Even picnic coolers underwent the same changes, until finally both the inner and outer liners were eliminated. Even the casual observer probably noticed that the early portable iceboxes, made of metal, began to rust through, not from the outside but from the *inside*. Some of the better iceboxes were galvanized, and this did prolong their life but did not eliminate the problem. However, with our conditioning to the idea that, given time, everything wears out, this was accepted. The usual solution was to purchase a more expensive model "next time," to insure a longer period of use before the inevitable replacement. One solution substituted aluminum for steel. Everyone knew that steel would corrode and that aluminum would not. Aluminum would pit, but not too badly, and with a little paint, even this could be stopped. Not so in practice!

Enter the aluminum boatbuilder. Ever cautious, he realized that for aluminum to serve well at sea it had to be properly alloyed. The aluminum manufacturing companies had not only done this but also had accumulated abundant data to back their claims. A good seagoing alloy does not need paint above the waterline except for cosmetic purposes. Below the waterline, aluminum presents even more problems than either wood or steel when one is applying anti-fouling bottom paint. These problems were solved with an eventually successful schedule of barrier coats of paint that isolate the hull material from the metallic compounds in the anti-fouling paint. Since corrosion of hull interiors was not seen as a problem some 15 years ago, there was no precedent for painting the interiors and insulation was applied directly to the aluminum without surface preparation. In those days, a likely choice of insulation was wither cork or mica, which require an adhesive if blown on—still the accepted method. Fiberglass, mineral wool, etc., can also be installed without too much trouble as long as there is an air space and ventilation to carry off the moisture accumulation (condensate). If there is insufficient ventilation, the aluminum will be attacked by "poultice corrosion." In some cases this could be severe. In theory, if the aluminum surface could be sealed, this problem would not arise since the surface would be airtight. Once again, foam seemed the answer—or was it?? Again, in theory, the foam bonds to the aluminum and, therefore, a sandwich is created, the outside of which is one of the best conductors of heat, and is prevented from absorbing that heat by the bonded-on material that is a poor conductor.

This was my thinking as I approached the insulation phase of our junk, *K'ung Fu-tse*. I even went so far as to inquire of the foaming subcontractor if it was necessary to prepare the aluminum to receive the foam—such as painting—which, for some reason, I thought I ought to do just for old time's sake. But I was reassured that it would be a waste of time and material, and that "the aluminum surface only has to be clean." I asked him to check with the manufacturer of the basic materials—just to be sure. Within a week, I was told not to worry; they always applied the foam directly to aluminum, and only with vast extremes in temperature could any problem arise.

Frequently in the life of a designer and boatbuilder schedules have been interrupted and unforeseen delays have occurred; so it was with the foaming. Instead of everything being ready by the first of August, it became the first of October. Then Dame Fortune smiled and the fickle finger of Fate held back. In quick succession, I had a chance to inspect an aluminum reefer trailer-truck, not of major manufacture, that was in a state of deterioration and several that were not, and then, an old steel-bodied one that was in good shape—all of them foamed. I developed serious doubts. (I am a great believer in having a belt as well as suspenders.) One foam failure by disintegration is enough to shake you, and I certainly did not want to be in the middle of the ocean if or when it occurred. So I began writing to paint companies, without getting any definite answers in reply. Then Dick Evanson, the regional engineer for Reynolds Metals Company, visited my yard, and we discussed the problem of insulating aluminum hulls with polyurethane foam. According to Dick, there was some suspicion that freon, the principal foaming agent, reacted with metals and, especially, with aluminum. This problem had first come to their attention in walk-in coolers and freezers, when it was discovered that there was some delamination at the interface of the aluminum and the urethane foam.

In the foam manufacturers' data file, they admitted that while their product is closed-cell foam, water *does* enter surface cells. Also, there is a further probability that some cells, although only a fraction of a percent, will not form in the foaming process. It is also probable that water vapor has a permeability through foamed urethane about four times greater than atmospheric gases. Thus, where differential temperatures are involved in metal hulls, the water vapor will condense at the interface. If a freeze-thaw cycle occurs, as it does from Daytona, Florida, northward, this alone will cause separation to occur. Furthermore, water vapor tends to carry fluorides and chlorides to the interface where these products of corrosion will also destroy the bond between foam and metal. Next, the corrosion products, being of greater volume, tend to separate the two components.

Finally, when water is present at the interface along with oxygen, then a typical oxygen corrosion cell could cause "poultice" corrosion.

Well, this is enough to scare one half to death. So back I went to the subcontractor and his suppliers. "Not so," said they. In short, "Believe us, and you will live happily ever after." I like a good story, but no longer believe in fairy godmothers. I have given them plenty of opportunity to help me at critical times—to no avail. So I mailed the subcontractor a sample of aluminum, just as the hull would be at foaming time. A couple of weeks later, the sample came back, fully encased in foam. My first question was, how to test it and then evaluate it? Having less than three weeks before my vessel's foaming day, I decided upon destructive testing. Dropping did nothing, nor did hammering, so I cut one edge, exposing the aluminum and, without too much pressure from me, the foam and aluminum parted company! Sweet words were not echoing through the shop at that moment, but, fortunately, it was Saturday.

By Monday I had calmed down enough to call Dick and ask, "What now?" Barring some persuasive new solution, I was determined to call off the foaming of the interior of my boat.

Dick said that the Swift Company near McCook, Illinois, made a product that was compatible with the foam *and* metal, and had been used recently on a shrimp boat. I was born in Chicago, and the only Swift Company I knew about was the packing house. I also knew from having toured the place that about the only thing not used was the last "moo," so I could only wonder with what part of the cow I was going to coat the interior of my hull!

Long-distance telephone is the fastest and best way of obtaining quick information. Several calls produced the discovery that the Swift Company is involved not only in meat processing, but also in chemical manufacturing. With great patience, the operator finally connected me with a staff chemist who was familiar with my problem and could give specific recommendations. He switched me to the vice-president for sales, who took the order and expedited shipment. I was now satisfied that the problem had been solved and that longevity and minimum maintenance of the foam could be achieved.

The material arrived via UPS and was applied long before the "spec" sheets arrived in the mail. In fact, the foam had already been applied without having the bonding instructions—I know that they usually are read only as a last resort. The adhesion was fantastic; the smell was horrible; and the application was an experience unto itself. I had been told to work with the chemical only in a well-ventilated area; however, even with three exhaust fans working, two intake fans, and a respirator, I had the dry heaves while applying it.

The "specs," when they arrived, revealed that "Swift's FOME-BOND

#64 RTM was developed to improve the adhesion of foamed-in-place urethane foam to metal, wood, hardboard and plastic surfaces." It was recommended for use in all types of refrigerated spaces, and the specs stated that "it provides excellent adhesion to aluminum surfaces which are normally difficult to adhere to, as well as to steel and reinforced fiberglass. When used, some or all of these benefits should result: (1) improve specific adhesion; (2) act as an elastomeric cushion; take up vibration, expansion and contraction of metal skins; (3) promote greater structural integrity and serviceable life; (4) provide the same coefficient of friction resulting in a more uniform density of the foam; (5) act as a flexible protective coating for aluminum, steel and rigid fiberglass, and further help to minimize the corrosive effects of chemicals."

So our new vessel, *K'ung Fu-tse,* was coated and foamed-in, preventing —for the most part—condensation, and also providing thermal insulation. I realize that by controlling condensation, in reality what I did was apply a thermal barrier. However, it would be possible to apply enough foam to keep from drowning in my bunk from condensation, and still not have enough to keep us warm with only a small stove on a cold winter night. Thus, I see two distinct values. The foam did not *significantly* improve the acoustical characteristics of the vessel as would, say, fiberglass batts. It lowered the decibel level by only one decibel; still, this is about a 26 percent reduction from the original noise level, and every little bit helps. More importantly, when combined with regular acoustical materials, the foam does not create any new problems.

The procedure in preparing an aluminum hull for foamed-in-place urethane goes like this:

1. Complete all welding in the areas to be foamed, inside and out.

2. Wire-brush all welds with a stainless steel wire brush, removing *all* traces of "smut."

3. Vacuum all dirt and splatter and all loose particles.

4. Wipe entire interior surface with Tauol or Taulene, a degreaser and cleaner.

5. Use a mild detergent and wipe down, following with a fresh water rinse. If any area of the surface does not show complete wetness, then oil, grease or wax still remains, and this area must be cleaned again. Prepared mixes such as phosphoric acid etch, followed by rinsing, or applying alodine followed by rinsing are alternate cleaning methods.

6. Dry out the hull. Clean dust-free air is the best, but high summer temperatures and direct sun will also speed the process.

7. Apply FOME-BOND #64 RTM to a thickness of one to two dry mils. If the protective coating is for steel, or if severe conditions are expected (frequent freeze-thaw cycles), then three to four mils are better— i.e., two coats.

8. Apply urethane foam. It should be thicker for an aluminum hull than for the same hull in steel—say 1¼ to 2 inches for aluminum and ¾ to one inch for steel.

9. The foam hardens in a matter of minutes and seems to cure in about 48 hours—that is, becomes rigid.

Evidently, the more experienced the operator, the more uniform the coating thickness; thus, less cleanup time. I've never claimed professionalism in foaming, but I've never skimped on using the material. Therefore, my cleanups have always been mostly cutting away the excess where it might interfere with interior joiner work or acoustical insulation. In removing excess thickness, you lost some of the benefits of the original hard skin that forms a protective coating, and expose the new, rougher surface cellular structure to possibility of entrapping moisture. On the other hand, it is desirable to paint the entire surface with a flame-retardant paint anyway since the foam, while somewhat self-extinguishing, will burn if subjected to enough flame, and will produce noxious if not fatal gases. I have been told that this is cyanide gas.

It's natural to wonder if the operation was a success. In the short term, yes. In no area have we found delamination. Where the FOME-BOND #64 RTM was inadvertently sprayed and was not wanted, it had to be removed with solvents, or scraped and sanded off. Where the urethane foam was inadvertently sprayed on bare metal, it peeled off easily. The interior of the hull is easy to heat. When the temperature outside is 5°C, three light bulbs totaling 350 watts will raise the temperature to 16°C, which is quite comfortable in winter weather. With milder temperatures, the hull interior has often been maintained at 24°C, which has eliminated having to wear long underwear!

No record was kept of all the freeze-thaw cycles we experienced, but one recent winter we had −8°C, and often a nighttime temperature of −1°C, and up to +10°C during the day. So we have had ample opportunity to observe defects in foam application. To date, none has been observed. We have had many days when the exterior of the hull was actually sweating in rivulets, but the inside remained bone dry. To me, long-term results means 10 to 20 years, so we will have to wait to see what the future holds.

There must be at least an implied moral to every story, so I am led to say that it is incumbent on any builder to use the best materials, technology and skills during the construction of any vessel; that often subcontractors and their suppliers are not aware of the side effects of their products in conjunction with other products and the builder's application; and, that when a hunch indicates something may be amiss, then in spite of the inconvenience, the builder must satisfy himself from every possible source that his anticipated procedure and application will not cause a possible disintegration of his vessel.

Gone are the days when the builder was on a first-name basis with the original manufacturer of each piece of equipment or product he used in the construction of a vessel. It is a loss that we all miss. Today, companies are so remote from the end use, through conglomerate control, that boat-building is now an impersonal business rather than the highly personal enterprise it was when I started.

8

---·◆·---

The Dinghy

A dinghy is an essential item of equipment for a cruising vessel, and one of the most difficult to select. A dinghy that is satisfactory in the average U.S. harbor or anchorage is often inadequate or even dangerous in a cruising environment. The majority of cruising vessels, as designed and built, are not capable of handling a proper dinghy for extended cruising. This is a fault that must be remedied sooner or later, so it soon becomes apparent that two dinghies are desirable for any cruising vessel, and become almost mandatory for large crews. (Incidentally, a dinghy is *not* a lifeboat!)

The most common fault of dinghies is that they are too small and too light in construction. For two persons, eight feet is minimum. As for construction, one pays by the pound, but it is wise to remember (as I've noted before) that first class adds only 10 percent to the cost. Don't fall in with the false idea that a dinghy must be light to be easily handled. This is true only when the dinghy is carried on deck. At all other times, weight has the advantage, especially if it is accompanied by length.

A proper dinghy should: (1) carry the entire crew at one time in a good chop, say, two-foot waves; (2) row and scull well; (3) power well; (4) sail close to the wind and be stable downwind; (5) tow in rough seas as well as calm; (6) be suited for remaining in the water for weeks at a time; (7) be able to lay safely alongside a vessel (without banging up either hull) or a concrete seawall, and to be beached on sand, rocks or coral; (8) withstand an abnormal amount of pounding; (9) be stable and easy to get into; (10) have a dry compartment for cameras, mail, watches, etc.; (11) be easy to launch and stow; (12) be simple and economical to maintain. A tall order!

A dinghy too small for the entire crew means too many trips ashore. A few hundred yards is no inconvenience, but a few miles is a nuisance and so time-consuming that one tends to either anchor in a possibly less-protected anchorage close to shore, move the vessel back and forth on go-to-town days (perhaps having to leave someone on board), or just pass up the area. The latter, of course, is not acceptable in a cruising philosophy.

If more than two persons are cruising, a second dinghy appreciably increases the freedom of all. It need not have, or even attempt to have, all the attributes of the first dinghy, although the closer it comes to it, the better, in case the first dinghy is lost or destroyed. Out of a group of 15 vessels in he same anchorage in 1975, two had lost their dinghies *and* outboards; three had broken, or lost through capsize, one or both oars; two had broken rowlocks, and one dinghy was holed. The attrition rate *is* high.

Without question a hard dinghy fulfills more of the requirements than the soft (inflatable) dinghy, which neither rows well, tows well, nor sails. However, as a *second* dinghy, the inflatable has considerable merit in that it is easy to get into, has excellent stability, serves well for skin diving, and is easily carried over rocks or coral or up on to a beach. The inflatable does not ding up the topsides when tied alongside; it powers well, and it takes up little room when stowed. If used as the primary dinghy in the tropics, it will have a short life, say 15 to 18 months; but used as a second dinghy in the tropics, three to five years is not unusual.

Hard dinghies have a life of five to about 15 years, depending on strength of construction and usage. All types require frequent repairs. Most common faults are loss of bow eyes, followed by breaking of gunwales, loss or destruction of rowlocks, popping of thwarts (in cheaper models), splitting of the transom, holing and disintegration of the hull material—caused by worms in wood, ultra-violet in fiberglass, or electrolysis (through faulty repairs) in metal.

While eight feet is the minimum for two persons, 10 feet for four, and 14 feet for six—as always, the larger the better. For my designs, I have usually specified a pram for the simple reason that it is a better carrier for its size than a sharp-bowed dinghy. (If the sharp-bowed dinghy is very full, she will probably evidence all of the pram's faults.) The main fault of a pram is that in a good chop it is wet, and is often stopped in a head sea. It cannot be rowed or sculled as well as the same size sharp-bowed dinghy. Sailing ability is about equal if she is V-bottom, but less if flat bottom when it pounds badly in a step chop. Sailing ability is a must if any distance is to be covered, as dependence on outboard power assumes plenty of fuel and no mechanical failures.

As to stowing a dinghy, right-side up is better than upside down because the dinghy then holds all its own gear plus other accumulated odds and ends. However, this does require more vertical clearance. On small vessels, to ship a sea into a dinghy stowed upright would instantly reduce the vessel's stability. Upside down storage poses other problems: Enough deck room is required. If located over a skylight, thus allowing the skylight to stay open, the dinghy can solve a ventilation problem, especially during a rainstorm, and help eliminate the leaks for which skylights are famous. To accommodate the dinghy, the rig and occasionally the deck structures have to be modified so as to allow sufficient boom clearance and deck room in which to work the vessel.

A dinghy in aft davits requires more freeboard at the stern than is customarily found on vessels less than 40 feet long on deck. Vessels that have an after cabin trunk and steer from amidships can often elevate the dinghy high enough to be safe, or stow it partially on deck, especially if the after deck is raised or flush. The width of the stern also influences the size of a dinghy—up to twice the width of the vessel's transom, but not more than the beam of the vessel in extra-wide-stern vessels. Double-enders are the most difficult type for carrying a dinghy over the stern and, unless canoe-sterned, the davits must be too far aft to be made safe in a seaway. A dinghy in davits presents more problems to a vessel coming alongside a wharf than any other appendage to the vessel.

Side davits are pretty much limited to large vessels, say, about 55 feet; on smaller vessels they foul most of the running gear. Also, if the dinghy is secured overboard, it is too high; or, if swung inboard, it hinders easy passage forward on deck.

A vessel making long, consecutive passages can, if necessary, get by with a smaller dinghy than a vessel that spends longer periods in each cruising locality. This somewhat eases the problem of stowage as sea convenience is then the foremost consideration. The stowage problem can often be overcome by towing the dinghy through the cruising grounds, stowing it on deck only for the ocean passages—hence, the requirement that the dinghy have good towing characteristics under rigorous conditions.

Perhaps some dinghy manufacturers could be prevailed upon to offer a heavier duty version of their stock dinghies, especially reinforced for cruising. There are many fine models available.

I want to repeat that a dinghy which can be sailed, rowed and powered allows one to extend the exploring and gunkholing in any area. (By the way, a powered dinghy is not allowed in the Panama Canal Zone unless it has a special license.)

A watertight compartment of some sort should be built in to the dinghy for carrying a purse or wallet, ship's papers, mail, camera, etc. Even in such a compartment, it's wise to wrap these items in waterproof plastic.

Our faithful dinghies, which served in extended voyages for everything from bathtub to lighter, might not be usable in United States waters now, at least to carry persons to and from the vessels. The new Coast Guard regulations would eliminate 99 percent of them because the weight of the occupants on the gunwale would capsize them, or because they do not have decals that tell the occupants where to sit or step. Careful reading of the law does not make it believable. There is one way out, since most dinghies are fitted with sail and they are exempt from the law while sailing. Otherwise, throw away the rudder and use an oar in a sculling notch for steering and scull—never row or motor. Or, swim ashore, towing the dinghy with your dry clothes in it—this way, there is no need for you to have to carry your PFD (personal flotation device) around town. We will be safe on the water, but have mercy on us ashore!

OUTBOARD MOTORS

Most serious cruising vessels carry an outboard. There are a number of prerequisites for a good outboard, among which are reliability, repair-

PHOTO 8-I. The British Seagull outboard motor, one of which is used aboard *Kung Fu-tse,* usually on the hard dinghy.

PHOTO 8-2. An Avon inflatable Sport Boat, of the type used aboard *Kung Futse* as a second dinghy.

ability, neglectability, light weight and a low price—to name a few. The only outboard I know that comes close to meeting all these qualifications is the British Seagull, which has enjoyed decades of well-deserved praise. The Seagull was standard on most of the cruising vessels I built, and I have used it on all my own vessels since World War II. Repair is well within my limited mechanical capabilities.

The British Seagull, however, is a low-speed, heavy-duty motor, and while it can be used on any type of dinghy, it is not particularly effective on high-speed (hard or inflatable) dinghies. When planing is necessary to achieve top dinghy performance, then the problem is to find a motor that has the many good features of the Seagull and can also offer the r.p.m. and horsepower required.

I have nothing against U.S. outboards such as Johnson, Evinrude, Mercury, etc., except they are complicated for the indifferent mechanic to repair. Parts are critical and made to close tolerances, and can seldom be jury rigged. Also, parts are seldom available (outside the United States and Canada), except in the largest ports, and even there they may have to be specially ordered. So, owners of many cruising vessels shy away from these engines, especially when they observe the frequency of breakdowns.

In recent years, many outboards manufactured outside the United States have come onto the market. They are used elsewhere in the world because of their reliability and ease of repair. Among these are the Penta, Honda (four cycle), and Mariner.

Aboard *K'ung Fu-tse,* in addition to our British Seagull, we have an eight h.p. Mariner outboard for our 12-foot Avon Sportboat dinghy. This engine was in constant use for six months when I commuted to *K'ung Fu-tse* daily, propelling me at about 12 knots. Required maintenance has been no more than for the Seagull, perhaps even less. More importantly, it is an easily worked-on motor, with everything in clear view. I highly recommend it.

As to horsepower, one should remember that an outboard burns approximately one gallon per 10 h.p., per hour. The availability of gas and the amount that can be safely carried aboard must determine the appropriate horsepower, along with the push required by the dinghy. Four or five persons aboard my inflatable and eight h.p. give about the same performance as a Seagull. With two aboard, we can plane the dinghy, and with only one aboard we can get about 14 knots. I based my choice on economy, limited fuel stowage, and the fact that fuel would be scarce in some of the areas we would visit. An outboard of 16 h.p. would have given better performance under specific conditions, but only a marginal increase under our normal operating requirements.

9

—◆—

Weather

At a loss for other conversational topics, people often discuss the weather; authors have written volumes about weather. A study of the subject suggests that the reviews and general acceptance of all this writing on meteorology are based more on the number of graphs, charts, tables, maps and mathematical formulas presented than on the usefulness of the information to the reader. I suppose this graphic material is all right for the TV meteorologist trying to impress his viewers. For the sailor, it is generally worthless, usually being too cumbersome to use.

Most "scientific theories" about the weather only confirm the centuries of seaman's lore based on the acute observation demanded by necessity. A sailing vessel is absolutely dependent on the weather—not only today's but tomorrow's and next week's. It is the wind that propels the vessel and the sea—rough or calm—upon which she sails. Therefore, the blue-water sailor always has his "weather eye" on the clouds, the sea and the sky.

I'm not suggesting that one should not read books on weather. Through reading, it is possible to condense learning time to a fraction of what would be required by experience. "Bowditch" covers the subject of weather concisely, as it does so many other subjects. I would like to suggest, however, that the old lore, passed down from generation to generation, in the form of jingles, gives one a quick reference upon which a sailing decision can be made.

As my father duly passed on these jingles (with an explanation) to his children, modified a bit to suit our gaff schooner, I, in turn, have passed them on unchanged to my own children. I believe that this lore will be of interest to those who have not had a seafaring background and are preparing to go cruising:

"When the glass is low
Prepare for a blow.
When it rises high
Let all topsails fly."

This refers to the behavior of the barometer (glass), which measures the pressure or "weight" of the atmosphere as it passes over the earth in waves of high and low pressures, the crests being the highs and the troughs being the lows. Like sea waves, they are in continuous motion. In the North Temperate Zones, these pressure waves always move in an easterly direction. On the U.S. East Coast, the center of the lows, or troughs, usually pass through the Gulf of St. Lawrence. The exceptions to this rule are the lows that form in the tropics, move into the Gulf of Mexico and then up the Atlantic coast. These lows, when extreme, cause hurricanes. The "waves" are not parallel, as are those seen from a beach, but end-on, and are of various depths and speeds.

High pressure areas are those of dense or heavy air, while the lows are of rare or light air. The flow of air is *to* the low pressure area *from* the high pressure area, and the velocity of this movement is wind. In the Northern Hemisphere, wind in a low-pressure area always revolves counterclockwise, inward toward the center of the low. The winds in a high-pressure area always revolve clockwise, out from the center. The relative difference in intensity and distance from their respective centers determines the velocity of the flow of air between them—i.e., a very high pressure to a very low pressure that is close produces the strongest winds.

In the Southern Hemisphere, lows always revolve clockwise towards the center and the highs counterclockwise away from the center. Remembering these hemispheric differences of rotation, and the similarity—wind in lows *always* revolves *toward* the center and in highs *always* revolves *away* from the center—will be important when discussing the laws of tropical storms.

Ashore, many daily papers print a complete weather map for the United States and occasionally for the whole of North America, showing the locations of the centers of the lows and highs and, in some instances, the barometric readings at the center as well as outward from the center. When all the same readings are connected by a line, the line is known as an *isobar*. When temperature readings are also given and these readings are connected by a line, it is called an *isotherm*. The drawings of the isobar shows, first, the relative position of the highs and lows to each other and, second, the steepness of their slopes. The slope is referred to as the *barometric gradient*. Similarly, the *isotherm* produces a *temperature gradient*. At sea, one only needs to know that such pressures exist, for if the barometer is falling, a low is approaching and the rate of fall indicates one's approximate distance from the center. The same holds true about the rate of rise for a high.

The most common type of barometer used today is the aneroid. It consists of a bellows that is partially exhausted of air which expands or contracts as the pressure varies, actuating a hand that moves across a graduated dial. The graduations are in inches, millimeters or millibars. Inches are used in U.S. weather forecasts; millimeters have been more or less confined to continental Europe, and millibars to England until lately when millibars have become standard except in the United States and will be standard everywhere as of 1978 when U.S. weather goes metric.

The other type of barometer is the mercury barometer. This one balances a column of mercury against the weight of a column of air in a glass tube which is inverted in a bowl of mercury, allowing the column to fluctuate from a height of 30 inches of mercury, this being the normal atmosphere. The rise and fall of the mercury indicates higher and lower pressures than normal. One must remember that the readings on all barometers refer to the height of mercury in a standard mercury barometer. If the barometer reads in inches, it is inches of mercury; in millimeters, it is millimeters of mercury. However, if it reads in millibars, it represents a centimeter-gram-second unit of pressure. Conversion from one type of barometer to the other can be done by using Table 14 in *Bowditch*.

At sea, one should read and record barometer readings at fixed intervals, such as at the end of each watch. A single daily reading is of little value and often is misleading. If bad weather is anticipated, making hourly readings is a good practice. The barometer not only foretells changes as much as 24 hours in advance, but also indicates the weather at present.

Unless some phenomenon indicates that a change is likely to occur, one can assume that existing weather will continue.

"First rise after a low
Indicates a stronger blow."

This sums up the wave theory, for once the vessel leaves the center of a low, it begins to work into a high which is feeding the low.

When using a barometer, it's important to know whether the rise or fall has been gradual or rapid; or, if stationary, how long it has been so. One must also remember that there is a semidiurnal barometric rise and fall, the highs occurring about 10 A.M., and 10 P.M., with the lows occurring about 4 A.M. and 4 P.M. (standard time). A normal fluctuation is .03 inch to .06 inch or one to two millibars (MB)—and this translates as a steady barometer.

It's customary to tap the barometer glass before reading. Usually, when you do this the hand will jump slightly, the direction it moves revealing the tendency to rise or fall. While a stationary barometer indicates a continuance of existing weather, a rapid rise or rapid fall indicates that a strong wind is imminent, *along with* a change in weather. The nature of the change is dependent on the direction of the wind:

> "Long foretold, long last;
> Short notice, soon past."

How rapidly the storm is approaching and how intense it is, is indicated by the rate and amount of fall in the barometer. A fall of .01 inch (.3 MB) per hour is considered a low rate, while a fall of .02 inch (.6 MB) per hour is considered a high rate. A very intense storm may cause a fall of as much as .10 inch (3.3 MB) per hour, and rates of .20 inch (6.6 MB) per hour have been recorded.

In the tropics, a rapid fall exceeding .02 inch (.6 MB) per hour is considered dangerous. Under such conditions, it's possible to determine the distance from the storm center by the average fall. If the fall is:

.02 inch (.6 MB) to .06 inch (2.0 MB), the center is from 250 NM to 150 NM away;

.06 inch (2 MB) to .08 inch (2.6 MB), the center is from 150 NM to 100 NM away;

.08 inch (2.6 MB) to .12 inch (4.0 MN), the center is from 100 NM to 80 NM away;

.12 inch (4.0 MB) to .15 inch (5.0 MB), the center is from 80 NM to 50 NM away.

When the barometer shows considerable fall without any apparent change of weather, there is a distant violent storm in the offing. The barometer always falls lower for high winds than for heavy rains:

> "When the rain's before the wind,
> Halyards, sheets and preventers mind.
> When the wind's before the rain,
> Soon you may make sail again."

In the Northern Hemisphere's mid-latitudes, the barometer falls to indicate southerly winds, SE by S westward, indicating wet weather, stronger winds or more than one of these changes—except occasionally when rain or snow and moderate winds are from the north. When the barometer falls slowly for several days in fair weather, one must expect considerable rain.

A falling barometer usually is accompanied by stormy weather with wind and rain at intervals, but rain probably will not fall in great quantity.

When the barometer is low and the weather is fine and calm, one must be wary of a very sudden change.

Conversely, the barometer rises to indicate northerly winds, NW by N eastward, for less wet or drier weather, less wind or for more than one of these changes—except occasionally when snow, hail or rain from the north is accompanied by strong winds.

When the barometer and thermometer both rise, fine weather is coming.

The continuous rising of a barometer in wet weather foretells fair weather of some duration, often arriving in a day or two. A barometer reading about 29.50 inches (999 MB) is very low; 30 inches (1,016 MB) is normal or average, and 30.50 inches (1,033 MB) is high.

The following rules are worth remembering:

- A gradual steady rise indicates fine weather;
- A gradual steady fall indicates wet or unsettled weather;
- A very slow rise from a low indicates high winds and dry weather;
- A very rapid rise foretells clear weather with high winds;
- A very slow fall from a high indicates little wind, wet and unpleasant weather;
- A very rapid fall foretells high winds or sudden showers, or both;
- A NE wind is usually associated with a falling barometer and the air becomes colder and drier;
- A SW wind is usually associated with a falling barometer and the air becomes warmer and wetter.

When the wind is between NE and E with a steady fall of the barometer, the storm is SW or S, its center will pass near or to the S or E of the vessel in 12 to 24 hours, and the wind will back to the NW.

When the wind is between SE and S with a steadily falling barometer, the storm is approaching from the NW or W. Its center will pass near or to the N of the vessel in 12 to 24 hours, and the wind will veer to the NW.

When the wind rises with the sun, it will more than likely go down with it, but when the wind rises with the setting sun, it will probably blow all night and the day following.

> "Evening red and morning grey
> Are certain signs of a fine day."

Wet weather on both coasts of North America generally begins when the barometer is falling. The exception is that, in the summer months, thunderstorms usually occur at the change from a falling to a rising barometer.

It is possible to foretell rain by the use of a hygrometer, which measures the humidity of the air, but this instrument is seldom carried on small vessels.

Sound travels best through moist air, thus:

> "Sound traveling far and wide,
> A stormy day will betide."

Moist air also causes excessive refraction, making distant objects sharply visible, and often raised above the horizon; therefore:

> "The farther the sight,
> The nearer the rain."

During winter months, winds from the ocean are warmer than the land, so that onshore winds are often rain winds. The land temperature being colder, the precipitation (rain, sleet or snow) usually begins at the coast line. Basically, it is warm, moist air being condensed by cold land masses.

In the summer months, the opposite is the case. This is because the ocean winds are cooler and, while moisture-laden, need the warmth of the land to form rain. When easterly summer winds increase on a falling barometer, the approaching low from the west foretells rain in 12 to 48 hours.

> "Red sky in the morning
> Sailors take warning.
> Red sky at night,
> Sailors' delight."

This jingle condenses the theory that a red sky at night indicates that the low has already passed and lies to the east; whereas, a red sky in the morning indicates that the low lies to the west and has yet to reach the vessel.

Frequently the traditional red sky can also appear in the form of a rainbow, which is produced by refraction of the sun's rays being bent by raindrops. The center of the "bow" is opposite the sun. Close up, most or all of the colors of the spectrum are visible; however, as the distance increases, more colors are lost, finally leaving only red.

In the summertime, rain is usually accompanied by thunderstorms, which can be forecast only in general terms for any given locality. For example, on the U.S. East Coast thunderstorms usually move from west to east. Surface winds alone give no indication of their approach; however, the movement and form of clouds will sometimes give a few hours' warning. A summertime thunderstorm that does not depress the barometer usually will be quite local, brief and of no great magnitude. However, winds 40 or

50 knots may blow for brief periods. With a high barometer, only rarely will a storm occur; they are most common with a low barometer. A scorching sun breaking through morning clouds is an early indication of an afternoon thunderstorm.

Dew is an indication of fine weather. In hot weather, lack of dew foretells rain, while heavy dew indicates continuing fair weather. Fog indicates fair weather and is usually caused by warm, moist air passing over a body of water of lower temperature. Frost seldom lasts when it immediately follows a heavy rainstorm.

The moon is one of the best weather alerts. A halo or ring around the moon is usually caused by water mist or ice crystals in the upper atmosphere, and it indicates bad weather in the offing, probably within 24 hours. When the moon is quite visible in the daytime, fair and cooler weather follows, with winds most likely from the northern quadrant.

Clouds have always been used as storm signals. One must remember, however, that the movement of clouds in one place foretells storms, while the identical movement in another area indicates fair weather. After a period of fine weather, the sky will begin to change in a rather constant pattern. The first signs of change are light streaks, curls and wisps or patches of white clouds, followed by increasing overcast vapor that develops into clouds, indicating wind or rain in the offing.

Clouds prevent and contain radiation from the earth. A clear sky foretells the minimum night temperature. When clouds form over air saturated with moisture, the clouds unite and the moisture descends through the moist air below, to fall as rain. The higher the cloud, the larger the raindrops. When high upper clouds move in a different direction than the lower clouds, the change of wind will be toward the upper direction. The best way to check this movement is when the clouds across the sun, moon or stars, for then the movement is not affected by the motion of the sea or the course variations of the vessel.

Light scud clouds moving rapidly across heavy clouds indicate wind and rain, but seen alone, they usually indicate wind only. Misty clouds that increase in size or are descending foretell rain and wind, but if they are rising or dissipating they indicate that the weather will improve or become fine. Fine weather is usually indicated by soft, ill-defined clouds. The softer their appearance the less wind can be expected; however, hard, rolled, fingerlike and ragged clouds warn of strong winds.

Clouds of unusual hues, with sharply distinct outlines, foretell rain accompanied by strong winds, while hard-edged, oily-looking clouds foretell wind.

There are many methods of classifying clouds into a total descriptive picture, and these are given in *Bowditch*. However, for general weather forecasting, it is essential only to remember the principal types; one can combine them to be more precise.

CIRRUS clouds are the most elevated and are thin, drawn-out, feather-like or fleecy patches, known at sea as "cats' tails" and on land as "mares' tails." They are high-speed clouds. In summer, their average speed is about 65 miles per hour, and in the winter, about 80 miles per hour; in fact, the speed of these clouds has been known to exceed 200 mph.

CUMULUS clouds are hemispherical in shape on top, and flat below, and they pile up on each other, often indicating rain and thunder with gusty winds. These are medium-speed clouds, moving about 35 miles per hour in the summer, and about 50 miles per hour in winter.

STRATUS clouds are layered or banded horizontally, and are slow, moving at about 15 miles per hour in summer and 25 miles per hour in winter.

NIMBUS clouds are gray, quite uniform in color, with ragged edges. These are the rain clouds, and cover the sky during the rainy season.

CIRRO-STRATUS clouds are the cirrus clouds coalescing in long strata, sometimes covering the sky completely.

CIRRO-CUMULUS clouds are also high clouds and cause what is termed "a mackerel sky." They portend fair weather; however, they thicken and lower preceding a storm.

CUMULO-STRATUS clouds, between the cumulus and stratus, usually have a black or blue-black tint at the horizon.

The ditty for all of this is:

> "Mackerel sky
> Twelve hours dry;
> The higher the clouds
> The finer the weather;
> When clouds appear like rocks and towers
> The earth's refreshed by frequent showers."

LIGHTNING

Of all natural weather phenomena, I suppose thunder and lightning are most feared. Thunder claps, because of their sudden loudness, are often startling. Understanding the cause of these storms may lessen the dread of them. Lightning is an instant electrical discharge and, as it travels through the upper to lower strata clouds, it rolls. The thunder is almost instantaneous with the lightning, but the lightning is seen seconds before the thunder is heard, due to the different speeds of light and sound. The apparent lag is useful in calculating one's distance from the lightning. The rule of thumb is one mile for each five seconds between the lightning and thunder. When lightning flashes are seen but no thunder is heard, the distance to the lightning is greater than 15 miles.

There are many types of lightning, classified as follows: *Heat lightning* occurs below the horizon; its flashes are illuminating upper strata clouds and it's too far away for thunder to be heard. *Streak lightning* is a broad, smooth flash. *Beaded lightning* is a series of bright beads along streak lightning. *Sinuous lightning* is a flash following a general direction. The line is sinuous—i.e., bending from side to side. *Ramified lightning* (also referred to as "forked") is when part of the flash branches off from the main stem of the flash. *Ball lightning* wanders about without a definite course and forms irregular loops.

The moon may be a great inspiration to song writers and poets, but the sun from earliest times has been worshipped as the great sustainer of life. One of the things it does is regulate the weather. The sun's elliptical path north and south of the equator causes the changes of seasons. Due to evaporation caused by the sun, aqueous vapor rises into the atmosphere; cooling, it forms clouds which then yield rain, snow, fog and hail. Differences in atmospheric pressure are primarily caused by the sun; therefore, the sun also produces wind.

The sailor's use of the sun is first for navigation and then for weather forecasting. This he does by noting the colors:

- A diffused, brilliant white sun before sunset foretells a storm.
- A purple sunset and a bright blue zenith assures fine weather.
- A bright noon sun will be red at night.
- A rose-colored sunset, regardless of whether cloudy or clear, foretells fine weather.
- A whitish yellow sky after sunset, especially of great height, foretells rain during the night or the next day. Clouds with distinct outlines and unusual or gaudy hues indicate rain accompanied by wind.
- A bright yellow sky at sunset foretells wind.
- A pale yellow sky at sunset foretells rain.
- A seasick green sky indicates wind and rain.
- After a fine day, the sun setting in a heavy bank of clouds and the barometer falling indicate summer rain or winter snow during the night or by the next morning. If setting in dark clouds, rain will not come before noon of the following day.
- A dark red sky indicates rain.
- A dark blue sky, gloomy in appearance during the day, indicates light winds.
- A bright blue sky is the sign of fine weather.

• A solar halo foretells bad weather, and rain follows shortly when the sun appears to draw water.

Sunrise has been previously covered by a ditty. However, dawn (or first light) is equally important. There are two kinds: a *high dawn,* when first light is seen above a cloud bank, indicates wind; and *low dawn,* when first light breaks on or near the horizon: If it is grey, the day will be fine; if red, wind and rain are likely.

Without question, weather satellites are performing a valuable service, observing and recording the weather at regular intervals. They transmit the data to ground computers, and it is assimilated, analyzed and sent out as weather information. This data certainly aids in weather forecasting; however, there is a time lag of six to 24 hours between the satellite's observations and the broadcast of the information. The coastal weather stations—162.55 MHz—are good, but have limited coverage. WWV and WWVH —2.5, 5, 10 and 15 MHz—give pertinent weather information regarding major storms. Local AM and FM radio stations often use only what they get from the major wire services. Over a 14-year period, our local weather stations have a batting average of about .200—hardly enough to stay in the minors, let alone reach the majors. Quite often, we have been sailing in a fresh nor'easter when the local stations are saying "so'westerly five to 10."

Marine radio telephone stations also give weather information. We no longer listen to them but we did at one time, and we had a favorite marine operator on the East Coast. She had a charming Southern accent, clear and slow, and careful enunciation of the name of each vessel called. The weather forecast, however, was rattled off at what seemed 500 words a minute! She was duly (but fondly) dubbed "Ex-Lax Liz."

As weather watchers, it behooves each of us to use whatever data is available and to remember that the immediate area is what is of utmost importance. Reliance on our own observations and judgments based of experience is as valid in forecasting weather as in other aspects of cruising.

In the northern hemisphere, with one's back to the wind, the high pressure area will be to the right and slightly behind; the lower pressure will be to the left and slightly ahead. In the southern hemisphere, with one's back to the wind, the high pressure will be to the left and slightly behind; the low pressure will be to the right and slightly ahead. This relationship is absolute and applies not only generally but also specifically to the high and low pressure areas which are normally associated with severe gales.

The different kinds of winds are covered in *Bowditch*. My preference is for the older editions, which are more oriented to sailing vessels and low-powered steamers, and give greater detail on all topics applicable to small vessels at sea. The orientation of the new editions is toward naval vessels and those with sophisticated equipment.

PILOT CHARTS

Pilot charts are the most valuable asset we have for planning a voyage. The United States was the first to compile all the weather information on a chart and, to this day, these charts are the best obtainable in the world. The subjects covered in pilot charts are barometric pressure, percentage of fog, air temperature, wind's average duration and force, percentage of calms, major storm tracks, percentage of gales, trade wind limits, ice limits, equatorial rains, a statement of past average conditions, and steamship tracks.

Pilot charts do not become outdated. I am of the opinion that, on the older issues, the wind roses are of greater accuracy than on the newer charts because they were compiled from logs of sailing vessels. I doubt if all reportings received from steamers today are as accurate as those earlier logs, since wind is no longer a common means of propulsion and, therefore, is not so carefully noted today.

In using the North Atlantic Pilot Chart for a voyage commencing June 1, I would use the information given for both May and June to generalize probable wind, current, percentage of gales, etc. However, if the voyage is to begin June 10, I would refer only to June.

The one caution needed in using U.S. charts concerns the wind rose. The arrows indicate the direction of the wind, their length and the percentage from that direction; and the feathers at the end of the arrows indicate the *average* velocity by the Beaufort Scale. What are not shown are the percentages that make up the averages. For example, if the arrow shows NE, Force 3—a gentle breeze, it could be made up from an average of 50 per cent Force 2, a light breeze; 20 per cent Force 1, light air and 30 per cent Force 6, a fresh breeze. The low is six knots and the high about 30 knots with a mean of 16 knots. So one must be alert to the percentage of gales and calms for that area; that percentage will give an indication as to whether the winds will be significantly higher than the average or nearer the mean.

The British pilots show the *actual* percentages making up each wind direction, and leave no doubt as to how the average is determined. It has been my practice to use the U.S. charts and then, if in doubt, to check with the British charts. The back of many of the pilot charts contains useful information in great detail on many nautical subjects, which is well worth reading.

I have had the misfortune to experience (and the good fortune to survive) a number of the revolving storms that, depending on the area in which they originate known as hurricanes, typhoons, cyclones, etc. These are the most severe gales to be met at sea, and because of their distinctive characteristics they are easily distinguished from ordinary gales.

Revolving storms rarely occur between latitudes 10° north to 10° south. They move *away* from the equator. From the point of origin in the *northern* hemisphere, the typical storm moves westward, then curves northwesterly to north, then northeasterly, and blows itself out. In the *southern* hemisphere, from the point of origin, the storm moves westerly, then curves southwesterly, to south, to southeasterly and blows itself out. In either hemisphere, the currents of air within the storm disc move in concentric circles around the center of a low pressure area, the air moving in a counterclockwise direction in the northern hemisphere, and clockwise in the southern hemisphere. When the observer is facing the wind, the center of the storm, therefore, will be approximately ten points (112°) to the right or on the right-hand side in the northern hemisphere, and approximately ten points (112°) to the left or left-hand side in the southern hemisphere.

The storm disc is always divided into right and left halves along the axis of and in the direction of the storm track. These halves are labeled "navigable semicircle" and "dangerous semicircle." The navigable semicircle is the side toward the equator. The proximity to land has an effect on the storm, as land tends to flatten the storm as its center moves toward the land, thus somewhat altering the circular wind direction in relation to the storm center. Local atmospheric disturbances, such as secondary highs and lows, also can alter the course of the storm.

One point of clarification should be made: If the winds were true circles about the storm center, the center would be exactly eight points (90°) to the observer's right or left, depending on hemisphere. A discrepancy of 8–10 points allows for the spiral *inward* path of the wind toward the center. In some cases, an allowance of 12 points (135°) is the proper allowance when the storm is being flattened by a land mass.

A good *storm alert* considers the following:

1. The time of year—June to November (with greatest frequency in September and October) in the northern hemisphere; and, September to May (with greatest frequency in February and March) in the southern hemisphere.

2. A long swell from the direction of the storm, which is usually the first physical sign.

3. Radical changes in the normal diurnal activity of the barometer. While the barometer does not necessarily give long-range warnings, after the commencement of the storm it will indicate your distance from the center and the speed of approach.

4. An unusually clear atmosphere and surface visibility—often with oppressive temperature and a high barometer.

5. A restless barometer, often visibly rising and falling because of atmospheric disturbances.

6. The sky becoming overcast, with a cirrus haze which gradually grows

denser, darkening into true revolving storm clouds which rise over the horizon.

7. Clouds detaching themselves from the main cloud mass, having squalls of wind and rain associated with them, increasing in strength as each successive one passes. The first rains are occasional light showers, but as the center approaches, frequency and amount increase. The rain area always extends farther to the front of the storm than it does to the rear.

These storms travel at five to 20 nautical m.p.h. in the tropics. However, they sometimes become stationary or end their "lives" traveling at 50 nautical m.p.h. Within the tropics, the storm diameter is small, and it is unusual for violent gales (Force 11–65 knots) to extend more than 150 miles from the center.

If, from all indications discussed above, it seems probable that a storm is approaching, there are four steps to follow: *first,* determine the character of the storm (from barometer and sky) and locate its center; *second,* determine the position of the vessel in the storm—i.e., the semicircle in which the vessel is located; *third,* determine the approximate direction in which the storm is moving, and *fourth,* decide what to do with the vessel to escape the center, or to take advantage of fair winds, whichever may be easier or possible.

The rule for determining what to do in regard to whether the vessel finds herself in the right or left semicircle is the same in both hemispheres, and is easy to remember: *right semicircle,* the wind changes to the *right*—heave-to on the *starboard tack. Left semicircle,* the wind changes to the *left*—heave-to on the *port tack.*

On the storm track, run before the wind. If the vessel is ahead and *on* the track, or *near it* on either side, she probably will not experience a change of wind, but have a falling barometer and an increase in wind velocity and sea height. If, on the other hand, she finds herself *behind* the storm center, she faces a rising barometer and gradual moderation of the weather. In any case, the vessel must be put before the wind on a compass heading for several hours to determine, by wind changes, into which semicircle she has run.

Even though the pilot charts do show storm tracks, there is no certainty that every storm will behave in an identical manner. To determine a probable track requires two or more bearings of the center, a known course, and a speed-and-time interval. The greater the angle between the bearings, the more accurate the results. At the time of each bearing, the vessel *must* be hove-to and, if possible, remain hove-to for several hours between bearings in order to obtain *true* wind direction. During these times, vectoring apparent wind is subject to sufficient errors of estimation that one's judgment could err and place the vessel in jeopardy.

In the northern hemisphere, in the *right* or *dangerous* semicircle, sail by the wind (close-hauled) on the starboard tack, carry sail as long as possible and, if obliged to heave-to, do so on the starboard tack.

If in the *left* or *navigable* semicircle, bring the wind on the starboard quarter, note the vessel's heading and steer that course. If obliged to heave-to, do so on the port tack.

If *in front* of the storm center, and *on* the storm track, run before it, note the course, and keep it. As the wind draws on the starboard quarter, trim the sails and, if obliged to heave-to, do so on the port tack.

If *behind* the center, and *on* the storm track, run off with the wind on the starboard quarter and, if obliged to heave-to, do so on the starboard tack.

In the southern hemisphere, if in the *right* or *navigable* semicircle, bring the wind on the port quarter, note the vessel's heading, steer that course and, if obliged to heave-to, do so on the starboard tack.

If in the *left* or *dangerous* semicircle, sail by the wind (close-hauled) on the port tack, carry sail as long as possible and, if obliged to heave-to, do so on the port tack.

If *in front* of the storm center, and *on* the storm track, run before it, note the course and keep to it. As the wind draws onto the port quarter, trim the sails and, if obliged to heave-to, do so on the starboard tack.

If *behind* the center and *on* the storm track, run off with the wind on the port quarter and, if obliged to heave-to, do so on the port tack.

Successfully using the above rules to avoid or escape storms is always dependent upon the ability to carry sail and on having sea room. If sail cannot be carried or the vessel is too close to land, then the vessel is *always* hove-to—on the starboard tack in the right semicircle, and on the port tack in the left semicircle; and *never* any other way.

When hove-to on the port tack in the left semicircle in the northern hemisphere, and on the starboard tack in the right semicircle in the southern hemisphere, a vessel will be heading *toward* the storm center. There is no danger in this, as head-reaching under these conditions is minimal and she will not approach the center, thus endangering herself, since each shift of wind will put her head up to the sea, making her ride safely. However, if she were on the opposite tack, with each wind shift she would fall off, eventually bringing the seas on the beam or quarter, a position which might cause serious damage, if not foundering.

It's been said: "Ill blows the wind that profits nobody." So, there are times when even a revolving storm can be used to advantage. However, care must be exercised in case the storm stalls or reverses direction. With that caution in mind, *one can run with a storm under the following conditions: In the northern hemisphere,* when behind the storm center and on its axis (wind on the port beam); when anywhere in the right-rear quadrant

THE BEAUFORT WIND SCALE, BASED ON A 36′ WATERLINE CRUISING VESSEL

Beaufort Number	Description of Sea	State of Sea	Close Hauled	Broad Reach	Velocity in Knots	Force In Lbs/Sq Ft
0	Calm	Smooth, mirror-like.	All sail; 0–1 knot.	All sail; 0–1.5 knots.	0–2.6	.03
1	Light Air	Smooth, small wavelets.	All sail; 1–2 knots.	All sail; 2–3.5 knots.	6.9	.23
2	Light Breeze	Small waves, crests breaking.	All sail; vessel heels moderately. 3–4 knots.	All sail; 4–6 knots.	11.3	.62
3	Gentle Breeze	Foam has glossy appearance; not yet white.	Working sail and topsails. 5–6 knots.	Working sails; topsails & light sails; 6–7 knots.	15.6	1.20
4	Moderate Breeze	Larger waves, many "white horses."	Working sail only; Lt Displacement vessels reef. 6–7 knots.	Full working sail & topsails; Lt Displ. hand topsails; 7–8 knots.	20	1.90
5	Stiff Breeze	Waves pronounced; long white foam crests.	All vessels reef; Lt Displacement double reef. 5–6 knots.	Working sails only; 8–9 knots.	24.3	2.90
6	Fresh Breeze	Large waves, white foam crests all over.	Deep reefs. 3–4 knots.	Hvy Displ, small reefs; Lt displ, deep reefs. 8–9 knots.	29.5	4.20
7	Very Fresh Breeze	Sea heaps up; wind blows foam in streaks.	Hvy Displ, deep reefs; Lt Dis, min. working sail. 2–3 knots.	Deep reefs in largest sail; 8–9 knots.	34.7	5.9

Beaufort Number	Description of Sea	State of Sea	Close Hauled	Broad Reach	Velocity in Knots	Force In Lbs/Sq Ft
8	Moderate Gale	Height of waves & crests increasing.	Min. balanced canvas; emer. only. 1–2 knots.	Run off—storm jib or bare poles. 7–8 knots.	41.6	8.40
9	Strong Gale	Foam blown in dense streaks.	Lying ahull; sea anchor or drogue out; side drift.	Run off—under bare poles and warps. 3–5 knots.	48.1	11.50
10	Very Strong Gale	High waves; long over-hanging crests: Lg. foam patches.	Lying ahull; sea anchor or drogue.	Run off—bare poles & warps; 3–5 knots; speed too great; danger of broaching.	56.4	15.5
11	Violent Gale	High waves	Lie to sea anchor.	Bare poles; sea anchor, warps, drogue; vessel must be slowed down.	65.1	20.6
12	Hurricane; Typhoon	Streaking foam; Spray in air.	Lie to sea anchor.	Lie to sea anchor.	78.1	29.6

(wind on port side, abaft the beam); or, when abeam and to the right of the storm center (wind aft).

In the southern hemisphere, when behind the storm center and on its axis (wind on the starboard beam); when anywhere in the left-rear quadrant (wind to starboard, abaft the beam); or when abeam and to the left of the storm center (wind aft).

Years ago, in the twilight of sail, the powers to be saw fit to alter the names and descriptions of the various wind conditions in the Beaufort Scale. Thus, the old Force 8, a "moderate gale," was reduced to Force 7, which used to be a "very fresh breeze"—hence the term a "yachtsman's gale." Regardless of what one calls it, the actual pressure in pounds per square foot that wind exerts on sails is our concern. This can be expressed by the formula $P_N = -.0004 \, AV^2$. P_N = Pressure per unit; 0.004 is the constant for knots; A is the Area (usually unit = 1 square foot; and V is the Velocity of the wind in knots, squared.) Note, for example, the pounds of wind pressure exerted by a "normal" 15-knot breeze, and, one, say, of 35 knots.

Therefore:	5 knots =	.10 lbs.	35 knots =	4.90 lbs.
	10 knots =	.40 lbs.	40 knots =	6.40 lbs.
	15 knots =	.90 lbs.	45 knots =	8.10 lbs.
	20 knots =	1.60 lbs.	50 knots =	10.00 lbs.
	25 knots =	2.50 lbs.	55 knots =	12.10 lbs.
	30 knots =	3.60 lbs.	60 knots =	14.40 lbs.

Fifteen knots, Force 4, is a fine sailing breeze with four-foot seas; 30 knots, Force 7, is double the wind velocity of Force 4 and *quadruple* the wind pressure, and seas are 13 feet; whereas, 60 knots produces a quadrupling of wind velocity and a *sixteen-fold* increase in wind pressure—with seas to 40+ feet.

Perhaps when reading the accounts of early blue-water voyagers, one can feel some compassion. To them, a moderate gale was 34 to 40 knots of wind; today, a moderate gale is only 28 to 33 knots. So, the old-timers' heaving-to in a gale indicates no inferiority in hull design or lack of courage. It's just that *their* gales exerted *one and one-half times* as much pressure per square foot, as ours do today. Only, later, someone changed the name of the game!

10

Survival

Man, through social evolution, has become a creature dependent upon others to perform for him a multitude of services which he reciprocates with those of his own talents. This has brought about a bonding in clans, tribes and countries for mutual interest, protection and collective survival.

The blue-water sailor is (and probably always has been) a mutation of this evolution—a loner, who may at times attempt to make the adjustments necessary to conform, but who rarely has been able to accept the limitations imposed by society. Collectively, blue-water sailors can be considered a clan, but one so scattered and individualistic that it does not pose a threat to any other group. At best the blue-water sailor is tolerated, but is usually ignored.

Blue-water sailing is not just a momentary performance—it is a way and philosophy of life which requires thorough understanding of dozens of subjects, and the ability to make decisions required by oneself, by one's vessel, and by the environment. These are the arts of the sailor. To study and learn any subject and ignore all but one detail is myopic and distorts the validity of any conclusion. Survival, for example, cannot be discussed only in terms of life rafts, emergency rations or "great storms." First, a definition of survival is needed; then one must consider several possibilities which may require specialized and varied equipment to achieve survival in dangerous situations.

Survival does not depend only on an ability to weather hardship, but also on the capability to endure an infinite combination of mental and physical stresses brought about by dangerous situations at sea. One must recognize that though he cannot control events he has some control over his reaction to them. That's possible through the application of experience, knowledge and logic—with a small dollop of hope that fate will provide some luck.

Ashore or afloat, most of us are involved in surviving every minute of life. Most people apply "survival" only to living through catastrophes. When this concept is applied to voyaging, it's quite clear that cruising is one of life's safest pursuits.

Newcomers, like experienced voyagers, must question the many assumptions advanced by contemporary designers, boatbuilders and writers about what constitutes a safe and "proper" vessel for ultimate situations. By closely examining the "pseudo" facts presented in an effort to sell products, it usually turns out that many of them are mere suppositions—frequently, mixtures of fact, fiction and optimism. One must learn to differentiate fact from nonsense.

Herewith, some unreal characteristics—not necessarily in order of importance—in which the inexperienced buyers are asked to put their faith:

NONCAPSIZABLE.   *Any* vessel can be capsized or pitchpoled, but with proper design and good seamanship such an event is unlikely.

SELF-RIGHTING.   This can only be accomplished if the vessel maintains watertight integrity (hatches, vents and portholes closed and sealed), the ballast does not shift and structural damage does not occur at the time of capsize. Design stability calculations are assumed for smooth-water conditions and a predetermined center of gravity; all come under scrutiny when applied to rough water conditions and the variable loads imposed by heavy weather.

NONSINKABLE.   This can be true only if the vessel is properly subdivided and then is holed in the "right" location. In a one-compartment subdivision, a fracture or hole on a bulkhead will flood two compartments, and the vessel probably will sink. There are exceptions, of course, among which are unballasted mono- and multi-hulls, but even these can be sunk if their stores and outfit are over a permitted weight.

OVERSIZED RIGGING.   For this, one should ask, "Compared to *what?*" The late Uffa Fox suggested that the total strength of the shrouds on one side of the vessel should be capable of lifting the vessel, using as a yardstick the working strength of the wire. This is normally a safe rule of thumb. The exception would be a truly stiff vessel (great beam, high ballast-displacement ratio, or both) in which size should be related to the maximum righting arm. In some vessels, this would yield a wire strength three times displacement. Actually, the wire diameter may be quite small in multiple-masted vessels due to the additional shrouds required by the rig.

EXTRA-HEAVY CONSTRUCTION.   Again, compared to what? The only valid comparison is with an identical vessel or with one of similar size, type and purpose. Increases in structural weight are "bought" at the expense of reduced ballast, and/or a reduction of water, fuel and furnishings.

HIGH BALLAST-DISPLACEMENT RATIO. This indicates light-shell construction, coupled with sparse furnishings, small fuel and water capacity—all limitations important in racing. The exact opposite is true in cruising, where freedom from rules and fads allow the designer maximum use of hull shape as well as ballast to achieve required stability.

SEAWORTHINESS. This is not a function of design, but of man. *Seakindliness,* on the other hand, is a function of design. Thus, we find good and bad in all types of hulls and rigs. There is no inherent virtue in any particular design, by itself: It is impossible for all double-enders to be sea-kindly, all vessels with long overhangs to be fast, or all vessels with keels to gripe.

Selecting a vessel against the probability of loss is not difficult. Since over 99 percent of all disasters occur not in deep water, but on shoals, reefs and beaches, seagoing capabilities seem not to be a primary consideration. For the remaining less than one percent, the causes of loss are so diversified that no one feature could significantly lower the probability of loss. A few of the more prominent causes of loss, in their approximate order of importance, follow:

The principal cause of loss can be attributed to *hull, rig or equipment failure*. Vessels putting to sea with poorly maintained hull, rig or equipment are often manned by a lackadaisical crew that can compound bad situations with poor seamanship. A fully found vessel is one in which hull, rigging, sails and equipment are in very good to excellent repair—the minimum expected of proper seamanship.

Next is being *overwhelmed by the elements*. Years ago, the possibility of being overtaken by wind, wave and ice was much greater than it is today, with radio and weather satellites to give advance warning; chances of being surprised by hurricanes or typhoons are rare. Under "normal" conditions one can still experience freak waves, which are usually a combination of several wave systems; however, these occur infrequently and in fairly well-defined areas, such as Cape of Good Hope and Cape Horn. Normal storms at sea (gales) may be uncomfortable but are of small concern to a well-found vessel. Quite often, running too fast before a gale will cause broaching or capsize or pitchpoling. However, running too slowly can cause pooping or a capsize. Again, proper seamanship is the critical ingredient. Fortunately, the majority of sailing while voyaging is between the tropics and temperate zones—small need to worry much about heavy icing.

Collision at sea. Today, because of updated weather routing, steamers can evade weather systems and, therefore, may be met anywhere on the oceans. In the past, steamers pretty much stuck to the standard routes described in *Ocean Passages for the World* and shown in pilot charts, and one only worried about collisions when crossing these shipping lanes. Then as now, sailing vessels adhered closely to the long-established passage routes that promised most favorable winds. The possibility of a collision always exists, but when sailing in a confluence zone or its approaches, the probability increases. Most collisions happen not only in fine and clear weather but in daylight. A proper lookout reduces the possibility of collision to almost zero, but that is easier said than done.

Flotsam and jetsam are most likely encountered in areas where there is transport of logs (Pacific Northwest), off the mouth of great rivers such as the Amazon, Mississippi, Yellow, Yangtse, and Ganges, or in major ocean currents such as the Gulf Stream. For example, Peter Tangvald lost his *Dorothea* in the Caribbean due to collision with an unseen object.

Whales have inflicted losses, but having sailed amongst pods of them, I feel this borders on the freak incident rather than the common occurrence. Caution rather than trepidation is the rule.

Losses have also occurred through piracy, explosion, fire and sickness. "Extra-terrestrial phenomena" and other rare (nonexistent?) possibilities, such as the hazards of the Bermuda Triangle, make good fiction but are of little real concern to a voyager.

One must conclude that good seamanship—not the vessel—sharply reduces the possibility of loss at sea. As land is approached, safety diminishes. The more intimate one is with an area, the greater the chance of loss; prudence is often neglected because of familiarity.

The vast majority of losses are attributable to only a few factors. Acknowledging these greatest dangers and defining them may help to make one take appropriate preventive action as they arise in the cruise:

Fatigue is probably the foremost cause of accidents, strandings and loss of vessels. With physical exhaustion, reflexes and mental reaction time are impaired and slowed down, sometimes causing one to lapse into a stupor or even become unconscious. Most people have a warning sign by which the body signals that rest is needed and that it can not tolerate much more exertion without relief. (My signal is given to me in the calves of my legs.) This does not mean that we can't push our bodies further, but that the more we push beyond this point the greater the exhaustion and the longer it will take to recuperate. If one does not know his sign, then, under controlled conditions, a doctor can help him recognize it; it is worth discovering. Fortunately, ocean voyaging is a vigorous life which promotes good health and thus protracts the time before fatigue becomes evident. Diet certainly is an important factor in stemming fatigue. The time-honored misfortune of being seasick the first few days at sea, until one acquires his sea legs, in my opinion, is mostly a bodily way to expel the rich foods and fats accumulated in the typical shore diet. Vegetarians seem to have the least trouble adjusting to early days at sea and have more stamina, perhaps because they usually carry less body fat. Muscles tire quickly the first few days at sea due to the constant motion, so short voyages are inherently more fatiguing than long ones.

Lee shore is second among causes of accidents and often closely related to fatigue. The scenario goes: I am tired; the weather is worsening; if I can get into a calm anchorage or make harbor before dark, I'll be all right. Not so bad a choice if one is entering a large bay such as the Chesapeake, but it can be disastrous if the route to such safety is past jetties, through reefs, into river mouths that have breakers, rocks and other dangers on either side, or is by ill-defined channels. In a downwind situation, one has the ability to carry sail or at least make controlled headway. In the event of miscalculation, however, there is probably insufficient power (sail or auxiliary) to beat back into deep water. Take any of the world's infamous graveyards, such as the Goodwin Sands, Scilly Isles, Cape Hatteras, Sable Island, etc. The vessels lost were—with few exceptions—unable to work to windward because of the ferocity of the elements, and were forced by wind, wave and currents onto the shore. Proper seamanship dictates that one either heave-to *before* the danger of being driven ashore, or alter course to a safe port. Some islands are large enough so that their opposite side affords a safe lee, clear of dangers (coral heads, rocks, shoals). If this is the case, then it's wise to seek out such a haven. One should remember, however, that in areas where there are prevailing winds such as the Trades, the lee afforded by an island during a storm will usually become untenable during settled conditions; one should be prepared to move as soon as the storm abates.

Loss of power. In spite of the reliability of most engines, they are, inadvertently, contributors to groundings, strandings and even the total loss of vessels. An engine rarely fails because of a manufacturing fault. It is usually the result of a comedy of errors, any one of which is a nuisance, but which, combined, lead to a stoppage in a moment of crisis. It may go like this: A dealer promotes the idea that an engine with greater horsepower is a safety factor. Usually it *is* necessary, to run all the additional auxiliary equipment on the engine. The vessel designer, trying to achieve optimum performance under sail, specifies the smallest propeller for least drag. Between owner and engine dealer, the builder is forced to install the large engine in an inaccessible and perhaps restricted space. Dirty fuel clogs the engine. This happens at the fuel dock, which got the dirty fuel from the refinery. Such stoppages could have been prevented by the addition of a couple of fuel filters, but there was insufficient room because of the extra equipment and tight engine compartment. Now the owner keeps trying to force bad fuel through by mashing down the starter button, and this quickly depletes the battery. Since the engine is such high horsepower, it does not have a hand-starting capability. Even if there is provision for doing so, there is no elbow room for cranking. Up to this point, no calamity has occurred, but now a storm is coming up and he is entering a narrow channel. Certainly tired and probably flustered, with the anchor not ready to go, he perhaps stays on the right side of the channel although it is the lee side. He is making leeway, is being set to leeward by the current. About two seconds after impact, he will say, "That damned engine!" I know of just such an accident happening twice in 1975, and four times in 1976. Fortunately, only two vessels were total losses.

Navigational errors are a large category. Losses should be less frequent than they are in U.S. coastal waters with their excellent system of buoys and radio beacons. In more remote areas, mistaken identification of an island is rather common, especially low-lying ones, especially when one is dependent on charts that have not been corrected for years. Mistakes are made because old landmarks are gone or new ones have been added; a roof has been repainted; a prominent tree has been blown down; the channel has silted up; an under-reading log causes one to arrive too soon; weather such as haze or fog, or small, stationary rain squalls obliterates the land or distorts distances; one adds or subtracts incorrectly; one applies variation or deviation backward; a compass is faulty; markers are passed on the wrong side (in the United States it is one way, in the rest of the world, another); or one is not competent enough in piloting and navigation.

Therefore, a vessel facing a survival test is, in reality, man confronting such a predicament that he must as a last resort depend on the vessel itself for survival. When the vessel fails, as it sometimes must, the crew must have an alternate means of survival. This is ultimate survival.

At sea, a proper lifeboat would be ideal. The minimum size would be 12 feet, and it would be equipped with a 10-day supply (per person) of food and water, oars, mast and sail, hatchet, etc., as required by the Convention for Safety at Sea. Unfortunately, few vessels under 60 feet can carry and handle the bulk and weight of a 12-footer, and a dinghy is usually an inadequate substitute. The advantages of lifeboats are their maneuverability and ability to make independent passages. Few dinghies qualify in this respect.

Few vessels voyaging are so small that they can't carry an inflatable life raft, which is lightweight, compact, self-inflating, and capable of carrying emergency food and water. Other virtues are stability, comfort, a canopy for sun and storm protection, ease of entry and safety. It must be remembered, however, that the inflatables are "drift" floats. They are not designed for passage-making against currents or prevailing winds, nor do they tow, paddle or steer easily. (I often wonder if the general assumption is that these limitations are unimportant because one would "naturally" transmit an SOS prior to abandoning.) These rafts need supplemental provisions for safety. *Survive the Savage Sea* by Douglas Robertson, and

PHOTO 10-1. An Avon liferaft with canopy.

Staying Alive by Maurice and Maralyn Bailey, give impressive testimony to how long one can survive in an inflatable. These rafts are expensive, but the difference in cost between the four-, six-, or eight-man size is not great; the largest size, I feel, offers extra benefits. On *K'ung Fu-tse,* we have an eight-person raft. Normally we have four in the crew, but my feeling is that, while I hope never to need or use the raft, if I ever do, I am going to be as comfortable as possible.

In the event of a collision, especially at night, the odds are, first, that you were not seen and, second, that you could not inflict enough damage on the larger vessel for it even to feel the crunch. If the bow of the ship is what strikes you, one must realize that this could be as much as 800 feet from its bridge and no last-minute shouting, noise or lights flashed on will be to any avail. The automatically inflating life raft, therefore, becomes of prime importance as a vehicle of survival. Initial cost certainly causes one to ponder its necessity since the chance of needing it seems perhaps a million to one. On the other hand, what are the chances of having a second chance at life without one? The life raft must be unpacked, checked and repacked every 12 to 18 months—another expense added to the "simple way of life."

Many ocean voyagers have been carrying for a long time UHF-VHF-

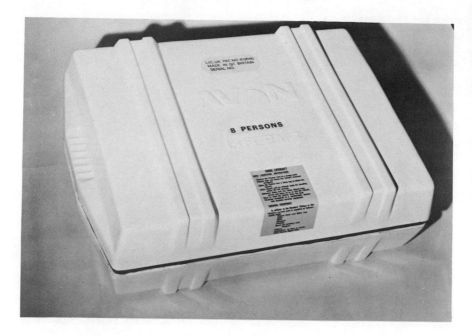

PHOTO 10-2. The Avon liferaft cannister for deck mounting.

transmitters, operating on 121.5, and 243.OMH$_3$ which is the aircraft frequency, although such units were not approved by the FCC for marine use. The FCC now has approved the unit, which makes a great deal of sense. Of course, the hope is that use of the transmitter will not become abused. If used in other than life-or-death situations, it could become a meaningless gadget and no one would pay attention to its signals. While I am not totally familiar with its range, I assume it is direct line-of-sight. With an aircraft flying at 30,000 feet, the theoretical visual coverage would be 1.15 $\sqrt{30,000}$ = 173 nautical miles radius; therefore, a diameter of 346 nautical miles and an area of 94,025 square miles—which means this transmitter could be considered essential. The most frequented cruising grounds now have (or soon will have) air strips as they become tourist meccas. Since the transmitter will work for 48 continuous hours on a self-contained battery pack and transmission can be had for a selected interval, all one would need to stow in the emergency kit (along with the transmitter) would be an up-to-date airlines schedule for the area cruised. I imagine the North Atlantic and North Pacific are so heavily crossed by aircraft that almost any time of day or night a signal would bring a response.

Equipment for survival is difficult to determine, as what you need depends on where the vessel is lost and how rapidly the loss occurs. If one decides to deal with three general situations—(1) loss at sea; (2) loss and almost immediate sinking on shore or a reef; and (3) gradual breaking up due to stranding, and eventual loss in shallow water—the task is somewhat easier. One should remember that the actual conditions or combinations of them leading to loss are infinite; therefore, there is no classic or textbook solution.

When a vessel is lost at sea, one must have, as mentioned, a suitable life raft, lifeboat, or both. Time permitting, food, water, medicine, tools, and clothing should be stowed aboard, along with ship's papers and other valuables. Water is the most important item, and a five-gallon gerry jug lashed near the liferaft is an excellent precaution. Additional lifeboat rations, which are available from most ship's chandlers, could also be stowed next to the water jug in a waterproof wrapping. A survival knife (described later) is desirable.

When a vessel is lost by stranding and rapid sinking, if the wind is onshore, jettison as much as possible after loading the raft, dinghy and lifeboat, just as for a loss at sea, particularly if the stranding occurs on what appears to be a deserted island. If it is a settled island, then one's valuables plus ship's papers, passports, etc., should be taken with you, with as much else as would be useful, including clothing. Extra water and food is of secondary importance here.

When a vessel is stranded and *not* sinking, one has several options. First of all, load into the dinghy or lifeboat all those things required for loss at sea—if it is a remote island. If it's a civilized island, get everyone ashore except one person to guard the vessel and then contact authorities and get permission to land stores, gear and valuables. Often, if this is not done, "Ali Baba and his Forty Thieves" take over. But face it: Even with permission from local authorities, one still can lose everything. This was the case with Gilbert Klingel when he lost his *Basilik,* only to find that he did not have a "permit to be shipwrecked." By the time he was released from custody, there was nothing left.

On deserted or only seasonally settled islands or shores, one must try to have everything required for survival on land. All the extra food and water possible is a must on arid islands or shores. Temporary shelter can be improvised from the remnants of the raft or lifeboat. The tools I'd want would be a buck saw, hatchet, machete, fish hooks and lines, knife and survival knife, and waterproof matches—lots of them.

The survival knife is the finest of all tools. I have one that was made by the Remote Survival Company of New Haven, Connecticut. Incorporated into it is a specially hardened knife, a saw, fuel and a striker, fish hooks and fish line, all in a case that can be worn on a belt or attached to a life raft. Furthermore, the knife can be flipped open with one hand if the other is incapacitated.

If anyone wishes to read a book on survival tactics, I suggest *Sea Survival, A Manual,* by Dougal Robertson.

Everyone who ventures upon the oceans has at some time considered the possibility of having to abandon his vessel at sea—and survive. These are not pleasant thoughts, but survival is a basic human instinct. Some who never go to sea claim authority on how it should be done—in "theory," but Dougal Robertson is an expert. He *has* done it and *did* survive. (His first book, *Survive the Savage Sea* described his family's 37 days in the Pacific in a raft and dinghy, until they were rescued.)

This, his second book, is a manual that gives step by step procedures—first, how to prepare for the possibility; and second, how to cope if possibility becomes reality. The book is well illustrated with simple diagrams, such as how to improvise a solar still, how to obtain fluids from the spines of fish, how to catch fish, how to make lures, the anatomy of a turtle, etc. Also included are sections on health, weather, navigation, surf, first aid and a very sensible discussion of drinking sea water.

The appendices cover: (1) suggested equipment for a survival craft; (2) birds (with excellent photos); (3) life in the sea; (4) navigational data, (including amplitudes, declinations and several star charts); (5) survival charts (three oceanic charts which show rainfall by the month; drift caused by wind; surface ocean currents; inhabited coasts, and magnetic variation) and a route chart (showing continental shelf areas, density of marine life, bird migration, tropical revolving storms and shipping routes) and (6) a compass rose on see-through plastic.

The surprising thing is that all this information is contained in a 5″ × 7″ volume of 148 pages, including the index—which is brief and concise. Should the unhappy time ever come when this book is needed, one will appreciate that it contains no B.S.—only facts. It rests in a waterproof wrapping in my survival kit. I hope I never have to use it.

11

Rules of the Road

"If you're overtaken by a gale, it's better to be at sea than closing a lee shore."

That was just one of the many axioms my father used to repeat when I was about to leave on a short cruise. On several occasions I did not heed his advice, usually to my regret. Life often seems to demonstrate—it appears to many of us—that there is little we can learn from our ancestors, until the moment when, after repeating their experiences, we ingeniously leap to their conclusions!

Several years ago, a group of cruising folk were at our dinner table in Miles, Virginia, when the subject of closing the land arose. We all agreed that the traffic of large merchant ships was our main hazard and concern, day or night. I, for one, have always maintained that one's chances of avoiding collision were better at night, because:

At night, observing the relationship of a large vessel's range lights will give an immediate indication of her course. If the lights are "opening," with each vessel maintaining her course and speed, there is no danger of collision. If, however, the lights are "closing" or one is over the other, danger of collision is imminent and action must be taken. That is no time to quibble over whether or not one is under sail, and which one is the burdened vessel. I know my running lights comply with the law—they are visible at two miles on a clear night (I have checked). And they are five feet above the water, but even if they were 50 feet up, they are still visible for only just over two miles.) The merchant vessel's side lights are 50 feet up, and her range lights 100 to 150 feet above the water. Her lights, unlike mine, are powerful and far exceed minimum legal requirements. On a night when my lights are visible at two miles, hers are visible for 12–15 miles. If she is traveling at 15 knots, she is closing at four minutes per mile to, say, my 12 minutes per mile. This is more than ample time for me to determine if collision is imminent. If it is, then a course at right angles to her is safest when head-on or overtaking. In a crossing situation, I will not cross her bow if I have any doubt about her distance off.

I never depend on being seen on radar, even though I know my vessel (aluminum) presents a fine target, as I am sure that constant surveillance—continuous observation of the scope—is just not practical on a merchant vessel. The mate still has other duties to perform while running his watch. I would rather count on a careful observation on his part—say, once every 10 minutes.

Lookouts? I have spent many an hour on the foc'sle in that capacity. The duty of a "lookout" is to report not only what is ahead but also everything around his visible horizon. Therefore, to see my vessel at two miles, the lookout must be looking well below his horizon, which is where he expects to see another mammoth that could harm him. In daylight and good weather, there are no lookouts except the mate on watch and, as noted, he must perform other tasks as well. No, give me nighttime—there's no confusion because of visible deck structures, masts or other silhouette clutter that might make it difficult to determine quickly if the vessel is coming or going.

Several years ago, having just completed a short cruise on which in one six-hour period we encountered 12 merchant vessels, I began to feel as if I were on Main Street. At a chance meeting with some ex-shipmates who are still merchant sailors, we discussed the frequently reported collisions of ships with small craft, not only at night but in daylight, despite radar. Their view was that many operators of small craft evidently panic and turn on their engines, light up the decks, if at night (becoming night-blind in the process), and then cannot make up their minds about which direction to turn. Some have been seen to start a zigzag maneuver that would do credit to a convoy trying to evade a submarine. This, of course, only confuses the men on the bridge of the merchant vessel, whether they are tracking by radar or by eye. If an erratic course is held long enough, there is no way the large vessel can evade the smaller one. Then, one can just hope for a little luck, or for the survivors to be rescued.

A sailing vessel may have the right of way, and the steam vessel may give it to you at sea if the choice is left to her. But a few facts often are overlooked: Most modern bulk carriers are oversized and underpowered; some are 1,250 feet long, 200 feet wide, have a draft in excess of 90 feet, a displacement of about 500,000 tons, a 45,000 shaft-horsepower engine and a speed of about 15 knots. This works out to .09 horsepower per ton—the equivalent of a one-horsepower engine on a 40-foot auxiliary!

Most of these vessels would find it difficult to make a tactical turn, 16 points (180°) in seven ship lengths, which was more or less the accepted rule of thumb in my years at sea in merchant vessels. Thus, when they are eight points (90°) off their original heading, they will have advanced 4,000 feet along their original course, and at the same time "transferred red" (moved at right angles) about 3,000 feet. What a slide! A crash (emergency) stop would require about 17 to 21 miles. To be sure, other types of merchant vessels are not only highly maneuverable, but also capable of speeds in excess of 30 knots when two of these behemoths meet. It's the same as passing a stationary object in an auto traveling at 70 miles per hour.

So it is no more than prudent for the ocean voyager to keep a sharp lookout when in shipping lanes. In heavy ship traffic, it is impossible for one person to both steer and keep a proper lookout. Fortunately, most sailing is done outside these pretty well defined shipping lanes.

It is also important to remember that, if a large vessel sees your stern light, it is an overtaking situation (stern lights should never be Fresnel or dioptric lenses). Once you alter course and a side light is visible, you have involved yourself in a crossing situation. Ah, these Rules of the Road are so concise and explicit! There is a lot of ocean which neither of you own, and a quarter of a mile is plenty of clearance—much closer than this might require the changing of pants!

Everyone who goes to sea should not only carry a copy of *The International Regulations for Preventing Collisions at Sea, 1972,* but also read, study and memorize all portions of the regulations to understand fully their meaning and implication.

Personally, I liked the *old* Rules of the Road which were easy to memorize. This was an absolute requirement for anyone who "sat" for a license. The new ones have many areas which are not to the benefit of the ocean sailing voyager, and can be very confusing, especially regarding restricted visibility; however, the intent and responsibilities have not changed.

Rule 2 (Responsibility) is (a) similar to the old Article 29 (Precaution), and (b) is similar to the old Article 27 (General Prudential), but in any case Rule 2 is the whole basis of the Rules of the Road at sea. It reads:

RULE 2

Responsibility

(a) Nothing in these Rules shall exonerate any vessel, or the owner, master or crew thereof, from the consequences of any neglect to comply with these Rules or of the neglect of any precaution which may be required by the ordinary practice of seamen, or by the special circumstances of the case.

(b) In construing and complying with these Rules, due regard shall be had to all dangers of navigation and collision and to any special circumstances, including the limitations of the vessels involved, which may make a departure from these Rules necessary to avoid immediate danger.

(a) covers everyone—the *vessel, owner, master* and *crew*—and further adds the *neglect of any precaution required* by ordinary practice of seamen. This implies seamen generically, not what you or Joe as seamen might do; furthermore, it makes it all inclusive by adding *by the special circumstances* of the case. You get it in this paragraph—one way or the other—*obey the rules!*

Well, then you read (b) and think, "Now I have an out." Not so—all it tells you is to obey the Rules. Someday you may have to depart from them to avoid immediate danger, but it is to be a last resort, and only when it is *necessary to avoid immediate danger.* In other words, don't wreck your vessel, but do obey the Rules until such time that, if you don't depart from the Rules (which means you are now obeying the Rules), you cannot *avoid immediate danger.* It's a fine line they draw. That's why I suggest that everyone aboard know and understand the Rules because Part (2) says every one of the crew must comply.

The implications and ramifications are fascinating, and if I were to be a lawyer, it would be in the field of Admiralty Law.

My disappointment in the new Rules is that some old things are lost, the worst being sound signals in restricted visibility. For sailing vessels, this used to be—at one minute intervals—one blast on the starboard tack; two blasts in succession on the port tack; and three blasts in succession with the wind aft. At least you knew it was a sailing vessel, what tack it was on and therefore his direction of travel, but not much more. Now the sound signal is "at intervals of not more than two minutes, three blasts in succession, namely one prolonged followed by two short blasts." But this signal does not tell you a damn thing about the vessel's direction and does not reveal that it is or isn't a sailing vessel. It is the same signal used for "a vessel not under command, a vessel restricted in her ability to maneuver, a vessel constrained by her draught, a vessel engaged in fishing, and a vessel engaged in towing or pushing" Rule 35(c). So this new form of the rule may very well turn out to be Hobson's Choice.

The Rules of the Road can never be learned from a book. They can be learned only at sea when, through constant use, recognition and reaction, they become automatic. A sailor must trust implicitly the Rules of the Road and know (and *believe*) that all other "vessels, owners, masters and crews thereof" are also obeying the Rules. If this were true, there would almost never be a collision at sea!

SNOWSTORM

(*A True Experience*)

We are four days out of Boston in a schooner bound for Barbados and have been lying ahull in a strong gale for the past 14 hours. Yesterday was spent hove-to, forereaching at two knots by the log in Force 7 and 8 winds, with heavy snow squalls. For December, the intensity of the storm is unusual; the temperature is between 10° and 15°. It is now four hours into the morning watch, and I am cold—almost numb—for I have been on deck the past two hours breaking away the ice accumulating on the hull, deck and rigging. Visibility is no more than 50 yards during squalls, and never more than a half mile in the lulls. About an hour ago, I was interrupted for the third time by a steamer's foghorn. She, like the other two, passed out of sight upwind, and I hope (but secretly doubt) that my horn can be heard. Yesterday I passed over Georges Bank and am now in the steamer lanes.

The fire has kept the cabin to at least 55° and my face feels prickly and drawn from the heat. I lost one of my mittens while getting the horn out of the deck box and fear frostbite, but notice that blood still flows from the cuts in my fingers. I have been 39 hours without sleep. I am tired. I am alone—and dare not sleep until the weather moderates or, at least, the snow stops. The screech of wind in the rigging makes it impossible to hear anything else, and every 20 minutes I force myself to have a good look around the horizon and listen hopefully—for nothing. Time passes slowly. Frequent checks of the clock show only minutes have passed when it seems like hours. Vigorous tapping of the barometer still does not budge the needle, which seems stuck in one place.

Time does pass, and morning twilight seeps over the horizon. The snow has stopped but wind and seas have not diminished. The water and sky are the same cast of gray, broken only when wave crests show white. I club down as much ice from the rigging as I can—it's not as hard this time—and go below, write up the log, and set the alarm for four hours.

Aroused by a distant ringing, I finally realize that it is the alarm clock. An eerie brightness fills the cabin, and I wipe the condensation from the porthole to find the sun is out in a clear sky! The motion of the schooner tells me the seas have moderated. I mechanically unchock my sextant and slide the hatch open, for the sun is nearing its zenith. Slowly and numbly I work out my latitude, wind the chronometer and tear out yesterday's page from the Almanac. I now work up my approximate position and enter it in the log which lies open before me. I am momentarily stunned by the last entry I made at dawn.

It reads: "Art. 16: Every vessel shall, in a fog, mist, falling snow or heavy rainstorms, go at a moderate speed, having careful regard to the existing circumstances and conditions.

"A steam vessel hearing, apparently forward of her beam, the fog signal of a vessel, the position of which is not ascertained, shall, so far as circumstances of the case admit, stop her engines, and then navigate with caution until danger of collision is over."

This is from the *old* Rules of the Road—there is nothing comparable in the 1972 Rules.

12

Navigation

It is an old adage that in the land of the blind, the one-eyed man is king. Before World War II, one was comparatively "blind" at sea because of being dependent solely on observations of navigational factors. One might assume, therefore, that the "new" electronic navigation that is not dependent on observation of celestial bodies would make one a "king." This assumption would be correct if electronic equipment offered 100 percent reliability and accuracy and were worldwide in application. Since this is not so, one must achieve maximum proficiency in, and rely on, the older navigational methods. With the *addition* of electronic devices (to be used as a convenience, not a necessity), one could indeed assume the role of the one-eyed man.

I am somewhat mystified (and even appalled) at the apparent neglect and belittlement—in modern navigation—of keeping a traverse table. Admittedly the modern navigation tables, using an Assumed Position (AP), do not require the precision of the older methods which require a Dead Reckoning position (DR). I well remember when the only charts aboard belonged to the captain, and the vessel's noon position was calculated by correcting course steered for deviation, variation, leeway, and current, as well as for the ability of the man at the wheel, and whether or not one was sailing in a high- or low-pressure area. Marking any chart was the prerogative of the captain *only*. The required noon position was given on a separate sheet of paper, reduced from the workbook, along with how far one had sailed and the course and remaining distance to destination.

The advent of radio for time ticks eliminated the need for correcting the chronometer by observation, just as the gyro lessened the need for frequent azimuths to determine compass error. No one really questions the convenience of all the navigational aids that have been developed in the last half century. The trouble is that often a reliable back-up system has either been forgotten or never learned.

Taking a look at electronic navigational devices, let's consider their usefulness in unlimited ocean cruising.

DEPTH SOUNDER. For certain types of bottom contours, this can be a convenient aid; it is certainly easier and faster than casting a lead line. However, it cannot sample the bottom or be used to determine current or drift. Knowledgeable users can often describe the bottom by the type of echo received on the light band, i.e., band width; however, digital and meter types can give only depth. A depth sounder cannot replace human eyes for shallow water sailing, especially around reefs and atolls, where depths change from a thousand fathoms to three feet above sea level in a cable's length. Also, the transducer has a limited life and must be recalibrated as it loses power.

DIRECTION FINDERS—RDF or ADF. These are useful over very limited distances. Corrections for greater distances are found in Table I in *Bowditch*. They must be calibrated as well as permanently installed if they are to be used as other than homing devices. Their usefulness is further limited to the areas of the world where radio signals are broadcast. Land effect, night effect and ambiguity are also critical factors in their accuracy.

CONSOL (Europe); CONSOLAN (United States). At one time, there were two U.S. East Coast stations, but now there is only one, so only a line of position is obtainable. The system is still widely used in Europe and many RDFs are equipped with a frequency band suited for Consol. Because it can be combined with an RDF set, it is a virtually free additional navigation tool. Its accuracy leaves much to be desired. A daylight range of about 1,000 miles and a nighttime range of about 1,200 miles can be expected. Errors at this range vary from 11 to 25 miles according to the area in which one is cruising.

SPEED AND DISTANCE RECORDING. The present devices are sophisticated adaptations of the old standard taffrail log, but without the nuisance of having to trail a line for the rotor and shifting it when tacking. Also, they do not become wrapped up in the propeller. However, they do collect sargasso weed just like their ancestors. All devices, whether rotating, pressure-sensing, etc., are subject to fouling and are usually the first items to give trouble, mechanical or electrical. Like the taffrail rotor, their loss is usually not mourned; most ocean voyagers can look over the side and determine the speed of a vessel $\pm$ .1 knot.

LORAN A. This device has gained enthusiastic reception from fishermen and is now frequently installed on ocean-cruising vessels. Using ground waves, during daylight the range is 700 to 800 miles, depending on whether one is in the Atlantic or Pacific Ocean. At night, the ground wave range is reduced to 450 to 550 miles. Using sky waves at night increases the range to about 1,400 miles. Loran A's main advantage lies in the accuracy which can be achieved by a skilled operator. Using sky waves 800 to 1,000 miles from the transmitter, one can usually expect to be within 300 yards of his position. Two miles is about the maximum error. Using ground waves, 100 yards is not an unreasonable expectation. Thus, with very few exceptions, Loran A can do all that a RDF or Consol can and with greater accuracy; however, it must all be done in the Northern Hemisphere—North Atlantic; North Pacific. There is some sky wave coverage from the New Hebrides to the Malay Peninsula—but none for the Indian Ocean and, of course, none for the Southern Hemisphere.

LORAN C. This is slightly more accurate than Loran A but is a lane-resolution system, so more adapted to continuous use than the selected or intermittent use of Loran A. For intermittent use, Loran C requires a very accurate DR position and has not found the favor enjoyed by Loran A. By 1977, a number of advances in Loran C had been made. First, the new sets can distinguish which lanes they are in, and now only an approximate DR position is required. After initial setting of the unit, it rates itself, finally locking into the correct lanes. This usually takes less than five minutes. The second improvement is that some of the sets will read out latitude and longitude direct. For my money, this is one of the most significant milestones in electronic navigation, for it eliminates the special charts which have Loran lines overlaid on them. Charts are costly and often the only updating (correction) on them is the change of price. After all, what we navigators are most interested in is latitude and longitude. The landfalls take care of themselves, even using old charts.

One must always remember that Magellan, Columbus, Cook and other great navigators made their own charts as they went along. I am mystified as to why charts are continually reissued without major corrections, or why, when a buoy or day marker is added, say, between No. 1 and No. 3, it could not be shown as No. 1, No. 1-B, No. 3, etc., which is self-explanatory and does not make a chart obsolete. Instead, they use No. 1, No. 3, No. 5, etc., which changes all the numbers and does make a chart obsolete. I guess the agencies operate like Columbus did. After all, "He left, not knowing where he was going; got there and didn't know where he was; returned, not knowing where he had been," all at government expense through taxes levied on the individual.

While on the subject of long-range navigation, Omega holds much promise, but for the present, it is very expensive. Its assumed accuracy is ± 1 mile daytime and ± 2 miles nighttime, (± 2 and ± 4 are more realistic) and it can be used worldwide. As this system develops, power requirements reduce. Basically, like Loran C, it is best used continuously; however, recent developments make intermittent use feasible.

Decca is extremely accurate but has very limited area of local coverage. For this reason, it is seldom found on vessels that are not consistently in the areas where its network is established.

RADAR. The price has been reduced enough so radar is now within the budget of many ocean voyagers, but it is seldom installed because its principal value is in coastal navigation and congested areas, and especially in fog. A range of about 15 miles is all that should be expected by the average ocean cruiser because of the difficulty of siting the unit high enough above the water and because of the power requirements for greater range.

For my money, the limitations of all electronic navigation aids require that we still rely on "regular" celestial and terrestrial navigation methods; therefore, accuracy in determining a DR position is worth cultivating. I am not against using electronics, but would not want to be solely dependent upon them.

NAVIGATION

My formal introduction to navigation was an old copy of *Bowditch,* price deducted from my pay, obtained when I went from AB to acting second mate. The captain's speech included, "Mister, everything you need to know is in here. You will now learn navigation." Well, it can be done with *Bowditch* alone, but it's about the most difficult way imaginable to learn that subject. Sort of like jumping down the well for a drink of water.

The only accepted method of navigation on sailing vessels then was the time-sight or Sumner Line. Several years later, I was introduced to HO 208 (Dreisanstok). Then, during World War II, I had HO 211 (Ageton); and also HO 214—which I did not like. On one voyage after the war, I used HO 249. More recently I have used HO 229. Depending on the mood I am in, I now alternate among time-sight, HO 211 and HO 229. The time-sight and HO 211 are worked from a DR position. Time-sight yields longitude as the answer. HO 211 yields an altitude intercept away from or toward the body on the azimuth. HO 229 is solved from an assumed position and requires plotting, especially with star sights where a different AP is used with each star; however, it is the quickest method.

For general navigation, HO 208 or HO 211 are really convenient, as one small book not only solves the problem but also occupies the least space aboard. I suppose World War II navigators learned and used HO 211 more than any other method.

Navigation at sea is called "a day's work," and always terminates at noon. I suppose that with all the other changes in the world, modern practice today would put termination at midnight. However, noon it used to be and noon it still is aboard *K'ung Fu-tse*. It goes as follows from noon: (1) In the afternoon, a sun sight is taken, and the Course(s) advanced to cross the line of position (LOP) of that sight which becomes the new dead reckoning position (DR); (2) at sundown, an amplitude is done to check the compass error; (3) at evening twilight, two to four (or more) stars and planets are observed and the DR is advanced, their solution resulting in a fix; (4) at morning twilight another round of stars is taken and the DR is advanced from the previous evening fix, using the previous courses and distance and a morning fix is obtained; (5) an amplitude is solved for compass error; (6) about mid-morning a sun-sight is taken, and the course is advanced to cross the resulting LOP; (7) time of transit (noon is calculated) and the course is advanced to noon, when the transit of the meridian is observed (noon sight). The result is the NOON POSITION, the end of one "day's work" and the beginning of another.

Unless exceptional accuracy is required, such as when sailing through passes, reefs and low islands, I seldom use stars but rely on the sun. On "normal" passages I use the sun in the morning, crossing this with the noon sight for my position. I have found this to be accurate to ± ½ mile. There are times when one is unable to get any sights and must place total reliance on one's dead reckoning ability. If one's DR position after 24 hours is more than a mile from his calculated position, he has made an error in the calculation or has been sloppy in handling all the factors which affect the DR position.

The notion of obtaining a latitude *and* a longitude by a meridian transit of a single body has been the perennial hope of thousands of neophyte navigators, often with the thought that it was an achievable dream— a method simply not realized by our forefathers—you know, those dunces of the past, and I suppose that includes me.

First of all, the method will only work in a few, isolated circumstances. Case No. 1 is when the declination of the sun is the same or *not more than* 3° of the vessel's latitude. The computed meridian transit should start a maximum of five minutes before the altitude is measured and the exact GMT noted. Within five minutes after transit the altitude is again measured and the exact GMT again noted. Then, using the *Nautical Almanac,* the GHA and declination are solved for each of the sights. Declination is then the latitude and the GHA is the longitude, with GHA + 180° = west or 360° − GHA = east. Correction to this would be for the direction of travel (course) prior to noon, less that portion of the distance covered after noon. The arcs of radii then plotted give two intersections, and you choose the one that looks best.

At other times the method is subject to very large errors for, as the difference between latitude and declination increases, the "hanging" increases, so that there may be several minutes when the sun does not change altitude. However, it *is* changing azimuth very rapidly, so even when plotting numbers of pre- and post-altitudes, it is impossible to designate an exact time unless, as in case II, the vessel is stationary. If the vessel is moving, regardless of its direction, no method of plotting will give an answer as there is no exact constant with which to work.

A preferred method is, again, one used on sailing ships. This solves for latitude and longitude from a *Simultaneous Observation of Altitude, Azimuth, and Time,* the formulae for which are:

$$\text{Long } t = \text{Sin } Z \cos h \sec d$$
$$\text{lat tan } \tfrac{1}{2} (90° - L) = \text{Sin } \tfrac{1}{2} (t+Z)\text{cosec } \tfrac{1}{2} (t-z) \tan \tfrac{1}{2} (h \pm d)$$

when $h = H_0$, L = Latitude, d = declination, t = local hour angle, Z = azimuth. Use +d when L and d are opposite; use −d when L and d are the same.

H.O. 249 finds favor with many ocean voyagers who want a modern method, especially in small vessels where space for navigation is usually at a premium. Consisting of only three volumes, it has some limitations, principally in the number of stars (Volume I) available. This is of little consequence because many people use only the sun. Therefore, only Volume II and III are required; and if one stays below Latitude 39°, Volume II is the only one needed. (This certainly saves shelf space.) The method is fast and, though not as accurate as HO 214 or HO 229, more than adequate for average small-craft navigation. (The maximum difference I have ever encountered in comparing HO 249 with other methods is ½ mile.)

Navigation is simple and requires a minimum of education, unless one finds it necessary for reasons of ego to comprehend the entire theory. In any case, one must understand and memorize the terminology, which can be found in *Bowditch*. Some modern authors change the names and the poles from which one observes the celestial sphere. Then time and arc are backward from all other standard methods and texts, and this leads to confusion. Believe me, nothing—absolutely nothing—is anticipated so much as that dot on the chart that represents the noon position!

NOTES

1. Pilot charts are necessary:
    a. Try to obtain British as well as U.S.
    b. U.S. are best.
2. Sailing directions are necessary; British are best:
    a. Generally gloom-and-doom books.
    b. Allow one to develop a chart from description.

    c. Total set for world = 75 (British).

    d. Index of World Charts—British and U.S. should be carried.

3. Ocean Passages for the World contains:

    a. Sailing ship routes.

    b. Steamship routes.

    c. Atlantic, Indian Ocean and Pacific routes.

    d. Index of sailing directions.

    e. World climate chart—Jan. and July.

    f. World surface currents.

4. Landfalls:

    a. Signs

       (1) Birds (learn their habits); insects.

       (2) Swells and waves.

       (3) Clouds; reflections in clouds.

       (4) Smell, sound.

       (5) Flotsam, sea weed.

    b. Always try to be to windward of port.

    c. Daylight entry.

       (1) Unlit ports.

       (2) Doubtful ports (where known changes have occurred).

       (3) Port for which there is no chart aboard.

    d. Time and date important; especially latter can mess up navigation.

       (1) Arrive in ports during working hours.

       (2) Avoid legal holidays.

    e. If port is also a lee shore:

       (1) Find an alternate port in case of bad weather.

5. Colvin Great Circle Distance Formula:

$$COS\ M = (\cos D \cdot \cos A \cdot \cos L) \pm (\sin D \cdot \sin A)$$

When M = great circle distance in degrees (1 day = 60 N.M.)

        D = latitude of departure

        A = latitude of arrival

        L = difference of longitude between departure and arrival

When A and D same name (N or S), use + (plus)

When A and D opposite name, use − (minus)

Only distance is derived from this formula.

6. Sound.

    a. Sound through water travels at .8 miles per second.

    b. Sound through air travels at .18 miles per second.

    c. Sound transmitted by vessel and echo results: Elapsed time is divided by two, which equals distance to object.

13

Junks and Junk Rigs

The rigging and sailing of the Chinese junk, and the adaptation of the junk rig to Western hulls is still in its embryonic stage here in the West. From earliest times, the Western seaman, shipbuilder or designer has been a very knowledgeable individual; he not only designed, built and rigged his vessels, but also sailed them. Furthermore, each change he made was for a *reason,* and was recorded. Western sailors, builders and naval architects have a rather complete record by means of which we can analyze and compare isolated features of hull designs and rigs—not so the Chinese.

Chinese builders were not sailors, and vice versa. Moreover, neither group had the technical ability to trace from antiquity the virtues and faults of any particular vessel type. It seems that changes were made and, if good, were retained, perhaps with a continuous sequence of modifications continuing right up to the present. Yet, the whys or wherefores were not recorded. In amassing data on the Chinese junk, the Western designer must assume, first, that decadence in design did not start until after World War II, when motorization of junks began in earnest; and, second, that the scant information available on hull shape must be analyzed from junk to junk, and no attempt made to compare Chinese hulls with those of any other culture, even though similarities exist.

The entire design concept of the Chinese junk's underwater lines runs contrary to most principles of our naval architecture. With regard to rig, we *can* develop a valid comparison by installing the Chinese rig on Western hulls and then comparing the results—*if* the comparison is made on identical hulls. The one weakness of such comparison is that the designer must choose the *correct* chinese rig and proportions for the experiment.

Perhaps the whole concept is summed up best in the words of the late G.R.G. Worcester, who spent decades studying the Chinese junk, especially the riverine type:

"Nobody could have designed the Chinese sail, if only for fear of being laughed at. A device so elaborate and clumsy in conception, yet so simple and handy in operation, could only have evolved through trial and error. It is indifference rather than difficulty that has caused Chinese sailing craft to be so little studied in the West, but the difficulties are formidable enough. There have probably always been more varieties of sailing craft in China than in all the rest of the world put together.

"The study of everything connected with the Chinese junk is complicated by contradictions. No sooner is an apparent solution found, or a rule permitting of a classification arrived at, than along comes an exception so formidable as to wreck all previous conclusions."

Several commonly held assumptions should be corrected before any serious discussion of the rig itself can be contemplated; the uninformed have a tendency to use isolated half-truths as the basis for dogmatic pronouncements:

1. "Seaworthiness is a function of design, construction and seamanship." There are many types of Chinese hulls developed for ocean service as opposed to coastwise and riverine work. Most of the ocean-voyaging, cargo-carrying, and fishing junks have design features to meet conditions of their home ports, even though they trade or fish in a common area with vessels of entirely different hull shape. Each shape conforms in its own way to the basic requirements needed for seaworthiness.

2. "Windward ability is a function of rig and hull." If all vessels are of similar rig, when windward ability is a function of hull only. The Chinese invented the leeboard, centerboard, daggerboard, drop rudder and balanced rudder, and they were the first to use free-flooding compartments and watertight compartments. One or more of these features may be incorporated in ocean-sailing junks. The use of the daggerboard (or boards) or leeboards seem to appear most often when the area of the midship section is more than six times the area of the lateral plane of the hull (including rudder), and if the sail area is greater than six times the lateral plane of the hull (including rudder). This is similar to Western practice. Furthermore, the emphasis on windward ability is dependent more on real need for it than on the Western notion that all else can be sacrificed to achieve it. Reliable observers are almost unanimous that, generically, junks point as high as Western rigs, though, if shoal draft, they do make more leeway.

3. "Junks do not use standing rigging." Many junks do not, but many ocean-sailing junks *do,* and evidence indicates they have done so for centuries. All vessels with unstayed spars will develop a rhythm with the hull in a seaway causing them to whip—thus, probably very early, the Chinese learned the need for some type of shrouds to prevent this whip. Because of the minimal strains imposed by the rig, it is almost certain that their rigs were not set up with anything near the tension of Western rigs.

4. "All Chinese rudders either drop and/or have holes within the body of the rudder, and the holes destroy the hydrodynamic flow, causing excessive drag." Again, some Chinese rudders drop and *some do not.* Only a few types have holes in the body, and such a rudder is very efficient—more so than a streamlined rudder or one without holes. What happens is that the rudders with holes are proportionately very large for the vessel. If one will admit that a sailing vessel must, except when running, make some leeway, then he will also have to admit that there is pressure on the rudder. The Chinese, in order to reduce the size of the rudder stock and the weight of the whole assembly, as well as to relieve the effort required to steer, put holes in the rudder. When the helm is put over, pressure is on one side of the rudder blade. *Some* water passes through the holes. From the study of hydraulics, it can be shown that when water is flowing through an orifice, the resistance is greatest at the commencement of the flow and decreases when the flow is established. Thus, when the rudder is first put over, the increased resistance causes an additional increase of about 35–40% in the hole area, added to the solid area. Once flow is established, there is a decrease of pressure on the helm, and the negative side of the rudder is relieved of its bubble, reducing the braking action so common in Western rudders. Such a rudder requires less angle when sailing. The holes are rhomboidal —i.e., twice as high as they are wide—and this shape is significant. A round hole would induce an entirely different and less effective flow.

5. "Deep forefoot and long straight keel make a hull slow in stays." This is true of most Western hull forms, but not of the Chinese. Much of this burden can be overcome with very efficient rudders.

6. "High full sterns cause the hulls to yaw and bury the low bows." Nothing could be further from the truth. Junk sterns are high by Western standards, but their shape is such that they develop little lift compared to a typical Western counter stern. The bows are not low in freeboard in comparison with Western vessels. It is just that they are the reverse of what we are accustomed to seeing—i.e., bow higher than stern. However, from the Suez eastward, the high stern is a common feature, and junks and dhows lie ahull quite close to the wind without sail aloft; whereas, most Western hulls require sail in order to lie ahull. Some of the so-called "modern" Western underbody profiles and hull forms cannot ever be made to lie ahull and must be run off in heavy weather.

The balanced lug rig has been, and is used in many parts of the world, but the Chinese have, through the centuries of continuous use, developed it to a point where it is one of the most efficient rigs in the world. The secret of the Chinese lug rig lies in its flatness, and the ability to control the shape of the sails. (Figure 1 shows a typical South China sail.) Flatness is achieved by the use of four to 32 bamboo log battens, each running the full length of the sail. Vessels with the fewest battens generally are ocean-going junks, while those with most battens are riverine junks. Contrary to popular opinion, these battens do not allow any type of foil section to develop in the sail—i.e., they are not tapered. Quite the opposite is true—constant-section dense bamboos are sought. From the meager data available, it appears that bamboo size is proportioned to the nominal wind force of the trading route. For example, on ocean-going junks, a batten, say 30 feet in length, would deflect no more than six inches in Force 8 winds (about 42 knots), which exerts a pressure on the sail of 8.4 pounds per square foot. Therefore, given a constant sail area, the sail with the fewest battens will have the largest diameter bamboos. Undoubtedly, the use of more bamboos on the larger junks results from the available size and quality of bamboo. In large sails, several bamboos may be overlapped and fished to achieve the required length. The shaping of the sail is done by attaching to each batten a line or bridle which gives the appearance of a spider web, called collectively, "sheetlets." The sheetlets eventually terminate in a block or blocks called a "euphroe" to which the sheet is attached. For the Chinese the euphroe is the actual boom of the sail, as far as sheeting is concerned. The battens are not arbitrarily placed for esthetic reasons, but have a mathematical relationship to each other and to the sail as a whole, as well as to the cumulative effect of the sheetlets as they are rove to the euphroe.

The Chinese sail also consists of a yard that is hauled aloft with a halyard. The yard is held to the mast by an adjustable loop called a "snotter." When the sail is fully hoisted, no adjustment is necessary as the snotter comes home taut. However, adjustment *is* required in the length of the snotter when reefing.

The battens are held to the mast by parrels which are spliced through the sail immediately aft of the mast; they lead to the forward end of the batten on the fan-shaped sail as, in lowering the sail, all the battens move aft. In the parallel-batten sail, the parrels often go only a foot or two ahead of the mast. Large sails often require, in addition to the ordinary parrel, a "hauling parrel" which permits the sail to move aft and, when under tension, acts as a shock absorber. The basic purpose is to shift the position of the sail and to maintain a straight luff. The lowermost batten has nothing in common with a Western boom, other than being at the bottom of the sail, though it does provide a "fixing point" for the lazy-jacks. Battens are attached not in pockets, but to the *outside* of the sail on the side toward the mast, with a chafing strip on the opposite side. They are seized through the sail at intervals of one to three feet, most often with wire, rattan or split bamboo.

The Chinese sail is extremely heavy. Indeed, there is no practical way of making it light without destroying its efficiency. What is lost in ease of hoisting is made up many itmes over when lowering; the sail never hesitates to come down when the halyard is released.

The Chinese lug can be reefed either up or down. Normal seagoing practice is to reef down. However, there are times (when sailing in rivers) that reefing up is a better solution, especially with high banks that block the wind or, on small vessels, when an awning is rigged or visibility is otherwise diminished. When reefing up, lazy-jacks are set up, and the required number of battens are hoisted upward. No other adjustments are required. When reefing down, the lazy-jacks are tightened to a point where the lowermost batten is parallel with the final batten to be reefed, or at least set up so that the sail does not drag on deck. The halyard is then slacked away until the desired amount of reef—usually one complete panel—is achieved. The snotter is then adjusted and the sheetlets shortened. The whole process can be accomplished within two minutes.

Regardless of the number of battens, sheetlets are independent of the sheet; otherwise ability to shape the sail would be destroyed. My personal preference is the South China rig of six battens, which are rigged as in Figure 2. The euphroe, in this case, is single and permits the sheet to be attached directly to it. When the southern method of attachment to the sails is used, it is necessary in tacking to toss the sheetlets aft and around the leech of the sail because of the tremendous roach cut into the sail, unless they are sheeted way aft. With a large crew, this is not difficult; however, the shorthanded yachtsman would find this complication a nightmare. Also, with single sheetlets the possibility of jibing is almost nil since there is only the moment when the tossing can be successfully accomplished. If you fail (in anything but light airs) the result is broken battens. When tacking, the Chinese move the sheet block to the weather side, setting up the sheet for proper trim. Nevertheless, the southern rig with its broad sails sets the maximum amount of canvas for a given mast height— thus, for the Western blue-water sailor, double sheetlets and sheets are mandatory. This is occasionally seen in China. When used, they are set into the sail eight percent to 10 percent and, so rigged, seldom foul and are self-tending when short-tacking.

An eight-batten rig has many complications built into it. With regard to the sheetlets, as shown in Figure 3, unlike the six-batten arrangement, control of all battens is not possible through a single euphroe. The advantage of being able to control the upper half or lower half of the sail by sheeting makes it somewhat more complicated *and* slightly more efficient. When used on a narrow sail plan, this system would lend itself to single sheeting, but the sail would still benefit by having the sheet transferred on each tack to the weather side.

A downhaul pendant is sometimes fitted to the lowermost batten, which aids in keeping a taut luff. This is not required on large sails and does prevent the sail from crawling in puffy winds, thus increasing the loading of the mast. Downhauls on the various battens are neither required nor desirable. The foresails are each fitted with a bowsing line that leads from the forward end of the lowermost batten to the mast. Its function is manifold. If left slack, when pointing, the vessel will make considerable leeway—i.e., in Force 4, about one knot ahead and one knot sideways. Bowsed a little aft, the vessel moves ahead. When running wing-and-wing, it can force the foot of the sail overboard about 30 percent of the foot length. Such a versatile line is seldom, if ever, seen on any Western rig. The man at the helm need only tell a crewman to heave or slack it, and with no other trimming of sails the vessel can fall off, go sideways, go ahead or, with practice, make sternway. Thus, for centuries, maneuvering in crowded situations was accomplished with great ease. The only rig that I have sailed with that permits greater maneuverability than the Chinese rig is the square rig; however, other limitations of the latter rig make it, I think, inferior to the Chinese lug rig.

Sailing the Chinese rig requires one to *unlearn* almost everything learned with other rigs. Because of the rig's balance, there is no luffing action, *so the rig never stops sailing,* and the leading edge of the sail reveals nothing of significance. The common practice is to learn the approximate setting of each sail for the apparent wind, and the shape required of the sail for this condition. For example, close to the wind, the leech wants to be as straight as possible with a minimum angular difference bewteen the yard and the lower battens. While broad-reaching and running, the center of the leech wants maximum belly. This is accomplished in the first instance by pulling the euphroe down toward the lowermost batten and, if necessary, adjusting the tension of the various sheetlet leads. Since the sheetlets are of finite length, and the euphroe and Chinese dumbbell blocks are often sheaveless, friction then holds everything as set. When broad-reaching and running, the euphroe is lifted upward toward the center of the sail, causing it to belly.

The Chinese junk rig will not heave-to. This is of small moment because the rig can be reefed to a greater degree than any other fore-and-aft rig. In a three-masted, six-batten rig, there are 343 combinations, and 180 of them result in an acceptable degree of balance. A four-masted junk has 2,401 combinations, of which at least 700 result in an acceptable degree of balance. It's important to note that combinations that balance in, say,

Force 3 do not necessarily balance in Force 6 or 7. Inevitably, weather conditions will deteriorate so that carrying any sail at all will not be prudent. Unlike Western rigs, all that is then required is to let go the halyards. There is no need to round up; within a few moments, with all sail off the vessel, the high stern causes the hull to come up into the wind. The bow, being lower than the stern, does not have the tendency to fall off. The Chinese do use sea anchors, and the hull form rides well to one. Under strong-to-violent gale conditions, there is little else to do than go below and eat and sleep, and many junk hulls provide a most comfortable motion in such weather.

Mention should be made of the adaptation of the Chinese rig to Western hull forms. My personal experience with one to four masts on Western hulls showed that in all instances the Chinese rig is equal to or better than the conventional Western rig for the *same* hull. There is no way I know to compare apples and oranges. Most of the cruising hulls of my design which have been converted to the Chinese lug rig have been schooners. I have retained the jib, which is used in light to moderate weather. When reefing is required on a two-masted Chinese lug schooner, the first task is to furl the jib and double-reef the main, at which time the vessel is perfectly balanced and is sailed in the same manner as a two-masted junk—with fewer combinations of balance but still with more than a Western rig.

Is the Chinese junk the hull for everyone? No. Not every Westerner can learn to sail one or will even wish to try. Should all cruising vessels be Chinese rigged? Again, one would have to answer "No." While it's true that most Western hulls can be adapted to the rig, very often they do not have the stability to carry the heavy rigs; to modify the Chinese rig to the lighter hulls spoils its most important safety feature—that is, it always comes down. The use of three masts, true Chinese fashion, is almost impossible on vessels without a deep angular forefoot, and even then they must incorporate the Chinese cross-head so as to have sufficient spread to the rigging. It's important to remember that there is a large quantity of running rigging in this rig, and this alone requires more deck room than is available in most modern yachts.

Having sailed almost every other type of rig, I still agree with others of similar experience who say that the Chinese rig is the handiest one in the world. Also, the Chinese ocean-going junk has as much if not more comfort at sea than any type of Western hull. After 12 years of sailing junk rigs and now owning and living aboard an ocean-cruising junk, there are no regrets—only the desire to learn more about the Chinese hull and rig through continuous experience, and to achieve the expertise of a *loada* (Chinese junk sailing master).

14

Sailmaking in General, and Chinese Sailmaking In Particular

The first decision is whether the sails will be made of cotton or Dacron. There are economic factors which favor cotton and for many the availability of cotton may be a deciding factor. From personal experience, a good cotton sail will last as long as one made of Dacron and be infinitely easier to sew. However, when sewing cotton sails, it is necessary to make what is called a "stretch allowance." In Dacron, this is not needed. Throughout this description, both materials will be referred to when it is necessary to switch from one to the other. (In the tropics, cotton will outlast Dacron two-to-one.)

The sail plan shown encompasses all of the sails that would be normally carried on a Chinese junk, plus a conventional Western jib. This last is the only difficult sail to lay out and sew. It is suggested that those who want to make their own sails consult a book on sailmaking, such as *Make Your Own Sails,* by Bowker and Budd, St. Martin's Press, New York. It's impractical to describe all of the multiple variations that are possible within the scope of the plan given here.

MATERIAL

If the sails are to be cotton, the best choice is Vivatex—boat-shrunk, mildew-resistant, and water-repellent. The following is a table for determining the weight and size of Vivatex to use:

		Oz. per Yd.	Oz. per Sq. Ft.	Unsupported Panel Width	False Seam +1″ Reg. Overlap	Unsupported Panel Width
(1)	31″	8.98	1.120	30″	4.0	13 ″
(2)	31″	11.23	1.404	30″	5.0	13 ″
(3)	36″	10.38	1.153	35″	3.89	15½″
(4)	36″	12.98	1.443	35″	4.85	15½″

600 sq. ft. regular sails use (4), false-seamed.
600–1,000 sq. ft. regular sails use (2), false-seamed.
500 sq. ft. Chinese sails use (3), no false seams.
500–800 sq. ft. Chinese sails use (1), no false seams.
800–1,000 sq. ft. Chinese sails use (4), false-seamed.
1,000–2,000 sq. ft. Chinese sails use (2), false-seamed.

The general guide to determine appropriate weight of fabric is to take the largest sail as the criterion, and carry this weight throughout the *working lowers*. Topsails are then made of a lighter cloth, if available. Chinese sails under 800 square feet need not be false-seamed. However, if the vessel is fitted with a jib (as on the vessel shown), then the jib—if made of cotton—must be false-seamed. It need not be false-seamed if made of Dacron.

For general sailing, the jib should not be roped except on the luff, and approximately 12-inches back along the foot and down on the leech. In the clew, it should be roped approximately three feet in either direction. *For ocean cruising, this sail should be roped all around.* It would be false economy and make extra labor to put wire luffs in the jib as, with the Chinese rig, it is impossible to set such a sail taut enough without pulling the remainder of the rig out of shape. Regardless of the intended use of a Chinese sail, once it exceeds 1000 square feet in the largest sail, the sail must be roped all around. They should not, under any circumstances, be machine-roped, but must be hand-roped.

Choosing an appropriate type of rope for this purpose today, the possibilities are sisal, manila or Dacron. Sisal has a short life expectancy, and manila of a good quality is almost unobtainable today. So, the economics appear to favor Dacron—*never nylon*. It also seems impractical to use less than the $\frac{5}{16}$ inch size for roping. Actually, $\frac{3}{8}$ inch is more than strong enough to be good on sails up to 450 or 500 square feet. Above this, $\frac{7}{16}$ inch would be better. The difficulty of using small sizes such as $\frac{3}{16}$ inch or $\frac{1}{4}$ inch is that the stitches fall too close together and it takes forever to do the sewing job. In really large sails (over 1,000 square feet), it's advisable

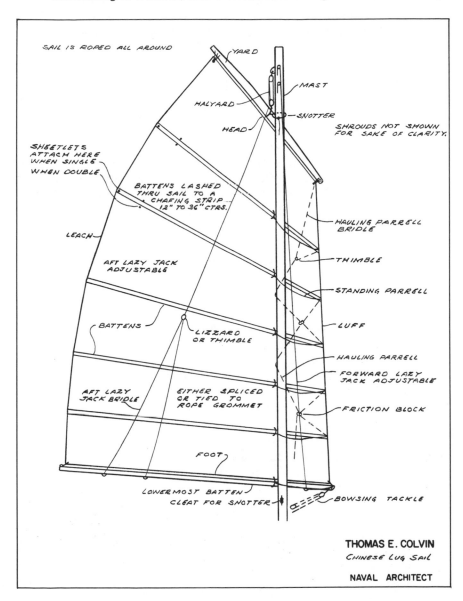

FIG. 14-1. The Chinese lug sail.

to use three different sizes of rope, the heaviest being along the luff, lighter along the leech, and the lightest along the foot and the yard—on Chinese sails. In sails that are roped all around, it is mandatory that somewhere along the foot of the sail a long splice is made to join the starting and finishing ends. The long splice should be approximately two feet in length for $3/8$ inch rope. A useful formula for length of splice is: The number of eighths of the diameter of the rope, times eight, equals the minimum length in inches of a long splice for that particular rope. Dacron rope does not stretch more than canvas. In fact, its stretch is approximately equal to Vivatex. So, in sewing a Dacron rope to a canvas sail, it should be sewn on slack; this particularly applies to the leech and foot of the jib as $3/8$ inch Dacron rope stretches approximately one inch for every 36 inches of length when 100 pounds of weight is applied. In Western sails, the tension on the luff would have to be precalculated to determine the allowance that should be made in roping the sail. In Chinese sails it is immaterial, other than that the rope, if Dacron, should be sewn on slack to take care of most of the stretch allowance required by canvas sails.

SEWING

The use of zigzag versus straight stitching is not important. In Dacron, the advantage of zigzag is that it does flatten the seam, and provides a bit of stretch in an otherwise unstretchable material. Many satisfactory cotton sails have been sewn with straight-stitch machines. Hand-sewn sails are not difficult to make but the job is tedious. If the sails are to be made at sea, there is usually little alternative to hand-sewing, and a credible job may be done over a period of time. In hand-sewing, the general description in any of the sailmaking books should be followed. The only general hint is that the thread should never be more than $4\frac{1}{2}$ feet or five feet in length after doubling, as having to pull the excess thread through the material each time a stitch is made slows down the sewing process. On Chinese sails, it apparently is quite unimportant, as it has been known that stitches sometimes do not exceed 72 to the yard!

Material Weight	*Stitches Per Yard*
4 oz.	278
6–8 oz.	180
10–12 oz.	144

The bolt ropes at the corners of all sails must be double-stitched. Double-stitching should generally extend for at least half the length of the patch, except at the clew where it should run at least 1/12th of the length of the foot of the sail on either side. All corner eyelets must be sewn over a brass ring, and a brass thimble punched in. Generally speaking, a number 7 ring is about as small as is desirable on a vessel of 36 feet and up. Grommets of rope may be substituted, providing a brass thimble is inserted before the grommet is spliced. External cringles in the corners of all sails are not necessary until the area of the sail exceeds 1,000 square feet, in which case corners should also be leathered.

JIB

In cutting the jib, it may be either miter-cut or scotch-cut, following directions given in Bowker and Budd. The jib hanks should be spaced at 30-inch intervals with one hank being exactly on the miter, and the others being spaced up and down from that point. At the head of the jib, a large cringle must be sewn in, with a brass ring. Into this is fitted the halyard block and a long D-shackle which goes around the headstay. To this is attached the jib downhaul which leads to a block at the end of the bowsprit. The downhaul rope diameter should be the same size as the snotter. Because the jib is loose-footed, the clew patch should be extraordinarily strong. In a schooner-rigged junk, this is one of the sails that will be used in about Force 7 Winds going downwind. The luff tabling should be extra heavy, and the leech tabling should not be less than 1.25 inches in width for sails up to 150 square feet, and around 2.50 inches for sails of around 300 square feet. The foot tabling should be cut off and resewn to take care of the differences created by the gore. All seams in this sail should be triple-sewn and the roping along the foot should be quite slack.

Chinese sails are laid out as follows. The first cloth is laid parallel to the luff, and all other cloths are parallel to the first. What we normally call a boom is really the lowermost batten; it should be heavier than the other battens because the lazy-jacks must fasten to it, but it need not be of a dimension one would consider proper for a boom on a Western sail of the same size. The leech is on a bias; therefore, it is necessary to cut off the tablings for resewing, as each point is a straight line between batten ends. The width of the tabling should never be less than 1.25 inches on sails up to 400 square feet, and should be ¼″ additional for every additional 50 square feet. The sails are laid out on the floor, carefully stretched out, and the strike-up marks are made at six-foot intervals. The cloths are stacked as they would be for a normal Western sail; however, prior to lifting them, a chalkline should be struck for the batten mark or patch. This strike-up mark across the sail will eventually stagger up and down a little after sewing, but can be restruck after the sail is sewn together. Careful attention should be paid to whether the batten strike mark is the top or bottom of the batten. I always mark off the nominal top of batten.

It will be necessary to cut strips of cloth suitable for batten patches. The width of each batten patch will be equal to the width of the batten plus three inches. One-half inch (½″) of the edge is turned under, giving a finished under-patch of the batten plus two inches. This will then lie one inch above or below, depending on where the strike-up mark of the batten is located, and strike-up marks prior to sewing must be made. Before sewing the inner batten patch to the sail (which will equal in width the batten plus 1.50 inches) it should be straight-stitched along the center of the outer patch, and underneath. When the ½-inch fold-overs cover this, the fold-over will cover the edge of this patch by ¼-inch. For the first time around, it might be easier to sew under the edge of the outer patch as well so that the finished patch will go on in one piece, with the edges already folded over and sewn. The best way to make this patch is to add the total length of all patches needed, plus about 10 percent and sew it as one continuous strip *across* the cloth—not along the length. Make sure the under-patch seams are staggered from the over-patch. It is not necessary to do any more than just seam the pieces together about in the same manner and width as that used in sewing the sail.

It is better to cut the patch from edge to edge of the material on the bolt of the cloth, using either 31 inch or 36 inch pieces. While the patch will not lie exactly square to the weave of the other cloth, it does not seem to make any difference. In theory at least, the sail "stops" at each of these patches, the areas above and below being totally independent of each other. In the drawing, the batten patch is shown as installed, also the methods of sewing by machine, where triple stitching should be used, and where sewing is to be done by hand when only each edge must be done.

As for the grommets on the leading edge of the sail, which may be stamped-type spur grommets, each one should clear the edge of the batten patch above and below it by a minimum of ½ inch. Immediately after the spar, the dimensions given on the sail plan are for another row of grommets. These grommets should be set in reinforced-patches that are over-sewn and of the same thickness—i.e., double—the batten patch. These grommets also should be a minimum of ½ inch above and below the batten patch. There will be two grommets required at each batten, and through these a rope grommet made from three-strand Dacron should be made. The rope grommet should be larger than the batten grommet area, similar to that shown in the drawing. Whether it is a little larger than shown is immaterial. To this will be tied the parrel lines. These parrel lines are spliced through the forwardmost pair of grommets, with a tail long enough to span the mast when the sail is down, plus approximately one foot. The size of these parrels should be of rope the same diameter as the bolt-rope. It is well to note that the lowermost grommet must be *much larger* in diameter than any of the others as it must pass over the lowermost batten (or boom).

Eighteen inches (18″) in from the leech of the sail, or to the dimensions shown on the sail plan, is another pair of grommets. These are used for the attachment of the sheetlet, bridles, whips or standing end, as the case may be. The drawing shows the port line passing through the bottom grommet and spliced to the standing end of the starboard line, which in turn passes through the upper grommet and is spliced to the standing end of the port side. It's a good idea to have the major part of the strain taken by the upper grommet, but the bottom line should not be so slack as to receive no strain at all. Immediately forward of the grommet, a downhaul is passed to the lowermost batten or boom. It will usually serve to make a small eye-splice, which is passed around the lower boom or batten, and have the standing portion pass through the eye and down to the cleat. The length of the downhaul should be approximately two feet to the cleat, with a minimum of three feet of tail below that. This permits the tail to be passed through the batten grommets when reefing is required. Downhauls are not needed on larger sails, as the weight of the battens is sufficient to keep the sail from climbing and bring it down when the halyard is cast off.

SNOTTER

The yard does not have a grommet as do the other battens, but instead has a "snotter." The snotter is lashed with "small stuff" around the yard and just abaft the mast. A small tail is left out, into which a thimble is spliced. The long standing end then passes around forward of the mast, through the thimble and down to a cleat opposite the downhaul cleat on the starboard side of the mast. This line, or snotter, is used to adjust the sail only when reefing, where it must be adjusted continuously, more or less according to the vessel's sailing trim. In the up position, the snotter has but one adjustment, and that is to hold the yard as close as possible to the mast. In every case, the snotter must lead off the top of the yard—not the side or the bottom. It is usually passed at a point just aft of the halyard block, or it can pass forward of the halyard block with the final tie being made just aft of the block, thus allowing the bridle for the halyard block to prevent the snotter from sliding forward on the yard.

The grommets at the head and the foot should be spaced approximately 12 inches apart for small sails—never less than that; however, in larger sails, they need not be spaced closer than three times the diameter of the yard (or lowermost batten). The sail is laced to these with ¼ inch three-strand Dacron for sails up to 500 square feet; $\frac{5}{16}$ inch Dacron for sails 400

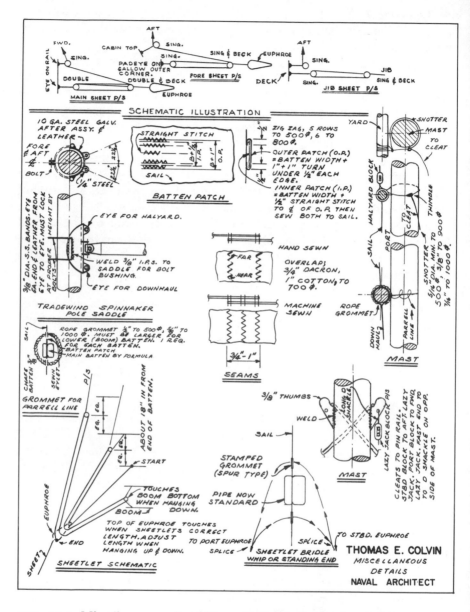

FIG. 14-2. Miscellaneous sailmaking and rigging details for the Chinese lug rig and masts.

to 700 square feet; and ⅜ inch Dacron for sails 700 to 1,200 square feet.

There are no rounds cut into the head, foot or luff of a Chinese sail. A minimum of five measurements is required to lay out the straight portion of the sail—i.e., the length of the luff total; the length of the foot total; the length of the yard total; the length of the leech total, and the diagonal from the throat to the clew. Batten positions are then struck, and the piece to form the roach—or leech curvature—of the sail is added from the clew-peak line and a straight line struck between these two points, forming the curvature.

The first cloth laid down in a Chinese sail is usually the piece forming the luff. It is then parallel to the straight line from the throat to tack line. Always allow sufficient extra cloth for the tablings. All cloths then go parallel to this first-established edge. In sewing up, the last cloth sewn is the luff. In laying down the sail, be sure that, after the initial unrolling, *the sailcloth bolt is turned around but never over.*

You'll need a bit of additional cloth to make the batten and corner patches. The battens themselves consist of two pieces—the *main* batten, on the starboard side of the sail, and the *chafing* batten, on the opposite side of the sail. These battens are fastened to each other with lacings placed on 12-inch centers. On sails to 500 square feet, two 3/16-inch bolts serve better. I suggest using stove bolts, *with the nut always set up inside the batten tube.* The excess length need not be trimmed off. The nut should be set up on a washer, but no washer should be under the head of the bolt. Round-headed bolts are better than flat-headed bolts that require countersinking, which weakens the thinner chafing batten. With cotton sails, it is desirable *not* to pierce the cloth by drilling, but merely run a pricker through it, opening up a hole in the cloth of sufficient diameter to pass the bolt. Because this bolt hole is in a completely sewn area, it can be quite easily made for ³⁄₁₆-inch holes. For the larger holes, such as for ¼-inch bolts, it is desirable to cut a hole with a grommet punch and seal the edges with a bit of epoxy to keep it from fraying. In Dacron cloth, it is desirable to burn the hole through. The heat seals the hole edges. I suggest that the battens be placed together and predrilled before being attached.

Battens can be made of almost any wood—ash, mahogany or Douglas fir. Sitka spruce can also be used if available. But the best material, I believe, is aluminum pipe—Schedule 10. Bamboo is the next best material, but must be fired first for hardening. Still, over the last ten years I've found Douglas fir to be entirely satisfactory. If made of wood, battens should be well-sanded, corners slightly rounded so as not to cut the sail, painted first with a sealer-primer, and then with high-gloss enamel. How long such a batten will last is uncertain, but since it works in the open air and is thoroughly painted, it's quite possible that one will last without rot ever setting in. The battens *are* subject to occasional breaking because of sudden bend-

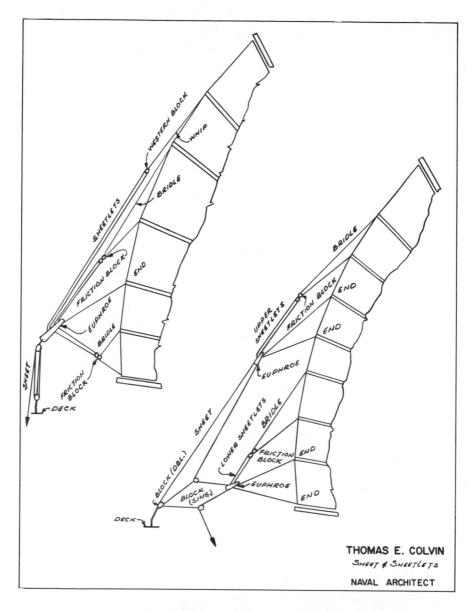

FIG. 14-3. Sheet and sheetlet details on the Chinese lug sail.

ing by the wind, and more frequently from being fouled when raising. Should a batten break, a repair is easy, by "fishing." At the first good opportunity, the batten should be replaced with a new one or a permanent repair should be made. On our 42-foot *Gazelle,* several broken battens were "temporarily" patched and served satisfactorily for several more years.

The lengths of the bridles are critical, but there is no formula for determining their proper length. Shown on the schematic that accompanies the sail plan is the approximate amount of drop required below the battens. It is the same problem with the length of the sheetlet; however, I've found that when the pendants and bridles are installed and the sheetlet is rove, the euphroc block tip *just touches* the underside of the lowermost batten, or boom. It is a good idea to have a sufficient amount of tail—originally at least—so you can make further adjustments if required. Drawings show the four homemade blocks and two euphroes required for each sail.

A further word on material for Chinese sails. Because of the great strength of the sail as sewn, the material used is rather unimportant. In a pinch, gunny sacks would prove acceptable. However, since it is assumed that the sails being discussed here are for yachting purposes, the owner is well-advised to use a good quality material, which requires no more labor than the cheaper material. And, while any material can be used satisfactorily in a Chinese sail for a junk, only the best quality cotton or Dacron is really acceptable for any *Western* style sail carried on a Chinese junk.

TOPSAIL

A triangular topsail is used in many true junks as well as on schooner-rigged junks. The advantage of a triangular sail is that it does not need to be lowered when the vessel is tacking. For us, it has turned out to be a really useful sail. It can be set scandalized, or in the normal fashion. It should be miter-cut, as with a jib, and done in the manner shown in the drawing. It is set flying, and is roped along the upper edge and down three feet on the foot and leech. In way of the clew, it should be roped three feet in both directions. The clew patch must be extremely strong. The weight of this sail should not be greater than that used for other sails, nor less than one-half the weight of the other sails. When purchasing the cloth, economy may dictate that it be the same material as the regular working sails.

TRADEWIND SPINNAKER

Also shown on the drawing of *Nor-Ann* is the tradewind spinnaker saddle. This is the proper type of saddle to be used with a tradewind spinnaker.

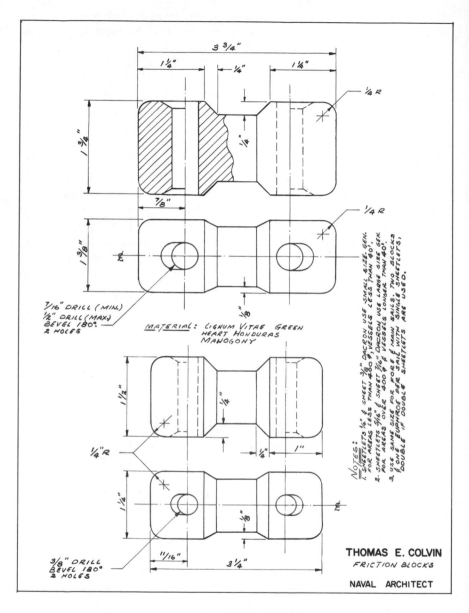

FIG. 14-4. Friction blocks.

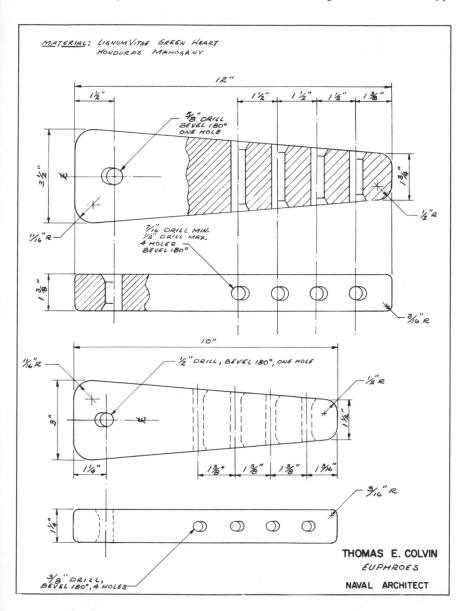

FIG. 14-5. Euphroes.

It is hoisted by the jib halyard or a separate halyard to a height where when set, it lies parallel to the clew of the tradewind spinnaker. It is desirable that these angles approach 90°, and the saddle must be fitted with a downhaul to maintain perfect tension on it. The saddle itself is made of 10-gauge steel for all sizes of hulls up to 60 feet in length, and must have a gooseneck welded on in such a way that the poles will move up and down as well as toward or away from the centerline. Tradewind spinnaker poles are always set so that the sail forms a 22½° angle with the centerline of the vessel. The poles are then shifted according to whether or not the wind is dead aft or as much as 22½° from the stern, port or starboard. It is imperative that this angular distance remain constant; however, because of the purpose of the poles and the method of setting them, they must swivel in all directions—i.e., up and down and athwartships. The length of the pole given on the sail plan is for when it is used on any one of the Chinese junk rigs. It is generally a poor substitute for the main working rig, and will be found to be more of a nuisance than an asset, as the Chinese rig is fully capable of working downwind about as efficiently as the tradewind spinnakers.

In setting a tradewind spinnaker, the following steps are taken: The foresail is lowered; the saddle is positioned on the foremast; the jib is lowered and its halyard swung aft and hooked into the saddle; the two ⅜ inch stainless steel bands are taken around the mast and pinned together with a bolt; the spinnaker poles are led forward and temporarily secured in place alongside the bowsprit with a loop-type lashing; the saddle is hoisted to its approximate position and the tradewind spinnakers are brought out on deck; the tack is secured to an eyebolt welded to the forward deck at a place predetermined from the drawings (forward of the mast and off the centerline); each spinnaker has its own halyard, which should not be secured; the clew is led out inboard and toward the centerline of the spinnaker pole and secured to its end; the spinnaker-pole sheet is led aft, outside of both the fore and main rigging (in schooners) to the end of the pole (it is not necessary to have any other purchase on these long whips); the guys are next led forward and through a separate pair of blocks attached to the end of the bowsprit; these guys are then led aft as far as the foremast; the sails are now ready to go aloft; as the first sail is hoisted, the temporary lashings must be slipped just before tension is taken on them; at this point, the spinnaker pole will lift toward the centerline and, as the sail goes up further, begin to swing outboard in a lazy S; then it will swing back toward the centerline; the second spinnaker is hoisted the same way; after securing the halyards, the vessel should be put dead before the wind, and both poles trimmed so that the sails make the required 22½° angle with the centerline; the guys are then adjusted to hold the poles in this final position.

In strong winds the mainsail may then be dropped by doing it all over-

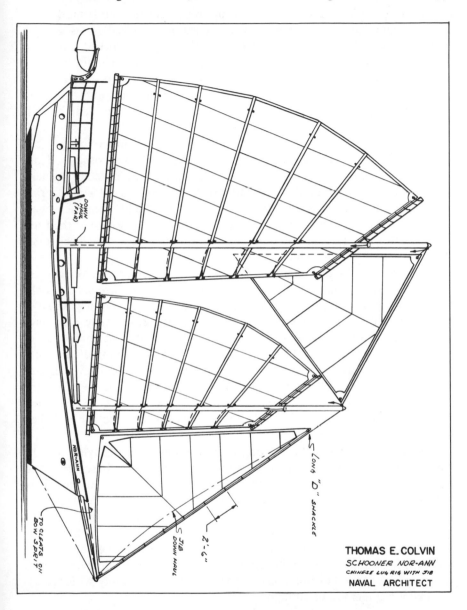

FIG. 14-6. Schooner *Nor-Ann* with Chinese lug rig and western jib.

board, using the lazy-jacks well-topped up to prevent the sail from dipping into the water, and then hauled aft and the boom stowed in its gallows frame. The vessel is then, by use of the sheets and guys, worked around to her desired course. Once she is on course, sheet and guys should be made secure. Chafing gear will be required on the sheet as it passes through a snatch block leading to the cleat. The rudder must be amidships, and lashed in that position. Subsequent change of course must be made by sails only, never by using the rudder.

In securing these sails—if the wind is blowing with any velocity—it is necessary to reverse the setting procedure, and not set any other sail but get the vessel going dead before the wind. As soon as the sails are on deck and muzzled, the jib should be hoisted quickly and the vessel kept bearing off downwind. As soon as the sails and poles are secured, then the vessel, using the rudder, may be brought into the wind by 20° to 40° and the foresail set. Once that's done, it will be possible to round up even closer to set the main or reefed main, whichever is indicated.

The total area of tradewind spinnakers must never exceed 60 percent of the working area of the original sail plan. In light displacement vessels, it could be as low as 50 percent and still be satisfactory. Tradewind spinnakers are not set on a stay, but are set flying; therefore, they may have either wire or rope luffs. Wire is preferable, but if rope, it should be of prestretched Dacron rope. This rope is pulled into the tabling of the cloth in the same way as wire, and should be oversewn and blind-sewn as one would do with wire. The foot and leech of the sail should be roped on the outside as with all other sails, except that the clew must be heavily reinforced with extra patches. The bolt-rope diameter should not be less than that of the largest sail on the boat.

The method shown in the drawing is an alternate way of laying out the Chinese sail. The more common way today of laying out these sails is to make the cloths parallel to the luff rather than to the leech. That way, there is less waste of cloth and a reduction in laying-out time. With Dacron, it is then possible to turn over the foot and, in the case of some sails, the head of the sail, too, without having to cut off and resew the tablings. The luff in any material is merely doubled under. It has also worked out that on the leech it is sufficient to double under this portion of the sail, even though it is on a bias. All other functions of normal sailmaking apply with the exception of the method of cutting.

NOTES

1. Pipe size is standard nominal size, not actual outside diameter.
2. Pipe is Schedule 10, 6063-T6 aluminum alloy.

3. Patch width = nominal size + two inches.
4. Dimensions given to upper edge of nominal size of batten. Patch edge is therefore one inch above dimension given.
5. Inner edge of grommets at nominal width of batten, Size #0.
6. Chafe battens fitted to opposite side of sail and to be nominal pipe size in width as follows:

$$1\tfrac{1}{4}'' \times \tfrac{1}{4}''$$
$$1\tfrac{1}{2}'' \times \tfrac{5}{16}''$$
$$2 \quad'' \times \tfrac{3}{8}'' \quad \text{(Douglas fir, spruce or any other}$$
$$2\tfrac{1}{2}'' \times \tfrac{7}{16}'' \quad \text{wood on hand.)}$$
$$3 \quad'' \times \tfrac{1}{2}''$$

7. Lashing grommets (size #0) are in pairs on 12-inch centers along the batten patch. Inner edges are the nominal width apart.
8. Chafe battens need not be of one continuous length, but may be of several pieces. Joints must fall clear of lashing grommets and butt against each other.
9. Batten ends are to be bolted with $\tfrac{3}{16}$-inch stainless steel bolts into inside of pipe, through sail and chafe batten—two or three per end.
10. Pipe may be spliced via welding, or sleeving and riveting.
11. Batten lashings are to be of at least five (5) passes of tarred yacht marline.

EXAMPLE: Given a two-inch pipe batten, outside diameter of pipe is $2\tfrac{3}{8}$ inches; width of patch is four inches; inner edges of grommets are two inches apart; chafe batten is $2'' \times \tfrac{3}{8}''$ fir.

15

---◆◆◆---

Flotsam and Jetsam

There are enough tasks confronting the ocean voyager to keep him occupied without his becoming a collector of anything, but by nature most of us are pack rats. Like many other voyagers, my whole family enjoys collecting shells, and over the years we have become amateur conchologists. I think certain specimens in our private collection are equal to or better than many shown in museums.

If you're a collector of nautical artifacts and memorabilia, when the time comes to make room for new additions to the collection by disposing of older items, why not donate them to a museum?

I am thinking of the many museums, not only in the United States but also throughout the world, especially maritime museums. Some of them are well endowed and send out field teams to search for new items for their exhibitions. Others, however, depend on donations or loans from private collections for their various exhibits.

If one is an avid collector, one often can get suggestions from the curator of a museum as to which of the museum's exhibits could be enhanced by compatible new articles. From experience, I know that the right photographs with descriptive captions can fill gaps, clarify or even correct existing exhibits or records. This is especially true of the rigging and handling of relatively unknown indigenous craft. Sailors spot differences in both areas that go unnoticed by landsmen.

Along the cruising track, I have seen in museums some boat models of native craft that were inaccurately rigged and crudely constructed in comparison to others I could have purchased, or at least photographed, but did not. Perhaps, I have been too busy rushing through life to pay attention to what, at the time, may seem trivial.

BOOKS

Learning and using old and even ancient methods of navigation is good mental exercise and, at the same time, produces a fuller understanding of the basis for "modern" methods. Often one will find that an "old" method is not any more time-consuming than a "new" one, and gives direct single solutions to problems which are now considered complex. "Old" books such as *Bowditch,* 1888–1925, have information in one volume which, for example, can eliminate the need for owning six volumes of HO-229, four volumes of tide tables, a radio and plotting sheets. Using time sights, meridian altitudes and traverse tables can eliminate the charts; however, coastal and harbor charts are always useful though not an absolute necessity. Another book is the *Raft Book,* a survival manual by Harold Gatty, George Grady Press, New York, 1943, which contains much useful information that can also eliminate the need for the sextant. Many of us in the merchant service had a copy of this book during World War II.

Separate from one's personal library is a "trading library" of paperback books. Most vessels are too small to carry more than 30 to 50 paperbacks —10 to 20 would probably be average. Occasionally, because of space, one builds a paperback library of favorite authors. Aboard *K'ung Fu-tse* we have nearly 1,000 volumes in the permanent library, and 60 to 100 in the trading library. The boys read 20 or so books a year. Jean and I read from 50 to 100 each. One cannot emphasize enough the amount of leisure time one has when cruising full time.

FISHING—SCUBA

Whether you eat to live or live to eat, it's a worthwhile gamble to keep a trolling line overboard most of the time. I would, however, hate to depend on what is hauled over the stern of my vessel; if I did, I would be much thinner than I am today. Have you ever wondered how much that mackerel, dolphin or mahi-mahi weighed? The best way of estimating fish weight that I ever heard about is to take the girth of the fish squared, times the length, and divide by a constant of 800; this will give the weight in pounds.

When diving for dinner, I have often wished the fish were as large on deck as they appear underwater. Fishing has never been a sport for my family. We approach all fish as fillet, chowder or *serviche,* taking only what we need at the moment. For reef fishing, my younger son and I use a lance, while my daughter and older son use the Hawaiian sling. Fortunately, reefs are usually less than five fathoms below the surface, and the majority of them are only two or three fathoms down.

A questions we're often asked is: "Do you use scuba gear for fishing?" My answer is an emphatic, "No." We carry scuba gear because both my daughter and I are certified divers, but when diving with our gear, we always use the "buddy" system. In my youth, I was trained as and did work as a professional shallow-water diver. As everyone should know, diving under pressure, even to depths as shallow as one fathom, can cause an embolism, and impure air can cause lung damage. We have found that free dives of about one minute are manageable and, after some practice, not tiring. The scuba gear we carry is strictly for emergency underwater repairs to the vessel, and only when shore facilities can assure us of pure, multi-filtered air for our tanks—and medical facilities, in case of need. My advice always has been that if you want to use scuba equipment, enroll in a class or take private lessons from a certified diving instructor before you start. There is more to diving than just donning and using the equipment. The enjoyment is increased tenfold when the inherent dangers of the sport— fear and panic—are minimized by formal instructions.

PETS

The desire to have the companionship of pets is another powerful impulse which carries over into ocean cruisers, but each year, the laws and regulations of the various countries regarding pets become more stringent. Regulations range from requiring quarantine of up to a year in England, to destroying all dogs in Australia. Joan Beak (*Wahine*) wrote from the Seychelle Islands in the Indian Ocean that *no pets* are allowed on board there, and must be either quarantined or destroyed if a vessel cruises those waters. Much of this regulation has been caused by the failure of owners to keep their pets aboard and to keep rabies vaccinations and other shots up-to-date. (Again, the conscientious pay for the negligent.) From an ecological point of view, the laws seem justified. Often pets escaping from vessels have no natural predators in their new environment and therefore multiply to the point of becoming a menace—for example, dogs and rabbits in Australia. It's well known that rodents leaving ships have ruined many an island. The introduction of foreign plants, birds and even fish into an environment may have the same disastrous consequences. So, those contemplating a cruise will probably find it more prudent to locate a good home for their pets before departure than to take the pets along at the risk of having cruising itinerary restricted, incurring fines and quarantine expenses or perhaps even losing their pets.

FIREARMS

Whether or not to carry firearms aboard is a question that doesn't produce easy answers. Many of us come from countries where hunting has always been a means of supplementing food supply and the possession of rifles, shotguns and even handguns is still so commonplace that it arouses no curiosity. From early colonial times, especially in North America, firearms frequently have been the only protection a home-owner had for his family and himself against predators. Statistics show that firearm possession in areas where it is common does not cause or increase crime. If anything, it is a deterrent, possibly because where all share a high degree of skill with firearms, mere possession of a gun does not confer any advantage on the armed man.

A vessel is one's home, so in countries where ownership of firearms is permitted, one might correctly assume that possession is not a crime. Most countries do not permit carrying concealed weapons without a permit, so by virtue of living aboard one could not go ashore with concealed or unconcealed weapons unless permission has been granted by the authorities. To deny the owner of a vessel the right to protect himself from piracy or hijacking can only encourage such practices.

I have always owned a weapon of some sort, but seldom use it now that there are supermarkets available. My list of the firearms that could be considered legitimate are hunting and target rifles of .22 to .44 caliber, shotguns, .22 caliber target pistols and other revolvers. Military weapons in limited number such as machine guns, bazookas or anything larger imply something quite beyond sportsmanship or defense. In the United States there is available in almost every state a program that teaches hunter safety and the proper use and care of firearms. In some states, such a course is mandatory before one can own a gun.

Occasionally one hears from reliable sources that a yacht crew has gone ashore and shot a farmer's chickens or pigs, or shot birds and mammals protected by law, but I believe such an incident to be very rare. The above not withstanding, a news item from *The American Rifleman,* August, 1974, is worth quoting:

JAMAICA, FAREWELL?

The first foreigner convicted in Jamaica's special new Gun Court turns out to be an American, a licensed private pilot who landed on a remote inland airstrip on Jamaica with *two rounds of ammunition,* news services report. Although he had no gun at hand, the court sentenced him to indefinite detention at hard labor.

The Gun Court was established earlier this year by a special act authorizing it to hold suspects without bail and try them in closed court before a single judge. One news report described the court, outside Kingston, as a "unique institution" with "all the appearances of a World War II concentration camp with its sentry booths and barbed wire. . . ."

Jamaican officials, who said a recent crime wave on the island was closely related to marijuana as well as firearms, claimed that the Gun Court has brought about a dramatic reduction in crime. It could also bring about a dramatic reduction in tourism. How many gun owners now yearn to vacation in Jamaica?

Some countries ask that firearms be declared and registered. Still others impound guns on a vessel's arrival and return them on its departure. Others require that arms be kept locked up with the bonded stores, and some may require a hunting license just as they may require a fishing license for the possession of a fishing pole. A friend in Bermuda tells me that possession of a flare gun is illegal there and that if you have one it is impounded during your vessel's stay at the island.

To keep informed on the laws of all countries is, of course, impossible, and fortunately not necessary. Except in rare instances, genuine courtesy, a sincere desire to be friendly and a polite inquiry from the vessel's owner upon or before entering will turn up any restrictions imposed on visitors. Needless to say, *all* countries have restrictions of one sort or another.

Much more now than formerly, we're seeing rudeness from yacht crews, with veiled threats of informing the tourist bureau, the consulate, or even the president if such-and-such is not done. Such behavior can only infuriate. In all the years and all the areas I have cruised, which includes North, Central and South America, as well as the Far East and Europe, I have never paid bribes or *morditas,* but *have* paid for services rendered. I've occasionally paid penalties for entering after hours or on national holidays. Oddly enough, the latter happened twice in the United States, and once in the Bahamas. A good try at observing the Ten Commandments seems to be about as good a code as any to cruise by; those who try to live by an eleventh, "Thou shalt not get caught," sooner or later are doomed.

PASSAGES

The adage "different ships, different long splices" applies to the comparison of voyages over the same route. Many factors must be considered (the most important being waterline length) if one were trying to establish rec-

most important being waterline length) if one were trying to establish records for fastest *or* slowest. At the turn of the century, the only comparisons necessary would have been with waterline length and rig, as few ocean cruisers had auxiliary power. Today, however, few vessels are without an auxiliary engine, and in many calculations of passage time, allowance has to be made for the number of hours under power. Some owners try to maintain an average and/or a schedule, so use their engines frequently. With others, it is a matter of pride never to use power except when entering or leaving port—often not even then—and their passage times are a matter of simple fact without modifying conditions.

Passage times, weather encountered, and month of voyage are important in planning a voyage. It is well to remember that consistency of daily runs is more important than a few bursts of speed and then being becalmed for a week. Some might question the value of the table that follows, especially since the pilot charts give a good indication of what to expect on any passage. That is certainly true but many of us have made voyages where the pilot chart has shown the frequency of gales to be less than one —and we have encountered two or three! We've also had trades predicted at Force 4, turn out to be Force 1, or come from a direction contrary to that given.

I've often felt that 20 miles a day would be a good pace for real enjoyment, and half that distance would still be fast for a true gunkholer. Schedules are the bane of most cruisers and, in our case, have caused us to bypass some of the most interesting cruising grounds.

On the following two pages is a short summary of passages made by seven different vessels, one of which was not my design (*Gouden Draak*).

Rig for each has been noted and I think this proves interesting as I've been "assured" by some nautical writers that any vessel with more than one mast is passé. Incidentally, both length on deck and waterline length are given. When actual passage time is known, full days and hours are used. Otherwise, day of departure and day of arrival are in full days and left blank if unknown.

FINANCES

Back in 1947, a man could depart on an extended cruise with only a few hundred dollars or some pounds sterling, and perhaps a letter of credit for emergencies or to prove he was "solvent" back home. Leaving a modest savings account behind, drawing three percent interest, he could return in five years or so, probably financially better off than when he started his cruise, if he had been frugal. Today, that's impossible; the old rules govern-

Vessel & Owner	LOA	LWL	Rig	Date	Departed
ALSANAL TOO (Alex Bell)	52′	44′	Ketch	Apr '72	Panama
				Apr. '72	Galapagos
				May '72	Guayquil, Ecu.
				June '72	Galapagos
				July '72	Hiva Oa
				Sept. '72	Bora-Bora
				Sept. '72	Rarotonga
				Sept. '72	Vavau
				Oct. '72	Suva
				Jan. '73	Auckland, N.Z.
				Mar–May '73	Brisbane
				May '73	Darwin
				June '73	Christmas Is.
				June '73	Cocos Keeling
				July '73	Mauritius
				August '73	Durban, S. Af.
WAHINE (Tom Beak)	45′	39′	Ketch	Jan. '73	Norman's Cay
				Jan. '73	Port Royal, SWI
				Feb. '73	Balboa, Pan.
				Mar. '73	Floreanna, Gal.
				Apr. '73	Nuku Hiva
				May '73	Papeete
				May '73	Pago Pago
				June '73	Suva, Fiji
				July '73	Palekula Bay, N.H.
				July '73	Port Moresby
MIGRANT (Dick Johnson)	42′	33′	Chinese lug sch.	July '73	Bellingham, Wa.
				Aug. '73	San Francisco
APOSTLE (Dick Dixon)	40′	31′	Gaff ketch	July '73	Walkers Cay
GOUDEN DRAAK (Nick Pleass)	46′	32′	Ketch	——	San Salvador
DELIGHT (Dave Heeschen)	34′	27′	Sch.	——	Morehead, N.C.
K'UNG FU-TSE (Tom Colvin)	48′	41′	Junk	July '76	Walkers Cay

Arrived	Passage Time	Wind Force	Notes
Galapagos	——	——	burned out crank shaft
Salinas, Ecuador	7 days	——	
Galapagos	4 days	——	
Hiva Oa, Marquesas	23 days	2–4	5 days under jury rig.
Papeete, Tahiti	9 days	0–4	
Rarotonga, Cook Is.	5 days	3–9	
Vavau Is., Tonga	2 days	——	fuel pump out.
Suva, Fiji	——	——	
Whangarei, N.Z.	9 days	3–4	one gale.
Brisbane, Aus.	13 days	2–3	light weather.
Darwin, Aus.	65 days	variable	via Barrier Reef Course—50 mile days.
Christmas Island	12 days	2–3	
Cocos Keeling Is.	4d, 10h	3–4	
Mauritius	14d, 15h	3–7	161 mi. per day
Durban, So. Africa	16 days	3–9	
Capetown, So. Af.	13 days	3–10	winter gales; hove-to 2 days.
Port Royal, SWI	3d, 12h	——	via Crooked Is. Passage.
Cristobal, Panama	4d, 16h	3–7	
Wreck Bay, Galapagos	12 days	0–3	via Ocean Passages of World Route.
Nuku Hiva, Marques.	31 days	0–2	except frequent squalls, Fc. 6.
Papeete, Tahiti	——	——	
Pago Pago, Samoa	12 days	0–4	
Suva, Fiji	5 days	0–8	
Port Vila, New Hebr.	unknown	2–5	
Port Moresby, New Guinea	11 days	3–5	
Port Darwin, Aus.	10 days	5	via Torres Strait
San Francisco, Ca.	10d, 2h	4–8	hove-to 15 hrs; bare poles 8 hrs.
Victoria, B.C.	14 days	——	usual headwinds.
Charleston, S.C.	3d, 12h	0–6	light weather.
Virgin Islands	7 days	——	headwinds.
San Salvador	6d, 12h	——	light weather.
Wilmington, N. C. (Southport)	3d, 10h	2–8	light weather except for 2 fronts.

ing the finances of cruising have to be modified to cover not only today's conditions, but to anticipate the future, the success of which I suppose depends on whether one is optimistically or pessimistically correct.

I can only pass along certain basics that one might want to consider prior to departure. In 1947, I built a 40-foot ocean-cruising schooner completely equipped and ready for sea, including dinghy, for $10,000. Today, to build her of the same materials and to the same quality would cost me $70,000. The first impulse is to think "costs have risen." To my way of thinking, that is not correct. What has happened is that *the dollar has decreased in purchasing power*. For example, a coconut, purchased in 1947 for a penny, today costs a dollar: The coconut was, is and always will be a coconut—thus is a constant; the variable is the value of money. This is important to understand, as the basis for cruising independence hinges directly on this fact.

The ocean voyager necessarily must live outside of, yet cope with, the world *system* of finance, politics and propaganda. His survival depends more on self-sufficiency than on being able to "buy" his way around the world. Self-sufficiency, of course, means living off the land and sea—not stealing. There are still many areas where money has no value unless it takes the form of gold or silver coins. Tradable merchandise is the only real "value" sought in many places. This has always been true—and a good trader has always been able to acquire the necessities. I don't wish to suggest that a good cruiser should be a floating warehouse, but only that one should realize that what may be surplus or scrap in one place may be a means of survival (or a luxury) in another. Free trading happens when each party feels that he has received equal value in the swap. Trading at gun point is done only by governments.

Inflation is a method used by governments to "steal" legally from their citizens. Since it is running at over 10 percent per annum in the United States and even higher in some other countries, it is quite possible that any savings account, cash, etc., you have accumulated will be completely valueless in five years or less. I think it was Ludwig Mies Van der Rohe who said: "Only governments can take a useful commodity like paper, print something on it, and make it totally worthless."

With this in mind, fitting-out requires six considerations:

1. Use only the best and most reliable equipment and gear in outfitting the vessel.

2. Spare parts should be carried for all items in addition to normal maintenance or expendable stores.

3. The maximum amount of long-lasting victuals should be brought aboard.

4. Whenever possible, food supplies should be replenished by canning, salting or other methods of preservation.

5. One should prepare himself to be totally independent, especially in the maintenance and repair of his vessel.

6. The vessel must be fully paid for and free of any encumbrances.

With whatever money remains—which should be considered a luxury and expendable as well as spendable—here are some thoughts regarding *its* use:

1. Add extra items that would prove useful in trading with natives of areas to be cruised.

2. Go to an established international bank, such as Chase Manhattan or Barclays, and arrange for funds to be deposited to your account in various countries within the planned cruising grounds. The sum need not be large; it merely indicates to the authorities that you are solvent. Whether the sum is in dollars or another currency depends on your astuteness about what may happen.

3. Although it is convenient to have cash on hand, large amounts may invite trouble. Loss of it by perils of the sea is a remote possibility, but search, seizure or confiscation is possible.

4. Try to have *some* currency of each country to be visited. This often can be acquired from other cruisers.

5. It would seem prudent, when departing from some countries, to convert paper money into their silver or gold coins. One cruiser of my acquaintance who has made a practice of this has one of the finest coin collections I have ever seen.

6. It is difficult to give advice regarding "continuing income," as any government can at any time restrict the outflow of currency from its shores; so one should probably not count on a continuing income from investments. Assets of real value can be stored with or administered by trusted friends or relatives at home. Stocks, bonds, commodities, futures, etc., are not one of my involvements. A friend of mine who is a stock broker labels that an "Alice in Wonderland" attitude and hardly conducive to establishing a dependable income if one is cruising.

Although I have never approved of credit cards per se, I have found it helpful to have either a Master Charge, Visa or American Express card, as, in all states and in some countries, such a card is accepted as identification and opens many doors.

Relying on obtaining employment in foreign countries is chancy as there are just too many "ifs" involved. If you are employed, that usually implies that some citizen does without that job. Sometimes, because you have special skills, a work permit may be issued. Teachers seem to fare well while cruising. To work without a permit invites confiscation of the vessel and even imprisonment—a poor trade-off in my opinion. If there is a firm rule about dealing with governments, it has to be that one should never violate their laws or become involved in their politics.

LIVING ABOARD COSTS

Some people, when calculating the cost of living aboad, note *every* penny spent, including the cost of air travel home to see the kids, tuition costs for children in college, and the like. My figures do not include such items but only food, dockage, fuel, boat insurance, haul-outs, repairs, maintenance, replacement of worn or broken equipment, new charts for a particular voyage, etc., in other words, cost of actual charges against the boat.

Since I believe my style of living aboard is comparable to shoreside living, then the costs can be compared item-for-item. When I calculate the cost of the house, I have to figure in city, state, county and personal property taxes, utilities, auto, telephone, maintenance, food, clothing, etc. So, setting up a comparison it looks like this:

Example
(Monthly Average)

Item	*Boat*	*House*
Food	$160.00	$200.00
Auto (fuel, tires, depreciation)	18.00 (fuel)	300.00
Telephone	10.00	40.00
Taxes	—	50.00
Insurance P/I	10.00	20.00
Insurance (fire, auto, etc.)	—	30.00
Utilities	13.00	200.00
Maintenance	20.00	100.00
Laundry & Cleaning	8.00	15.00
	$229.00	$955.00

Life insurance, dining out, entertainment, vacations, gifts to charity, etc., have nothing to do with cruising but only with one's life style.

RAGS

(*A True Experience*)

On December 7, 1960, I left Hampton, Virginia, to sail, mostly in the Intracoastal Waterway, to West Palm Beach, Florida. Jean was pregnant and usually had difficulty during the first couple of months, so she had elected to remain behind in Hampton while I started south in our 40-foot ketch *Apostle*. It was just as well she did not accompany me because on the first 10 days of the voyage the temperature in the cabin never rose above 27°.

Anyway, the evening of December 28 I anchored just off the Waterway, abeam of Hutchinson Island—a nice spot with about seven feet of water. In spite of anchoring late, I was up two hours before dawn for a quick breakfast and the ordeal of discovering if this was going to be a day when the engine would start. On many mornings I wondered what sins I had committed to be condemned to that Jonah of an engine. I usually used ether to start it, and I am positive that on many mornings a doctor could have taken out my appendix without giving me additional anesthesia. But, no luck. Finally giving up on the engine, I weighed anchor in the morning twilight and proceeded under sail with a chilly fair wind of about Force 4. If the wind held, *Apostle* would make just as good time as she would have under both power and sail. All the bridges opened; the tide was fair; so, all in all, I had no complaints.

The northern portion of Jupiter Island passage was slow. The passage is narrow with dense vegetation on either side. Soon, however, Hobe Sound opened and, in the early morning hours, it was a pretty sight to behold. As you may know, Hobe Sound is where the "gingerbread" houses are—not real ones, of course, but quaint boathouses that look like they're right out of Hansel and Gretel. At the southern end of Hobe Sound is Hell Gate, which is the entrance to Jupiter Sound. This stretch is not very interesting except that in 1960, the hand-operated Jupiter Island swing-bridge was the halfway point which I would reach by mid-morning.

As I approached the bridge, *Apostle* was moving along at about three knots. I saw a man waving a red flag from the bridge. A look through the binoculars did convey any useful information. It was apparent, though, that the bridge was not going to open, but I could not tell why. I sailed right up as though I wasn't going to stop, and the bridgetender yelled, "Honest, Cap'n, I cain't git her open. Waitin' on the road gang now."

"How long?" I called back.

"Dunno . . . maybe two, three hours."

I came about. Rather than sail back to Hobe Sound and anchor, I decided to jill back and forth between Hell Gate and the bridge. I was hot and wanted to get out of my longjohns anyway, and I decided this might be a good time to touch up the paint on the doghouse, so I changed into my paint clothes. (Jean maintains that *all* my clothes are paint clothes, but I don't really consider them paint clothes until they look like Joseph's robe —that's when they are comfortable.)

Well, sir, luck was with me on the third return. I was waved ahead, and sure enough, there was the road gang going round and round, three men to each bar. One guard was sitting in the shade of the bridge house, and a really fat guard was under a palmetto tree on the mainland side. The wind had dropped but was sufficient. I would have liked a bit more, but I worked *Apostle* right up the Loxahatchee River into Lake Worth Creek. Seven more miles and Lake Worth opened up, along with a bit more wind. Within two hours I blew for the Flagler bridge and rounded up smartly, dropping the mizzen and jib, and worked into the marina under mainsail alone.

As I entered, I saw the dockmaster on his electric cart stop in front of an empty slip, so I assumed that was to be mine. To my liking, I found it was dead to windward and more or less blanketed from the main force of the wind; so as *Apostle* forereached right into the slip, I dropped a stern line over the outer pilings, and walked forward and actually lassoed a cleat at the end of the slip. Yep, one would have thought I was a cowboy instead of a sailor! I then lowered the main as the dockmaster's cart rolled out on the wharf. He leaned over the wheel, staring at me and *Apostle,* and finally said, "You alone?"

"Yep," I replied.

"Say," he inquired, "Does your owner know you dress like that—you know, out of uniform?"

I looked down at my paint-spattered clothes and said, "Well, I work for a woman, and you know they don't pay well, especially on sailboats."

"Ain't that the truth," he sighed and continued, "I've seen it many a time. They always spend everything on the boat and the poor bloke that has to sail 'em wears rags."

16

---◆---

Not So Useless Information

Wind is, of course, of utmost importance in sailing and I think some random information about wind, its velocity and flow, that I have picked up in my years at sea might be of interest to all sailors . . .

The rotation of the earth every 24 hours affects wind velocity as follows:

At 0° latitude, eastward velocity is 1,036 m.p.h.

At 15° latitude, eastward velocity is 1,000 m.p.h.

At 30° latitude, eastward velocity is 897 m.p.h.

At 45° latitude, eastward velocity is 732 m.p.h.

At 60° latitude, eastward velocity is 518 m.p.h.

At 75° latitude, eastward velocity is 268 m.p.h.

Regardless of hemisphere, air flowing from the Equator to the poles, moves eastward; air flowing from the poles to the Equator moves westward.

Warm air rises and is displaced by cooler air. Surface air flows from cooler toward warmer air. Upper winds flow from warmer toward cooler air.

Friction with the earth's surface tends to reduce wind velocity near the surface of the earth and causes winds to blow in gusts.

There are times when it is necessary to make a quick measurement of angles with no other tool than the hand. Here's a useful rule of thumb, or more exactly, a rule of fingers:

With arm outstretched in front of you, the angle of thumb and middle finger is about 15°; of thumb and middle finger spread apart as far as possible, about 19°; of thumb and little finger, about 22°; middle finger covers about 2°; palm-down fist is about 8°. This rule does not apply to double-jointed people.

Determining your speed by using a log line is easy when you have the right formula. Log lines are about 150 fathoms in length. From the chip log, about 15 fathoms of line marked with red bunting and called the *stray line* is tied to the log line to assure that the chip log is out of the vessel's wake. The remainder of the log line is tied with a knot every 47′3″. A knot is the relationship of distance to time, thus 60 min. × 60 sec. = 3600 sec., and 3600 sec. is to 6080 feet as 28 sec. is to *x;* therefore *x* = 47′3″. The log glass is always at 28 sec. except for high speeds when the 14 sec. glass is used and the knots are doubled. Readings are in knots and fathoms or approximate knots and eighths of a knot. Shown is a diagram of a chip log:

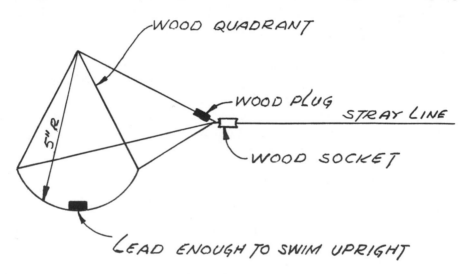

FIG. 16-1. Diagram of a Chip Log.

The ground log is used in shoal water to determine *drift* when you are out of sight of land or in a fog.

"Plumbing the depths" is not a matter of desperation to a mariner, but merely a method of keeping track of the depth of water by using a lead line. Lead lines are marked:

    2 fath. = 2 strips of leather
    3 fath. = 3 strips of leather
    5 fath. = a white rag (cotton)

    7 fath. = a red rag (wool)
    10 fath. = leather with a hole in it
    13 fath. = same as 3
    15 fath. = same as 5
    17 fath. = same as 7
    20 fath. = two knots

Intermediate soundings are called deeps.
Only fractions used in sounding are quarter fathom and half fathom.
EXAMPLE: "By the deep six;
             plus a quarter;
             plus a half;
             7 less a quarter;
             7."

When anchored near shore, a vessel needs window screens as much as a house does, and treated properly they add greatly to the crew's comfort. A mixture of used crankcase oil and kerosene applied to screens keeps out the very pesky "no-seeums." Screens should be washed every fortnight and the mixture reapplied.

At sea, where flying insects are a rarity, screens should be removed because they cut down air and light.

There are times when screens and sea breezes are not enough to stand off the insect assailants. Then an insect repellant is necessary. Avon bath oil is one of the best for personal use. Apply it lightly. It can remain on the skin overnight and comes off nicely during your morning swim.

English	French	Italian	Spanish	German
abandon a vessel, to	abandonner un navire	abbandonare una nave	abondonar un buque	ein Schiff ver lassen
abeam	par le travers	al traverso	por el través; través	querab; dwarsab
aboard!	à bord!	a bordo!	¡a bordo!	an Bord!
accept, to	recevoir; accepter	ricevere	recibir	annehmen; abnehmen
accident	accident; cas fortuit	accidente; accidente fortuito	accidente; caso fortuito	Unfall; Unglücksfall
account; bill	compte	conto	cuenta	Rechnung; Abrechnung; Nota; Faktura; Warenrechnung; Schein
address	adresse	indirizzo	dirección	Anschrift
afloat	à flot; déséchouement; renflouement	a galla; scagliamento	a flote; descencalladura	flott; schmimmend
agent	agent	agente	agente	Stoff
aground	échoué	incaglianto; arrenato	varado; arenado	gestrandet
ahead	de l'avant	di prua	de proa	voraus
aid; assistance; help	assistance; aide; secours	assistenza; aiuto; soccorso	ayuda; socorro; auxilio	Hilfe; Beistand
air mail	poste aérienne	posta aerea	correo aéreo	Luftpost
alee; leeward	sous le vent	sotto vento	sotavento	leewärts; unter dem Winde
all's well!	tout en ordre!	tutto in ordine!	¡todo en orden!	Alles in Ordnung!
aloft	en haut	a riva	arriba	oben
amount due	somme due	somma dovuta	cantidad débita	fälliger Betrag
approach, to	(s') approcher	avvicinarsi	acercarse	(sich) nähern

arrival	arrivée	arrivo	llegada	Ankunft
astern; to go astern; aft	en arrière de l'arrière	indietro! di poppa	¡atrás! de poppa	rückwärts! achteraus
avast heaving!	tiens bon virer!	ferma l'argano!	¡basta virar!	fest hieven!
avast veering!	tiens bon filer!	ferma catena!	¡basta filar!	fest stecken!
back, to	scier	sciare	ciar	streichen
			navegar atrás	
bar pilot	pilote de barre	pilota di barra	práctico de barra	Barrelotse
bill of health	patente de sante	patente sanitaria	patente de sanidad	Sanitärspass
boat harbor	port pour embarca- tions	porto per imbarca- zioni	puerto de botes	Bootshafen
buy provisions, to	acheter des provisions	comprare viveri	comprar provisiones	Proviant einkaufen
by mistake	par mégarde	per inavvertenza	por descuido	aus Versehen
call at, to	faire escale à	fare scalo a	hacer escala en	anlaufen
caution!	avertissement!	avvertimento!	¡aviso!	Warnung!
certificate of health	certificat de santé	patente sanitaria	patente de sanidad	Gezundheitspass
clear from the customs, to	dédouaner	sdoganare	sacar del almacen de aduana	einklrieren
clearance papers	papiers de douane	spedizione doganale	despacho de aduana	Zolipapiere
closed	fermé	chiuso	errado	geschlossen
close hauled	au plus près	stretto di bolina	todo a ceñir	beim Winde
come alongside	accostez	affiancare	atracar	längsseits kommen
compass reading	lecture de compas	lettura di bussola	lectura de brújula	Kompassablesung
complain, to	réclamer	reclamare	reclamar	beschweren
consulate	consulat	consolato	consulado	Konsulat
correct	précis; correct	preciso; giusto	preciso; correcto	genau; richtig
correct, to	corriger	correggere	corregir	verbessern
cruise, to	croiser	incrociare	cruzar	kreuzen
customs house	douane	dogana	aduana	Zoilamt
danger	danger	pericolo	peligro	Gefahr

Nautical Terminology

English	French	Italian	Spanish	German
declaration	déclaration	dichiarazione	declaración	Deklaration
departure	départ	andata	salida	Abfahrt
destination	destination	destinazione	destinación	Bestimmungsort
ease the helm!	mollissez la barre!	leva barra!	¡levantado!	komm auf!
fairway buoy	bouée de chenal	boa di canale	boya de canal	Fahrwasserboje
fall off, to	faire son abattée	abbattere	arribar	abfallen
fathom	brasse	brasse	braza	Faden
flag, quarantine	pavillon jaune	bandiera gialla	bandera amarilla	Quarantäneflagge
follow, to	suivre	seguire	seguir	folgen
fresh water	eau douce	acqua fresca	agua fresca	Frischwasser
full speed!	toute!	tutta forza!	¡toda!	grosse Fahrt!
give way port!	avant bábord!	sinistra voga!	¡boga babor!	Backbord, ruder an!
give way starboard!	avant tribord!	dritta voga!	¡boga estribor!	Steuerbord, ruder an
haul a vessel, to	touer un navire	tonneggiare una nave	atoar un buque	ein Schiff verholen
illness	maladie	malattia	enfermedad	Krankheit
in sight	en vue	in vista	a la vista	in Sicht
increase the speed	augmenter la vitesse	aumentare la velocità	aumentar la velocidad	die Fahrt vermehren
inform, to	informer	informare	informar	benachrichtigen
keep off!	vers le large!	alarga!	¡largar!	weit!
luff, to	loffer	orzare	orzar	anluven
lying to	la cape	alla capa	en facha	beiliegend
manifest	manifeste	manifesto	manifiesto	Manifest
money	argent	denaro	dinero	Geld
moor, to	s'affourcher	afforcarsi	amarrarse en dos	vermuren
mooring	affourchage	dell'ancora	amarre	Verankerung
name of a vessel	nom d'un navire	nome di una nave	nombre de un buque	Schiffsname

no anchorage!	ancrage interdit!	no ancoraggio!	¡no anciadero!	kein Ankerplatz!
no entrance!	défense d'entrer!	vietato l'ingresso!	¡prohibica la entrada!	Eintritt verboten!
no smoking	défense de fumer	vietato fumare	prohibido fumar	Rauchen verboten
open	ouvert	aperto	abierto	offen
pilferage	larcin	furto	ratería	Plünderung
piling	palification	palificazione	empalizamiento	Verpfählung
pilot	pilote	pilota	piloto	Lotse
port of call	port d'escale	porto di rilascio	puerto de recalada	Anlaufhafen
port of clearance	port de départ	porto di partenza	puerto de salida	Abgangshafen
port of distress	port de relâche	porto di rilascio	puerto de recalada	Nothafen
port of refuge	port de refuge	porto di rifugio	puerto de refugio	Fluchthafen
port of registry	port d'attache	porto di registro	puerto de matrícula	Registerhafen
port of sailing	port de départ	porto di partenza	puerto de salida	Abgangshafen
proceed to sea, to	quitter le port	uscire dal porto	de jar el puerto	auslaufen
ready about	parez à virer	allesta a virare in prua	listos a virar	klar sum Weden
ready for sea, to be	paré à appareiller	pronto per salpare	listo a zarpar	seeklar sein
receipt	quittance	ricevuta	recibo	Empfang
safe anchorage	bon mouillage	ancoraggio buono	buen tenedero	sicherer Ankerplatz
ship's clearance inwards	permis d'arrivée	permesso d'arrivo	permiso de llegada	Ankunftserlaubnis
ship's clearance outwards	permis de départ	permesso di partenza	permiso de salida	Anfahrtserlaubnis
ship's papers	papiers du bord	carte di bordo	documentación del buque	Schiffspapiere
ship's register	registre	registro	registro	Registerbuch
slow ahead!	en avant lente!	avanti adagio!	¡avente despacio!	langsame Fahrt
slow astern!	arrière lente!	indietro adagio!	¡despacio atrás!	langsamer Segler!
steady!	en route!	via così!	¡vía así!	recht so!
steady course	route stable	rotta stabile	rumbo estable	fester Kurs
tack	virer de bord	virare di bordo in prua	virar por avante	wenden

NAUTICAL TERMINOLOGY

English	French	Italian	Spanish	German
take in the slack	embrayez	ricuperare l'imbando	cobrar el sena	lose durchholen
thank you	merci	grazie	gracias	danke sehr
tidal amplitude	amplitude de la marée	ampiezza della marea	amplutud de la marea	Tidenhub
tidal current	courant de marée	corrente di marea	corriente de marea	Gezeitenstrom
tide is coming in	la marée monte	la marea cresce	la marea sube	die Flut setzt ein
tide is running out	la marée descend	la marea discende	la marea esta vaciante	die Ebbe setzt ein
tide velocity	vitesse de marée	velocita della marea	velocidad de marea	Gezeitengeschwindigkeit
time of departure	temps de depart	tempo di partenza	tiempo de salida	Abfahrtzeit
tonnage dues	droits de tonnage	diritti di tonnellaggio	derechos de tonelaje	Tonnengeld
tons measurement	tonnes d'encombrement	tonneliate di ingombro	toneladas de capacidad	Raumtonnen
tons displacement	tonnes de déplacement	tonnellate di dislocamento	toneladas de desplazamiento	Deplacementstonnen
tow in, to	remorquer dedans	rimorchiare in dentro	remolcar a dentro	einschleppen
tow off, to	déhaler en remorquent	disincagliare rimorchiando	desencallar remolcando	abschleppen
tow out, to	remorquer en dehors	rimorchiare fuori	remolcar fuera	ausschleppen
transit visé	visé de transit	visto di transito	visado de tránsito	Durchgangs-Visum
under sail	sous voile	alla vela	a la vela	unter Segel
under way	en marche	in marcia	en marcha	in Fahrt
veer and haul, to (wind)	adonner et refuser	ridondare e rifiutare	variable en dirección	raumen und schralen
vessel in distress	navire en détresse	nave in pericolo	buque en peligro	Schiff in Gefahr
vessel (the) is aground	le navire est échoué	la nave si è incagliata	el buque está verado	das Schiff sitzt fest

vessel (the) is bound for	le navire est destiné à . . .	la nave è destinata per . . .	el buque está destinado para . . .	das Schiff ist bestimmt nach . . .
vessel (the) is in danger	le navire est en danger	la nave è in pericolo	el buque está en peligro	das Schiff ist in Gefahr
warp	grelin	gherlino	calabrote	Warptrosse
warp, to	touer	tonneggiare	atoar	warpen
warp a vessel, to	touer un ravire	tonneggiare una nave	atoar un buque	ein Schiff verholen
wear, to	virer de bord vent arrière	virare di bordo col vento in poppa	virar por redondo	halsen
weather-bound	arrête par le gros temps	fermato del cattivo tempo	detenido por mal tiempo	durch Unwetter zurüchgehalten
weather forecast	prévision du temps	previsione del tempo	predicción del tiempo	Wettervorhersage
weather report	rapport météorologique	rapporto meteorologico	raporto meteorológico	Wetternachricht
weighing the anchor	dérapage	dritto	largar el fondo el ancla	Anker aufgehen
welcome, to	souhaiter la bienvenue à	porgere il benvenuto a	dar la bienvenida a	begrüssen
what ship?	quel navire?	che nave?	¿que buque?	wie heisst das Schiff?
yacht club	yacht-club	yacht-club	yacht-club	Jachtklub
yacht harbor	port de yachts	porticcio-panfili	puerto de yates	Jachthafen

Glossary

Ahull, lying.	Hove to, and driven before the wind broadside on or stern first, with all sail furled.
Anchor rode.	Anchor line (rope or chain).
Becket.	A small eye fitted to the end of a rope, that it may be tailed to reeve through a block.
Bowse.	To pull down on a rope.
Bridle.	A length of rope secured at both ends and controlled from its center.
Cat the Anchor.	Hoist the anchor to the cat head instead of to the hoist, where it is hung by a slip on the bow.
Cat Head.	A strong beam or metal support fitted to project from the bow.
Chip log	A wooden quadrant weighted on the curve so that it floats upright, and fitted with a bridle span to secure it to the logline.
Clew.	In fore-and-aft sails, the after lower corner; in square sails, either lower corner.
Cringles.	Rope loops or metal thimbles fitted into the boltropes of sails at the corners; strands of rope used to make a cringle.
Euphroe.	A wood or metal fitting from which a number of ropes form a crowfoot.
Fiddley.	The top of a boiler casing; the funnel casing. More often: A small searail affixed to a shelf or table to prevent things from sliding off.
Fish.	To strengthen a cracked or broken mast, yard or spar, etc., by lashing pieces of timber called "Fish" to it.
Full and By.	Sailing with sails full and as close by the wind as possible.
Gimbals.	A double concentric metal suspension fitting in which a compass bowl, primus stove, etc., may be retained in a horizontal position by counteracting the motion of the ship.

Gypsy.	A small drum attached to a winch.
Heart.	The center core around which the strands of a rope are laid up.
Leech.	The after edge of a four-sided fore-and-aft sail; both side edges of a square sail.
Lizard.	A wire or rope pennant fitted with an eye.
Nip.	A short turn or part of rope caught and jammed; to seize.
Parrel	A short rope-span that attaches a yard or the jaws of a gaff, etc., to a mast.
Practique.	Release from quarantine after regulations have been complied with.
Reeve.	To pass a rope through any aperture such as a block, ring, etc.
Roach.	The concave curve in the foot of a square sail; the curve extending outward of line, peak to clew, in the leech of a fore-and-aft sail.
Scandalize.	To spill the wind out of a sail.
Seize.	To bind two parts of rope together to keep them secure.
Snotter.	A rope loop to prevent anything to which it is attached from slipping.
Thimble.	A concave grooved metal eye around which a rope is nipped and spliced to make a hard eye.